THE SCOTT AND LAURIE OKI SERIES IN ASIAN AMERICAN STUDIES

T0373205

# THE SCOTT AND LAURIE OKI SERIES IN ASIAN AMERICAN STUDIES

# Letters from the 442nd

## *The* WORLD WAR II CORRESPONDENCE
## *of a* JAPANESE AMERICAN MEDIC

*Minoru Masuda*

Edited by Hana Masuda and Dianne Bridgman

UNIVERSITY OF WASHINGTON PRESS
*Seattle & London*

This book is published with the assistance of a grant from the Scott and Laurie Oki Endowed Fund for publications in Asian American Studies.

UNIVERSITY OF WASHINGTON PRESS
PO Box 50096, Seattle, WA 98145, USA
*www.washington.edu/uwpress*

All photos courtesy of family of Minoru Masuda.

LIBRARY OF CONGRESS CATALOGING-IN-PUBLICATION DATA
Masuda, Minoru, 1915–1980.
   Letters from the 442nd : the World War II correspondence of a Japanese American medic / Minoru Masuda ; edited by Hana Masuda and Dianne Bridgman.
      p.  cm. — (The Scott and Laurie Oki series in Asian American studies)
   Includes index.
   ISBN 978-0-295-98745-3 (pbk. : alk. paper)
   1. Masuda, Minoru, 1915–1980—Correspondence.   2. United States. Army. Regimental Combat Team, 442nd—Biography.   3. World War, 1939–1945—Personal narratives, American.   4. World War, 1939–1945—Participation, Japanese American.   5. United States. Army—Medical personnel—Biography.   6. Japanese Americans—Correspondence.
7. Medical personnel—United States—Correspondence.   I. Masuda, Hana, 1923–2000.
II. Bridgman, Dianne.   III. Title.
D769.31442nd .M36   2007
940.54'75092—dc22                                                    2007019487

Cover photo: Minoru Masuda writing home, Italy, 1945. Photograph courtesy of the author.
Design: Thomas Eykemans.

*To all those who fought for love of country, for liberty, and for peace.*

—Hana Masuda

# CONTENTS

# FOREWORD

The men of the 442nd, who endured the horrors and traumas of World War II, have a permanent blood relationship that binds those of us from friendly communities in Hawaii with volunteers from behind barbed wire, such as Min Masuda. The men of the 442nd, who left behind parents and loved ones in dusty, desolate internment camps such as Camp Minidoka, were a special breed. The question that has long endured in my mind is: "I wonder what I would have done? Would I have volunteered?" I would like to say yes, but not having been herded like cattle into camps such as these, I can't say what I would have done.

Daniel K. Inouye
*United States Senator, Hawaii*

# PREFACE

Work on this book began in 1989, when Hana Masuda asked me to collaborate with her to publish the letters her husband had written to her during World War II. At the time, I was working in the University of Washington Archives and had been assigned to process Masuda's papers. Hana and I worked together until December 1990, when she had a debilitating stroke. She died in 2000. Retired in 2004, I decided to resume work on the manuscript.

Hana and I selected 120 of her husband's 220 letters. We chose the most interesting and representative. First, we eliminated many detailed passages concerning Min's mail: the lists of letters from home, statements of plans to write back to various individuals, and references to delays of arriving mail. Next, we omitted frequent and elaborate descriptions of souvenirs sent to Hana, and acknowledgment of packages from her. Finally, we deleted personal messages to Hana. For authenticity, capitalization and punctuation were not changed.

The Medical Detachment Daily Log was divided to provide a chronology of events for the letters. Brief, frequent deletions were made: we eliminated military times, and date and place redundancies. To avoid a clutter of dots, we used no ellipses. Military abbreviations were standardized. We left capitalization and punctuation as is.

Hana wrote recollections of events to fill gaps and provide explanation. She also wrote Senator Daniel Inouye to request a foreword.

I wish to thank the University of Washington Archives for permission to print Masuda's letters and portions of the Medical Detachment Daily Log. I thank Professor Donna Leonetti of the University of Washington anthropology department for her assistance and kindness during the years since this project began. I also owe thanks to Pat Soden, director of the University of Washington Press. I am particularly grateful to Naomi Pascal, former associate director and editor-in-chief, now editor-at-large, of the University of Washington Press, for her encouragement, help, and patience. The Masudas' daughter, Tina Masuda Draughon, has provided much-appreciated help and support. Finally, I owe special thanks to John Carey, whose assistance in the final stages of the preparation of the manuscript made this book possible.

DIANNE BRIDGMAN

# ABBREVIATIONS

| | |
|---|---|
| AAA | Antiaircraft Artillery |
| AEF | Allied Expeditionary Force |
| AGF | American Ground Forces |
| AMG | Allied Military Government |
| APO | Army Post Office |
| ARC | American Red Cross |
| ASTP | Army Specialized Training Program |
| ATR | Antitank Rifle |
| BN | Battalion |
| CBI | China-Burma-India Theater of Operations |
| CP | Command Post |
| CQ | Charge of Quarters |
| DFC | Distinguished Flying Cross |
| EM | enlisted man (men) |
| ETO | European Theater of Operations |
| FA | field artillery |
| FFI | French Forces of the Interior (partisans) |
| G2 | Military Intelligence Section |
| IG | Inspector General |
| JA | Japanese American |
| KIA | killed in action |
| KP | kitchen police |
| LST | Landing Ship Tank |

| | |
|---|---|
| MAAF | Mediterranean Allied Air Forces |
| MIR | Mechanized Infantry Regiment |
| MIS | Military Intelligence Service |
| MP | Military Police |
| MTO | Mediterranean Theater of Operations |
| M1 | carbine rifle |
| ORD | ordnance |
| PBS | Peninsula Base Section |
| POE | Port of Embarkation |
| PRO | public relations office |
| PW | prisoner of war |
| PX | Post Exchange |
| QM | Quartermaster |
| RCT | Regimental Combat Team |
| RSO | Regimental Supply Officer |
| SP | self-propelled |
| TD | Tank Destroyer |
| T/3 | Technician Third Class |
| USO | United Service Organization |
| VFW | Veterans of Foreign Wars |
| WAC | Women's Army Corps |
| WD | War Department |
| WIA | wounded in action |
| WRA | War Relocation Authority |
| YW | YWCA |
| 88 | eighty-eight-millimeter artillery piece |
| 170 | 170-millimeter mortar |
| 155 | 155-millimeter artillery piece |
| 270 | 270-millimeter mortar |
| | |
| Mg | machine gun |
| ODs | olive drabs |
| repple depple | redeployment depot |
| Sp | separate |

# INTRODUCTION

During the last years of World War II, the 442nd Regimental Combat Team was well publicized in newsreels and newspapers. Knowledge of their service has continued through the years, with books, a movie, and a documentary celebrating their contribution. What has been lacking is a personal account written by a soldier during the war. This lack is addressed by this collection of letters Minoru Masuda wrote to his wife from 1943–1945.

Minoru Masuda was born in Seattle in 1915. He lived in Seattle's Japantown, where his family ran a small hotel. Encouraged to become well educated, he earned a bachelor's degree in pharmacy and a master's in pharmacology at the University of Washington. He and Hana Koriyama were married on May 28, 1939. They were interned in May 1942, first at Camp Harmony at the Western Washington Fairgrounds in Puyallup, Washington, then at Camp Minidoka, in a sagebrush desert near Hunt, Idaho.

In 1943 Masuda volunteered to serve in the segregated unit, the 442nd Regimental Combat Team. The 442nd, activated in February 1943, consisted of an infantry regiment, an artillery battalion, a company of combat engineers, a medical detachment, and a band. One thousand men volunteered from internment camps. They were joined by twenty-seven hundred Japanese American volunteers from Hawaii. They trained at Camp Shelby, Mississippi. Masuda was trained as a combat medic in the 2nd Battalion. In April 1944 the unit was shipped overseas.

Arriving in Italy, they were joined by the 100th Battalion, a former National Guard unit from Hawaii. The unit spent four months—June through September 1944—in Italy. There were two phases in this campaign. The first involved intense combat as the unit successfully advanced; the second was predominantly an exchange of artillery fire.

The 442nd spent October and November 1944 in the Vosges Mountains in northeastern France. There they continued the fierce fighting for which they were becoming well known. They liberated Bruyeres and rescued a "lost battalion" that had been cut off by the Germans.

December 1944 through March 1945 were spent on the French Riviera near Nice. The fighting there consisted only of sporadic artillery fire. The men enjoyed frequent passes to Nice. They called these months the "Champagne Campaign."

In April 1945 the unit was back in Italy. Combat was made especially difficult by mountainous terrain. As the Germans retreated, the 442nd pursued them northward through Italy.

After the German surrender on May 3, 1945, the 442nd processed eighty thousand German POWs at an airfield near Ghedi, Italy. Subsequently, they guarded POWs and supplies as the original soldiers returned to America to be replaced by new trainees. Masuda was among the last of the original volunteers to leave Europe. He arrived home December 31, 1945.

Although reluctant to return to Seattle, Masuda was persuaded by a former professor to return to study for a PhD at the University of Washington. He earned his PhD in 1956 and subsequently served on the faculty of the University of Washington School of Medicine as a professor of psychiatry. He and Hana became the parents of two children, Tina and Kiyoshi, born in the 1950s. During the 1970s, he became known as an advocate of minority rights. Masuda died of lung cancer in June 1980 at age sixty-five. Hana died in 2000.

This collection of Masuda's letters is a comprehensive account of his World War II experience: training, combat, postwar duties, and demobilization. The letters are vivid and lively. They emphasize Masuda's surroundings, his daily activities, and the people he encountered. For example, he describes Italian farmhouses, olive groves, and avenues of cypress trees. He writes of learning to play the ukulele with his "big, clumsy" fingers, and the nightly singing and bull sessions that continued throughout the war. The letters include descriptions of the plight of Italians who scavenged the 442nd garbage for food, and the mischief of French children who pelted the medics with snowballs.

The letters also include remarks describing the Masudas' rich personal life. Masuda had a tender regard for Hana. In addition to expressing his love, he encouraged her efforts in business school and teaching Japanese to soldiers preparing to serve in intelligence. The Masudas had a wide network of family and friends, so the letters are filled with comments about others' lives. For example, the birth of a niece prompts a dialogue regarding her name and behavior.

With the exception of references to food and infrequent expressions of indignation about prejudice, the letters do not reveal that Masuda is Japanese American. He and his buddies were enthusiastic participants in 1940s American popular culture. They liked popular music, movies, steak, and baseball. However, the letters reveal a subtle combination of American enculturation with Japanese cultural traditions, such as submitting to difficult circumstances and internalizing emotion. Masuda accepts the condition of war and his participation in it. He praises Hana for not weeping at their leave-taking and asks her to write about her daily activities rather than her loneliness. This adaptation is one reason the letters are valuable historical documents.

The letters are introduced by a prologue compiled from a speech and an article Masuda wrote in the 1970s. In it, he describes growing up in Seattle, internment, and volunteering for the 442nd.

Excerpts from the Medical Detachment Daily Log provide explanations of the military events that are the context for Masuda's letters. The log records the movement of the 442nd from town to town, the method of travel, and the status of the unit—in the front lines or at rest. It describes the intensity of combat and the number of casualties—light or heavy. The weather and the locations of the aid stations are also included.

Recollections by Hana Masuda describing her experiences during the war are included at appropriate intervals. For example, Hana relates her experiences living in Hattiesburg, Mississippi, near Camp Shelby, where Masuda was training; her move from Camp Minidoka to Minneapolis; and Masuda's homecoming in 1945.

A few brief paragraphs explaining tactics and goals are included.

An epilogue includes Hana's recollections of Masuda's homecoming and his account of their return to Seattle after the war. The afterword is a summation of the rest of Masuda's life.

DIANNE BRIDGMAN

# Letters from the 442nd

# PROLOGUE

## *Recollections*

I was born into the Japanese community in the heart of Chinatown, in Seattle. I grew up with it, was acculturated into it, and became a part of it. It was a bustling and hustling cohesive ethnic community, almost completely self-sustained, socially and economically. It had its own banks and a chamber of commerce, two Japanese-language newspapers, shops, fish markets, cleaners, hotels, restaurants, theaters, etc. The Nisei, my generation, the second generation, had its own English-language paper, its own athletic leagues, social functions, etc. In the thirties, then, it was an entirely different community than exists now, but this ethnic community was just as surely a ghetto as any other, even though not surrounded by stone walls. The community developed, as all immigrant communities do, because there was an internal need for people of a common language and custom and culture to band together in a strange land, and by doing so, they were buffered, isolated, and segregated, but protected from an alien, hostile, white American society.

As a Nisei, I was a part of a marginal group, pushed by family and community attitudes to strive to achieve by educational means. The scholastic records of these times attest to this devotion to education. [A very rough estimate is that 14 percent of Seattle college-age Nisei and 11 percent of all other Seattle young people earned degrees at the University of Washington in the late 1930s. Min received a bachelor of science degree in 1936 and a master of science degree in 1938, both in pharmacy.]

When Japan struck at Pearl Harbor on December 7, 1941, we were filled with anger and dismay at the turn of events. On that Sunday morning, a group of us had gone skiing at Paradise Valley on Mount Rainier and heard the news on the noon radio after a great morning run. At the shocking, incredible news, we gathered up and headed home, each of us sober and quiet, wondering what it all meant. Why had Japan done this stupid thing? What would happen to our parents? What would happen to all of us? It was a time for reflection and anxiety about what lay in store for all of us.

The FBI, from the evening of December 7, had begun to pick up and take away Japanese leaders in the community. In a matter of weeks, they had arrested dozens of our Japanese nationals—our Issei parents. Japanese language-school teachers, business leaders, Buddhist priests, and organization heads were among those suspected to be disloyal and taken away.

I remember telling my father that since he was not a citizen—he couldn't become one even if he wanted to—he might be taken away as the others, but for him not to worry about the family and the business (we ran a hotel in Japantown) because we—his sons—would keep the family and business together. I said that we were American citizens, that we couldn't be touched, despite all the furor, because we were protected by the Constitution and the Bill of Rights. I shall never forget what he said: *Wakarainai yo* (I wouldn't be too sure). Subsequent events were to prove that he had more wisdom than I in gauging the dark side of human nature.

Things were becoming more critical. Shortwave sections of our radios were removed. We turned in articles considered to be weapons. Curfew was imposed from 8:00 PM to 6:00 AM. But the real blow was the promulgation of the presidential exclusion order in February 1942. Now we were thrust onto the track that eventually led to incarceration.

It is strange, isn't it, and you will have to try somehow to understand this, how 110,000 people could so docilely and effectively organize themselves into being branded criminals and then to be led away to incarceration.

When General DeWitt issued his order of March 2, 1942, saying that all those of Japanese ancestry would be evacuated from Military Area Number One [western Washington, Oregon, California, and southern Arizona], the Japanese American Citizens League had protested vigorously along with other groups such as church people, university scholars, some business people, the American Civil Liberties Union, and the NAACP; but these were as small voices crying in the wilderness, inundated by the great mass and might of America. If you combine this with the cultural attitudes of fatalism, the acceptance of adversities, and the traditional bowing to authority, we have the answers for the bewildering but adaptive behavior of the Nikkei [Japanese American] people. They went and they survived.

My wife and I were reduced to a number—11704—as our identifying label. And with that label attached to our lapels, on that rainy morning in early May 1942, we took ourselves and what we could carry to Seventh and Lane streets to await the bus. And we were off to Puyallup, our temporary detention center.

Puyallup, our home until September, was the location of the Western Washington Fair. We had come to Puyallup—to these fairgrounds, to the wryly euphemistic "Camp Harmony"—stripped of our possessions, robbed of our dignity, degraded by epithets, and stigmatized as disloyal.

We lived, my wife and I, in Area B—in the parking lot to the east—a compound of long narrow barracks surrounding a central mess hall, toilet, shower, and laundry rooms, all enclosed by barbed wire six feet from the barrack walls.

Let me give you a short calendar of Camp Harmony events that I dug up from the *Minidoka Interlude* newspaper:

| April 30 | First movement from Seattle begins in the rain. |
| June 3 | Western Defense Command orders nightly check-up of residents (just as you do at a prison). |
| July 4 | July 4 celebration held in each area. Imagine celebrating Independence Day behind barbed wire! |
| July 13 | War bond drive starts. |
| July 18 | Japanese prints banned. Bibles and hymnals approved. |

It is a bizarre mixture of events symbolical of patriotism and oppression.

Life in Camp Harmony was the beginning of camp life that continued at Minidoka, Idaho [near the town of Hunt, about twenty miles from Twin Falls] in rattlesnake and sagebrush desert.

Minidoka was, like all the other nine concentration camps, located in the hinterlands, a prison set down in the swamps or desert where others would not live. Here the evacuees were to waste their lives for the duration—except for some students and workers, and those who went to war, some never to return.

The Minidoka Center rapidly became a self-organized community under the War Relocation Authority—a civilian authority composed of human beings under Dillon Meyers. Previously the evacuation was under military control. It was the philosophy of the WRA to relocate the people out to jobs or schools, and it is to their credit that they had our welfare at heart under these circumstances when clearances were still an army function.

What can I tell you of Minidoka? We were assigned to Block 16, Barracks 5, Unit F at one end of a long tar-paper barrack. There it was—tiny, studs exposed, shiplap floor, dusty windows, two stacked canvas cots, a black potbellied stove sitting on a bed of sand, and a lightbulb hanging from the ceiling. We didn't even have a place to sit down and cry, except the floor.

My wife and I worked in the hospital, which was run by an Idaho physician, but the staff and personnel were all evacuees. My job was as a pharmacist; the pay was a professional group pay, the highest pay scale, nineteen dollars per month. In the late fall, we went out to work picking potatoes, and others went out to harvest sugar beets. We went to work for a Mennonite family—lived with them and worked with them—and they were very sympathetic and friendly. We got to know them well, went to their church and went into town on Saturday night, as did all the farmers there, and it was a very enjoyable stay away from camp.

The physical hardships we could endure, but for me the most devastating experience was the unjust stigmatization by American society, the bitter reminder that racism had won again over the Constitution and the Bill of Rights, the perception that the American people had thrown us into concentration camps simply because of our blood. It was galling, infuriating, and frustrating. Scapegoats we were, and imprisoned scapegoats to boot.

At the same time, the stigmatization of being branded disloyal and imprisoned evoked a sense of shame, as if the wrongful branding and the unjust act were somehow valid because of its sanction by American society, an upside-down perception.

Added to the self-imposed cloak of shame was the altogether human defense of submerging anger and bitterness: allowing it to surface and bubble would bring forth pain too strong to bear and detract from the goal of survival and achievement in the postwar years.

Then, into this state of mind came the announcement that the army would be recruiting from the camp to form a segregated regimental combat team. The news fell like a clap of thunder on incredulous ears. How could the government and the army, after branding us disloyal, after stripping us of our possessions and dignity, and imprisoning us in barbed wire concentration camps, how could they now ask us to volunteer our lives in defense of a country that had so wrongfully treated us? The incredible announcement caused immediate turmoil and split the camp into two. One group reiterated the complete irrationality of the recruitment under these circumstances, and pointed out that once again the government was exploiting us and doing us in. The other group took the longer view and saw the threat posed to the future of the Nikkei if recruitment failed. A society as irrational and racist as the one that put us into Minidoka could as certainly be expected to follow by saying that the fact that there were no volunteers only proved their rightness in calling us disloyal and throwing us into camps.

I wrestled with the problem as both arguments tumbled around inside my head. It was a lonely and personal decision. I was older than the others. I was married, more mature, and had more responsibilities. It was a soul-searching decision, for the possibility of death in the battlefield was real, and, in the Nikkei context, almost expected. I admit, too, despite all the trauma, that an inexplicable tinge of patriotism entered into the decision to volunteer.

There were 308 volunteers for the 442nd Regimental Combat Team from the some six thousand to seven thousand people that were in camp.

The rest of the story is history: our induction, travel to Camp Shelby, Mississippi, our training with the larger Japanese American volunteer contingent from Hawaii, then overseas and the combat record of the 442nd.

MINORU MASUDA
*1970s*

Compiled from a speech given by Minoru Masuda, "Evacuation and Concentration Camps," n.d., Minoru Masuda Papers, Box 1, Acc. 54–12, University of Washington Libraries, and an article he wrote, "Japanese Americans, Injury and Redress," *Rikka* 6, no. 3 (Autumn 1979): 15–26.

# 1 AMERICA & ALGERIA

*August 1943–May 1944*

After the attack on Pearl Harbor, Japanese Americans in the United States were forbidden to serve in the armed services. Those already in the service were watched carefully. The only extant unit composed of Japanese Americans was a battalion of the Hawaii National Guard. Renamed the 100th Infantry Battalion, it was sent to Camp McCoy in Wisconsin. After much deliberation, the government announced the activation of the 442nd Regimental Combat Team on February 1, 1943. The unit was trained at Camp Shelby, Mississippi. Twenty seven hundred Japanese Americans from Hawaii joined one thousand men who volunteered from the mainland internment camps. The 442nd was composed of an infantry regiment, an artillery battalion, a company of combat engineers, a medical detachment, and a band.
—DIANNE BRIDGMAN

..................................................................................................................................

RECOLLECTIONS / HANA MASUDA, 1990

*Min's initial training was at Camp Shelby, Mississippi. During August and September 1943, Min was sent from Camp Shelby to O'Reilly General Hospital in Springfield, Missouri, for special medical training. I joined him there and then went back to Camp*

*Minidoka when he returned to Mississippi. I saved the letters he wrote me from this time until the end of the war.*

CAMP SHELBY, MISSISSIPPI
25 OCTOBER 1943

I finally got a letter from you today just as I'd hoped for—in fact, two of them. Boy, was I glad to get 'em. Don's the mail clerk, too, you know—he said jokingly that he was gonna hold my mail back for a week and I told him I'd kick him from here to hell and back if he did. But, it was so good to hear from you again. Please keep them coming, darling, won't you?

It's gotten pretty cold here and the nights are pretty bad. . . . We've two cute little stoves at each end of the hutment now, but haven't started to burn them yet. But, it won't be long now. We'd better or we'll freeze our ears off. And next week, we'll be out on bivouac—wow, will that be cold then!

Darling, you behaved very well at the station. I was proud of you. No tears, no fuss to make the parting a little easier. You saw me, didn't you, when the train started and stopped again? Then when we really got going and the train passed you, I could see you looking around for me—I waved and waved, but my last glimpse of you was your bewildered face looking frantically for me. I saw you, but you didn't see me. That wrenched my heart, too, for you looked so forlorn then. . . .

I'll tell Don to make an allotment out for you, so the gov't will mail you a check—I don't know how much. If I make it $85.00 to you, I'll have $36.35 left. I think I can use all of that—let's see how that works out. I can always change the allotment again. Okay?

I got a big chuckle, incidentally, when you wrote that the kids in Guilford thought I was handsome [Hana's sisters, Suzu and Tama, were attending Guilford College, in Greensboro, North Carolina]. That really was a laugh. . . .

Yes, darling, you must teach me a few things about life when next we meet. It would be quite interesting, don't you think. But, I can't be thinking too much of those things. No use reaching for the moon, so I'll just content myself with dreaming of you.

## 29 OCTOBER 1943

I've finally started to write this letter. The past fifteen minutes were spent in making an outline of what I was going to say. . . .

How's my little Kuso [Min's pet name for Hana] tonight—still the same wife of mine, I hope. . . .

The food here isn't so bad. It seems to be better than when I left or is it because I imagined it was worse? At any rate, it's not so bad, but I wish they could feed us a little more. Maybe I'm a chow hound, after all.

This week's work at the office has gotten me down. Just sit on your fanny doing paper work drives a guy nuts—there's no system at all it seems. I'm glad I won't be there long. In fact, I kind of look forward to next week's bivouac. I've had only one day of football and volleyball since I came here—the only physical exertion for a week. The others seem to play all day. Today I heard it was pretty rugged with drills and exercises and they ran the obstacle course. I haven't been on that thing once yet, what a soldier I'd make.

You can call me Sgt, but maybe you'd best address the mail as T/3 [Technician Third Class]—that would be more correct technically. I guess I'm proud of the stripes, too, but I'd like to be worthy of them and do more studying. I could use it.

I guess I've said plenty tonight, haven't I, honey? Talking to you like this helps ease the loneliness of the heart and gives me a chance to rest easier for the chat we've had, one sided though it may seem. But, I know you're listening way over there and you must know the feeling inside for you that is always within me. . . .

. . . And naturally, you must take care of yourself for me, for, darling, it won't be long before we'll be together again when we live in each others heart.

## 30 October 1943

It's only me piping up again, your dear husband (he is, isn't he?) with pen in hand to tell you how much he loves you and misses you. I hope you're feeling fine tonight, or is it day when you get this?

It's the weekend again—oh, precious two days—Saturday night and so it's a good feeling to know that the morrow brings a full day of my own time. Plan to go to church tomorrow with Doc and maybe Franklin if he shows up. In fact, I just got back from being out with your brother. He came over tonight as we'd planned when we met this AM, and we went to the Service Club. . . .

Saw Harribo Yana the other day—he's a corporal and so's Bako. All the other mainland boys seem to have been eased out so far as the ratings go due to their late arrival, that is, generally speaking. I don't know of anyone else who got higher than a corporal of the recruits—when you look at it that way, I suppose, neither did the island boys. So, I was pretty fortunate in getting such a comparatively high rating—the highest, I'm pretty sure, of all the mainland recruits. I don't say this in any bragging sense, just that the medics must have the technicians to do the work, and now I must live up to the rating. It's much harder to work up in the infantry and FA [field artillery] and such, but in our detachment, so newly organized, the chances are pretty good, as Hasegawa and I found out. We were talking tonight and he's pretty happy that we got the promotion—just as much as Abe is disappointed in not getting his. I hope he's enjoying his furlough right now. I think he is—how could one not?

One by one, I see the Hunt fellows in my meanderings and at the Dispensary. Saw Augie when he came through for his physical—looks all right. Saw Fat Yana, too, and oh, I guess you don't know most of them—Cowboy and his brother tonight and well, they just pop up. This place is full of Washingtonians, thank God.

Well, darling, I guess I've said my say in the daily report of my activities. Oh, I finally sent the T shirts that I'd accumulated to Hack via Sgt Hayashi when he went to town. Hope he likes them. . . .

Say, I was going to cease firing, wasn't I? But I can't, can I, without saying again that I miss you terribly. Every once in a while in the day's course I find myself daydreaming of you. And I have to plunge into the work again. There's no other way is there than that of my perpetual devotion of you.

31 OCTOBER 1943

Hello, darling, how's my little baby today? When you read this the 2nd Bn [Battalion]—and that's us—will be out on bivouac. We leave tomorrow morning around 6:30 for a smart little hike with full field pack for two hours. Then we ride the rest of the way—about 27 miles out, I've heard. It will be my first march in a long time and I don't know how I'll take it, but you can bet I'll be in there pitching. . . . We're taking a lot of junk out tomorrow—two blankets, comforter, OD's [olive drabs], longies etc. and even extra shoes—so the pack isn't too light. It's a good thing that the comforter and extra blanket and other junk will be carried by the ambulance.

Today was Sunday and Franklin didn't show up for chapel service, neither did Hasegawa, since he went into town today to get some things done. But, Sammy showed up and Ed Kiyobara and he and I went. . . .

A fellow just came in about a couple of hours and I was introduced to him—Walter Inouye—he's a Cpl [Corporal] Limited Service—was in the 100th Inf [Infantry] and when they went over he was assigned to Station Hospital as lab technician. We talked awhile of this and that and then it finally came out that he was Jun's brother—Mariko's brother-in-law. Wow, was I surprised. Knocked me off my feet— then we really had a gab session. We've been talking for a couple of hours now—he looks just like Jun and talks like him. We had a good time talking too. He's very amusing and more loquacious

than Jun. He's still here and I'm talking to him and writing at
the same time. It really is a small world. You can meet all kinds
of people here—relatives and such. They're from all over the country
and we seem to know the same people and places. This happens all
the time too.

Sgt Hayashi just told me now that we have to sit up with two hut-
ments of Co [Company] G boys with flu tonight—my shift is from
11:30 to 1:30—force fluids and stuff. . . . So I think I'll hit the hay,
darling. Take care of yourself and I'll see you tomorrow.


7 NOVEMBER 1943

Yep, it's your husband again stealing in to spread his little bundle of
cheer. Are you glad to see me? I know I'm glad to talk to you. . . .

Hana, I've been thinking quite seriously of having you come
down here. . . . That was one reason I went into town yesterday,
too, but I didn't say anything last night till I thought more about it.
I saw Howard Sakura in town last night and he urged me to have
you come here—Alice arrived last Saturday. I went to see the hostess
at the Aloha USO [United Service Organization] to find out things
about accommodations and jobs. . . . Jobs don't seem too difficult
to get, but that's incidental. She told me there were about fifty wives
here now dispersed over the town, one doesn't see them very often.
Being referred to the Billeting Office at the big Front Street USO,
the WAC [Women's Army Corps] there told me that sleeping rooms
are obtainable, but that kitchen privileges are hard to get. . . . The
advantage too, here is that the wives have an opportunity to get
together and have supper and you can always drop in at the Aloha
Center for companionship. . . . So far as my being able to see you,
I suppose that I could get a few more privileges so far as passes are
concerned. . . . I should be able to see you often enough and the
other girls here would help erase the loneliness. Besides, you'd have
the opportunity of seeing Franklin, too, and some of the others. Tell
me how you feel about it, Hana, as soon as possible. . . . If you do

come here, there's no sense wasting time, is there? I want you down here; my only concern is for your welfare. . . . I say "come", but don't until things are fixed up. So let me know soon how it is with you. Okay?

20 NOVEMBER 1943

Sorry I didn't say hello yesterday after we pulled in from bivouac all dirty from the Jeep ride, but one gets busy doing this and that and besides we went to the PX [Post Exchange] for some beer drinking— what a mess of guys with the same idea as us. So when I got back I just plopped into bed. We had to wash all the filth off us, too. We were really caked with dust the 1st, 2d, and 3d Bns pulled in and dog- gone it, out we go again on Monday. We begin the week's jaunt with a twenty-five mile hike—what a pleasant prospect that is. . . . Tomor- row (Sunday) morning I'm going in to look around for a place. I hope that God favors me with a smile on my search. Sgts Hasegawa, Kuwa- yama and I plan to go in the morning and go to church. I'll pray that I can find a place tomorrow. Maybe the prayer will be answered. If not, I'll try the YW [YWCA] at least for a bed. Then you can be here next week. You see, then, I won't be able to see you when you come in and not at all until the bivouac is over on Friday. That's the way things go. Maybe the next week we'll stay in garrison—I hope. Any- way, that's still better than nothing, isn't it? . . . Golly, your coming down here has got me a little excited. Everybody in 2d Bn medics knows you're coming and hope for the best. After all, I just can't keep things as joyous as this to myself. I'm wishing so hard to myself that my prayers are granted, yet I don't want to be disappointed, so I try not to get too het up, but what can a guy do when the one he loves will soon be in his arms again? I'm not made of steel, I just know that I love you and want you near me always. But, there's a little matter of a war in the way. We'll always be together, darling, no matter what, for though distance keeps our physical selves apart, it can never dull the memories and visions in our hearts.

RECOLLECTIONS / HANA MASUDA, 1990

*I was both happy and sad when I arrived in Hattiesburg from Camp Minidoka. It was Thanksgiving, and since Min was on bivouac, he was not there to meet me. Instead, my brother Franklin took me to dinner. We thought about our mother, alone and still in camp.*

*Even so, right away I began to feel more cheerful in Hattiesburg— camp was far away. I felt so free. I could shop for groceries and cook rather than waiting in long lines for food I didn't choose and didn't like. I could shower and do my laundry slowly, knowing no others were waiting. Hattiesburg was colorful and varied, not drab and uniform like camp. The wooden houses had flower gardens and trees around them. At Minidoka only dust and more dust separated the rows of identical barracks.*

*We rented a house with another Nisei couple. Min and I had a small bedroom to ourselves, and we shared the other rooms. We were happy that there was a large dining room where we could entertain.*

*Our first bus ride was quite an experience. Min and I were aware of the segregation in the South, and wondered how we would be treated. There was an empty seat in the back of the bus, so I just sat down and Min kept standing. Then I was told by the bus driver to sit up front. But because I was exhausted, I didn't budge. Since we had been sent to camp, Min and I had talked about prejudice a lot. It really hurt to think there were others who had been treated worse than we had, and for so many more years.*

*After I was settled, I volunteered at the Aloha USO, writing letters and cooking. I met old friends from Seattle and from camp, and made new ones who had grown up in New York, Chicago, and Hawaii.*

*At first, some Japanese American Hawaiians and some mainlanders didn't understand one another. Later, especially during the months in Europe, they came to accept and respect one another. Many lifelong friendships were formed. No matter where these men*

Hana cooking at the Aloha USO, 1944. There she met old friends from Seattle and Minidoka and made new ones from New York, Chicago, and Hawaii.

*were from, they had one thing in common—they were determined to prove that America was theirs as much as anybody else's.*

*When Min had a weekend pass, our apartment became the "Masuda USO," because we invited soldiers for a home-cooked dinner and a chance to relax. We usually had several guests. We were so crowded some had to sit on the floor. A typical menu included chow mein, fuyo-ha, sweet-and-sour pork, teriyaki chicken, rice, tea, and tsekemono (pickled vegetables). The men brought their own beer. Some of the guests arrived early to help cook, and some always stayed to wash dishes. I remember one soldier who brought me red roses.*

*These were fun times, but it all ended too soon. Before the unit went overseas, they held a final parade at the camp. I watched, huddled together with a group of other wives. We all cried and wondered how many of our soldiers would come home to us.*

442D INFANTRY MEDICAL DETACHMENT DAILY LOG

> Final preparations finished for the Combat Team (less 1st Bn)
> 21 April 44.

22–23 Apr 44, we departed the "Dust Bowl" Mississippi via rail. Well trained combat EM [enlisted men] arrived at Camp Patrick Henry, Va on 24–25 Apr 1944.

The RCT [Regimental Combat Team] spent one week at this staging area, medics administering typhus, smallpox shots which took the major portion of their time. Final POE [Port of Embarkation] processing ended on 30 April 1944.

25 APRIL 1944

I've been spoiling to write this letter since we pulled in here yesterday (the "here" being a military secret—and that's no joke), simply because I dreaded putting my thoughts down here in black and white. I have to be rather careful of what I write now, because we are subject to military censorship. It's often difficult to distinguish between what we consider conversation and that which is information. I only hope this doesn't get to you in too cut up a form. It has been only a few days since we parted, but somehow it seems a long time ago. (Just when you'll get this letter I don't know, since it has to go to New York first and then to you and then possibly by then you'll have left for wherever you're going and it will take some time to catch up.) I ached to see you again the day we left, but I knew in my heart that it was better this way. There were quite a few wives in camp hanging around to see their husbands off and I can tell you that they looked none too cheerful. I miss you a helluva lot, darling. Every once in a while I catch myself mooning—I try to keep as occupied as much as possible. On the train ride over, every once in a while as I gazed out the window at the passing countryside, I can't help but get the old nostalgia and feel a dark bottomless feeling in the pit of my stomach—it's a lonely ache. That's none too healthy for a soldier, so I must need relegate such thoughts as much as possible to the deep corners of my mind, for I know that I can never banish them completely. I've been restless all day today in anticipation of writing this letter, why, I don't know—like a freshman entering college. I think you know what I mean and understand my subjugating my feelings for you—for to allow it to occupy my thoughts is to undermine my morale. I think time will help me out a great deal in this respect, but don't think that I don't love you nor miss you as much as ever—let's say that the passage of time will help to dull the sharp edge of loneliness for you.

The train ride was fine as train rides go. Us medics were fortunate (with the help of Lt Ushiro who likes his comforts, too) in getting into a compartment-Pullman with adjoining washroom and other conveniences which made us the envy of the other men who just had Pullmans. Kozuma and I slept in the lower together (with all the natural bandying about of words). Kuge slept on the couch while two infantry men occupied the upper. It was quite cozy all the way. We've just whiled away the time playing cards, eating, and sleeping—of course, we did expend some energies in the form of whistling and waving at people, especially the female variety. It was the most comfortable train ride I had.

I don't know just what I can say about this place we're at, but I'm of the opinion that the less said the better—it's rather difficult because I can't divulge anything that may be of military value. Suffice it to say that it's alright, even though it doesn't look like very much. All of us medics are comfortably situated together by the infirmary—and we're quite close to the Service Club, PX, Recreation hall and theatres, so the conveniences are handy. We're still in the dark, the usual state of what's going on, although you can imagine all the conjecture that makes the rounds. All the boys are here, Don, Dick, Sammy, Roy, Maekawa, Kamo, Speed, etc. See them all the time—at chow and since we're living rather close to each other—we bump into each other often.

Last night some of us trotted down to a Rec Hall to see the Camel Caravan—it was very good. Then after that to a show—*Andy Hardy's Blonde Trouble*. At least it helps while the time away.

Just as in Springfield, I have an upper (this time above Hayashi) and that's where I am right now as I write. Incidentally, the roof over my bed leaks in a couple of spots and I had to shift the doggone bunk out.

Even as I lie here and wonder what else I can say, I can see your face before me. You were so very good that morning when we said goodbye. I loved you and admired you for that—and you're voice was so forlorn when I telephoned you the last day—please don't allow yourself to think too much. Let me know all that you do for if you don't I'll worry about you and I know that you won't want me to do that. I know that I don't have to tell you how much I miss you and love you—you know that already. Please write as soon as possible, darling. I'll be waiting eagerly to hear from you. I guess you realize that, too.

PS A big "hello" to all the gals for me.


28 APRIL 1944

Your letter of the 21st reached me this morning. It was so good to hear from you. Darling, did I forget to have a card sent to you? It's a change of address card with my APO [Army Post Office] number on it. I wouldn't be at all surprised that I'd forgotten to. But, by now you must have my address.

I'm CQ [Charge of Quarters] at the dispensary and it's all quiet here now. Incidentally, I heard from Suzu today, too. She'd got my change of address card and written right away. She moans of a breakup between her and Ed as the world-shaking catastrophe it must be. It gave me a great deal of amusement. It doesn't take much to amuse me anyway.

I'm still addressing the letters to the same address, for I don't know whether you are still there or not. At least you'll get it sooner or later. For all I know you may be miles away from there at this writing. Just let me know as soon as possible of your plans. . . .

We're doing stuff and things which I can't write any gory details about, but we're occupied most of the time. But I still have plenty of time to be thinking about you. But, I think that I'm not as bad as a couple of days ago. I feel better—my morale is higher now. I still miss you, but a spirit—a sense of resignation has become subtly entwined in such a way as to cut the sharp edge off the longing for you. I'm glad of that. . . . The other night we went to see a double feature show *The Chinese Cat* and *Wyoming Hurricane*. You can imagine— the first was lousy, but the latter—God! the stuff Hollywood perpetrates on innocent audiences! It's the first cow opera I've seen in years and I wished to heck I'd never seen it. But, still, it passed the time away.

I think Suzu deserves an answer now for being such a good girl to write so soon. She's next on the list—so I'm stopping here, darling, it seems I've run out of words.

PS Almost forgot darling, today makes 4 11/12 years of marriage, doesn't it? I have a pang of nostalgia when I remember all our happier moments.


MEDICAL DETACHMENT LOG

> 1 May 44 the organization traveled by rail to the Hampton Roads, Port of Embarkation, and boarded ship. The vessels were of the "Liberty Ship" type and departed the continental United States in convoy (rumored to be the biggest convoy in the history of the Atlantic Ocean) on 3 May 44.

> On 13 May 44 the convoy crossed from the American Theatre of Operations to European-African-Middle Eastern Theatre of Operations.

> On 20 May 44 we entered the Mediterranean Sea. The voyage was thus far favored with fair weather and was without incident. Someone remarked, "Who said the Atlantic was rough, I still say Pacific got 'em beaten."

## 19 MAY 1944

After what seems an interminably long time here I am writing again to you. Events have happened so rapidly the past few weeks since last I saw you that the whole sequence seems kaleidoscopic and like in a dream and yet with a definite timing. I don't know, even as I write, when you will get this letter. You don't know where I am and I don't know just where you are. It seems we're lost from each other, but somehow I know that you're still at the end of the line. Since I have no address other than that of the USO, I'm sending this through that organization. You'll be notified of my new APO soon, but till then please write to the address on the envelope. And, darling, please remember, too, that what may seem a lapse of mind on this sheet or the others may be due to my remembrance of military censorship which I have to worry about.

By now you must have received my prior communications from the POE. Well, since that time a lot of water has passed under the bridge and as I said before, in an incredibly rapid fashion. Just how things occurred I mayn't mention, but as I am writing this on my bunk below deck, the weather being inclement outside, seas are rolling a little and the rain is coming down, but here on my top tier (you know Masuda manages to do all right for himself) it is quite cozy. We are rapidly nearing our destination as one can surmise by various activities on this boat and from the latrinograms which are always so prevalent. We've been some days on this tub—it seems funny that one day we're on terra firma and then the next on the deck of a rolling ship. The first four or five days found me feeling none too good—as mal-de-mer always affects me. Food was distasteful and just going into the mess area was a trial, but it wasn't so bad. On the whole the seas have been very good to us. Naturally, we've had some few cases of seasickness. Sgt Hayashi was sicker than a dog for a long time and so was Kozuma—you can understand that we medics at these times were uninhibited in our activities, for even on board military discipline is still the thing. Ah, but the past week now that the dear Sgt is feeling quite robust again his sweet voice regales us from reveille (yep, we still have that) till lights out. But, we still have plenty of free time on our hands. We've two meals on board, breakfast and an interval before dinner, then a snack in the evening. The food is rather good, we get enough to eat, chicken on Sundays and stuff. Naturally, the chow line and wash line is quite a problem in a boat such as this and it seems that we're always in line waiting for something or other. Then, too, the PX opens every other day to supply our other wants as candy, cigarettes, toilet articles, cookies etc. And miracle of miracles, the great American beverage— coke—makes its appearance on PX closed days. So you see how well the dear old Army takes care of your husband. Almost as well as you used to, but not quite—certain touches are lacking. But, hell, it'll have to do for awhile. To also illustrate how solicitous Uncle Sam is of our welfare, we receive games, cards, overseas magazines and the good Red Cross (Toledo Ohio Chapter, incidentally) presented us with a little kit bag filled with miscellaneous useful articles. To break the monotony of the sea voyage, we've had boxing tournaments and entertainment. The rest of the time is spent in reading, gambling and gazing out to sea with various conjectures about what lies ahead. Your husband has still enough money for things—in fact, he seems to have made some on the ship just playing around. Sick call helps to pass some of the time away, though that has diminished, too.

Judging from what I've told you, you can see that time can lie quite heavy on our hands. I'd have written sooner, for no matter when I'd written I still couldn't have gotten it off. So I've saved everything for this one longish letter, whatever there was to save. As I've said before all that has happened seems like some dream which we knew was inevitable and yet when it happened was somewhat nightmarish in character. As I sit on deck sometimes and gaze out to sea, I wonder if this isn't all a dream and I'd wake up to find you hanging around, but no such luck. I know that I am not alone with such thoughts. Every night I go up on deck before seeking Morpheus and in the blackness of the night and in the twinkling constellations, some-how you are nearer and yet so far away. It's beautiful up there on deck, in the gently rolling sea and as the ship surges forward, to see brilliant sparkles, somehow ghostly, of phosphorescent marine ani-mals in the foam. And gazing upward at the darkness of the sky, to see silhouetted against the stars, the mast and rigging as they sway and break with the deck for a pivot. It's calm and awe-inspiring then in those moments I feel more than ever the need and longing for you. It is then when I realize fully how much you are a part of me and how I miss you. Since the departure there is a void that time has yet to heal, and yet I know that it never will until the day I hold you in my arms again. But, I'm hoping that at least the temporary exigencies of war itself will busily dull the sharp edge of loneliness.

I know that you must be quite worried about my activities and whereabouts, but please don't. Of course, with the coming of this letter some of the trepidation will have been dispelled. You, of course, realize that this is not of my doing—that censorship is of such nature. As to your activities I am still in the dark I don't know when or where you will get this, but eventually it must. Please write as often and as much as possible—you can never know what it means to a soldier to hear from his loved one. Will you send me some air mail stationery and envelopes as soon as possible—stamps not necessary, I can send them COD. That's the way this is going. I'm trying to write every-body I can; I guess eventually I will.

Darling, a big "hello" to all my friends and to you all my love and I miss you very much.


MEDICAL DETACHMENT LOG

Arrived Augustus, Sicily 26 May 44, leaving the following day via Messina Strait.

28 May 44 found ourselves pulling into Naples' war torn harbor, less the Hq [Headquarters] 2 Bn Companies F, G, and H. Where-

abouts of the missing companies not reported. Wild stories floating. Speculating seems pretty heavy.

The following is the detail account of the whereabouts of this lost battalion. On 21 May 44—this battalion including the same battalion medics, left the convoy and stopped at Oran, Algeria. Bivouac at Staging Area #2, Oran.


## 25 MAY 1944

It's been six days now since last I wrote you. I hope you've received the last letter (the first, too, incidentally) I sent. A lot of things have happened since then. Unfortunately I can't reveal all the details; neither can I even mention where we are, not even the continent. But, suffice it to say, that we're now in the old world. It's a strange feeling to know that the age-old stamp of the centuries is upon this countryside. Naturally, as we neared our destination, we were all eager to gaze upon all the sights that had only musty recognition in dull history books, that, too, we mayn't mention. At any rate, believe it or not, we've landed on this foreign soil. As we passed various towns on the shores, they were closely scrutinized through binoculars. Our first impression of these were one of surprise for they looked compact, clean and modern—which only goes to show the utter narrow-mindedness of Americans who live only in their own worlds and look upon other countries with a superior attitude. When we did land, away we were frisked to our encampment. Passing through the town and seeing the quaint costumes and a variety of them, too, plus the novelty of the atmosphere and its strangeness was an experience. The town from a distance looks glamorous, but on seeing it at close range discloses that it's the distance that lends enhancement. There's a startling contrast of the old and the new—of donkey carts and new automobiles, of modern dress and old. To us, there's a strangeness in the land which is often incomprehensible being brought up in the Western manner. I must investigate the town a little more thoroughly—

a fleeting glimpse isn't much, even though it didn't seem too inviting. I guess we all miss our comforts.

The countryside is one of gentle rolling hills and valleys—not unlike that of certain parts of the Northwest. The view is quite agreeable—as one Californian put it, certain portions remind him of San Fernando Valley. Vineyards are in great evidence which can only attest to the amount of wine consumed, that also bears further investigation. The natives gaze at us with curious gazes as well they may, but not with hostility. Their raiments are varied—GI clothes seem to be a good part—white draped forms can be seen on carts and turbanned and fezzed individuals are in evidence. Naturally, the physical conveniences of home aren't here, making their absence very conspicuous and one can't help but feel the poverty and the unhygienic habits as we know them. Ragged street urchins look upon us GIs as their manna from heaven as sources of candy, cigarettes, chewing gum, money, etc—anything to them is a mild fortune and it's remarkable how rapidly they've caught on to the GI lingo as, "Hey, Joe, gimme candy" and all the while they're looking at you with appealing eyes. We try not to appease them for there's no end and it's remarkable how soon a little band can form.

We are encamped on a small knoll in rows of pyramidal tents. The sight as we first gazed upon it was none too encouraging, for this was to be our next home till God knows when. The terrain is rocky to the point of discouragement—it being difficult to even pound tent pegs into. The wind is a continuous thing from the sea and even though it may be a blessing to cool the feverish brow on a hot day, it can be a decided nuisance constantly whipping about the tent and dust into the air. Naturally, a fine coat of dust lies over everything. We don't mind too much, for we don't expect to become clean again until the war is over or some deserved rest comes. There's a GI shower about a mile away, alongside what is called an open air theatre. The former helps out our physical needs and the latter, our mental. We saw a show last night, sitting on the rocky hillside listening to and seeing Joe E Brown cavorting in *Casanova in Burlesque*. It helps to pass the time. Water is quite precious and we use it sparingly. I hate like the devil to drink it, for it has a repulsive, brackish taste, but one has no choice. It certainly felt good to wash ourselves in this water even though it precipitates the soap and makes for gumminess especially on the hair— you see the soap actually lathers—a sight we hadn't seen for some time. Speaking of hair, Minata gave me a haircut a couple of days ago and it's really GI this time, just like a hairbrush. I'm not quite used to it yet, for I feel cold and a trifle naked. Naturally, the fellows had to watch the harrowing operation with various comments as "rat bitten", "moth eaten" etc which did my sense of comfort no good. But it's satisfactory and I feel much better. I wish I could send you a picture of myself now. I may at that—who knows? So far as food goes, one can't kick, we get enough and the quality isn't bad at all. I've gotten used to eating dust with my meals, too. Hayashi, Momoda, Morimoto, Kuge and I occupy one tent and our floor is littered with rock fragments which help out during rain and are used to anchor down the tent flaps from the breeze. Right at my head is a tear in the tent. It comes in handy for ventilation (although we get plenty of that) and light. At night I can look right through at the dark blueness of the night and the myriads of stars. I think I've given you a more or less haphazard description of the impressions I've had and how we live. I'll expand from time to time as I find out more, provided, of course, that I can reveal it.

Golly, I was so glad when I got mail the second day of our stay here. I got your telegram saying that you were leaving for Minneapolis that night. Then, a letter from you know where, Aloha USO, a postcard (thanks for the blonde) from Minneapolis and a letter telling me of your woes in finding an apartment and all the various headaches that went with it. Yesterday came a card from you mailed out of Chicago telling of your stay with Mariko and Jun. A nice letter from your mother, too in *nihongo* [Japanese] wishing me "maney maney good luck", it did my morale no end of good. My sister, Ruth, wrote me, too (I've been doing fine so far as mail goes) telling me all of Hack's final rite. [Min's youngest brother, Hack, passed away during the spring of 1944.] She wrote of a photograph—I'll see that eventually. Do you recall the last letter I wrote to Nay from Camp you know where—well, she says that they all three had a nice good cry over it. That made me feel sober, too, for I know that their thoughts are with me, too.

I hope you don't have any difficulty in finding a place. Please write me one all about it. Our anniversary is in three more days. I've tried through a fellow to do something to let you know that it hasn't slipped my mind, but I'll have to wait my turn to town. You don't mind the lateness, do you; it does not detract one whit from the sentiment that goes with it. Don't send me anything yet (except the air mail stationery and envelopes). Just keep writing—a little piece of you in your handwriting is all I want to keep me going. Yesterday, cablegrams were made available to us and now should be on your way, as well as to my folks, your mom, Otas, Sakamotos, Mariko and Jun, Suzu—only sixty cents and well worth it. I hope it got there before this did. One never knows.

Chow has been called and I must go—this must go out in the morrow's mail and I won't have time tonight to finish. . . . I miss you very, very much. There's nothing more I can say on that, but you're the dearest thing on earth to me.

PS Am enclosing a 5 franc note as souvenir—the franc is standard here and worth two cents.

RECOLLECTIONS / HANA MASUDA, 1990

*After Min left Camp Shelby for overseas duty, I went to Chicago to spend time with my dear friends the Inouyes until I decided where to go. I finally chose to settle in Minneapolis, because several very close friends lived there. It was a beautiful city that reminded me of Seattle with all its parks and lakes—but with fewer and smaller hills than Seattle. I have fond memories of this lovely city and its people.*

*As soon as I could, I went back for my mother, who was waiting*

*for me at Camp Minidoka. She was cleared by the WRA for reloca-*
*tion out of camp because she would live with members of her family*
*away from the Pacific Coast. My sister Tama and her husband Harry*
*had also moved to Minneapolis, and my sister Suzu chose to attend*
*the University of Minnesota there.*

*I had been fortunate to find a duplex where the nicest landlords,*
*John and Helen O'Connor, lived upstairs. My mother, Suzu, and I*
*lived on the ground floor. Helen and John became sympathetic*
*friends who were sincerely interested in our welfare. We used to talk*
*to them for hours about our incarceration, the war, and other current*
*affairs. Helen comforted me many times when I was most worried*
*about Min because I hadn't heard from him in a long time. Helen's*
*ancestors were Polish, and John's were Irish. Helen and I teased John*
*by saying she and I were members of stronger lineages than he was.*
*He just laughed. Helen was an excellent cook, and we often enjoyed*
*picnics in the large backyard.*

*In spite of the war and family worries, we had a happy home in*
*Minneapolis.*

## 28 MAY 1944

Today is our day, but here it is a very miserable day. It has been raining fitfully since yesterday when I wrote last and it has driven us all
indoors into crowded quarters. It came down so hard last night, our
tent leaked in so many spots, that we were, that is, our cots, all clustered toward the center. . . . As you know, today was Sunday and
reveille was out, but I got up for breakfast and ate huddled under a
tent edge to avoid the rain. Then back to the tent again. What else to
do but to go to bed again and sleep. I fell into a heavy sleep and got
up for lunch—a good lunch of fried chicken and stuff. Very good. That
was our anniversary dinner. I hope you ate better. . . . It's still raining.
At noon when I awoke I found welcome letters from you. Evidently
you're having quite a time finding a place to light. I hope by this time
that you're settled. . . . Don't let it get you down, darling. Everybody's

having a tough time—you're not alone in that. Keep punching. But, so long as you're there that's home to me. Always remember that. . . . Golly, it seems that none of my correspondence has hit you yet. It'll get there eventually; must be chasing you all over the damn country. Be patient, your ever-loving husband hasn't forgotten you one bit. . . . Has your allotment come through? That should help out quite a bit. . . .

I'm sorry that I couldn't send you anything for this day. I tried sending roses, but no dice. I'll have to try when I get to town which should be soon. . . . I hope I can find something that is worthy of you (and incidentally, one that I can pay for) to send you. It will be a little late, but just forget the time angle and pretend that the day you receive it is our anniversary.

There will be other happier days and times when this whole thing will have blown over and we are together again. Even in these trying times let us look ahead till that day when we will meet again. Darling, je vous aime beaucoup.

## 29 MAY 1944

As I lay in my bed roll last night in the quiet darkness, penetrated only by Morimoto's nocturnal snoring, and the thoughts suppressed by the days activities prevent my sleeping, I can't help but think of you and how we are far apart. I guess we were born either too early or too late. And I damn all the senselessness of war and the crazy gyrations of mankind which leads to God only knows what. It wouldn't mean anything to me if only it didn't affect us, kept us apart. All these random thoughts in my solitude only boils down to this, that I miss you so damn much it often hurts.

## 1 JUNE 1944

Today is the first day of June already, time certainly doesn't drag its footsteps, does it? Quite naturally, it's raining again, making comfortable little patters against the tent canvas. . . .

I didn't write you yesterday for it was my turn to go to town. Five of us hied ourselves out yesterday (it was a good sunny day). We just got paid, too, to make everything that much nicer. About town, it's as I told you before only more so. We spent almost all the time meandering around and shopping. Of course, a couple of jaunts to the beer joints were purely to quench our thirsts. . . . The beer drinking wasn't good. Small orchestras play in "Joes Joint" or "Al's Place" and strangely enough all that they play is stuff like "Mairsy Doats" and "In the Mood". That's the way it should be, but in this strange foreign land to hear the people play our contemporary jazz borders on the incongruous. . . .

I did luckily find that I can send flowers and by the time you get this, you should have a dozen roses. Small though the outlay may be and late as it is it no less conveys that you're still my very best girl. I also sent a little coin purse for you. . . .

The American Red Cross is a boon to us GIs. They help out no end in all things and we took in a show there, *Lady in the Dark*, an interesting psychiatric film. We tried to have a sidewalk photo taken by a native, but he just ran out of paper and it was no go. I'd like to have sent one to you. We came home early, footsore, and weary, but it was to me, time well spent. I've still fifty dollars left—it's not enough to send home for I've still a month yet to go 'ere next payday. I hope you got your allotment by this time. I know it could come in handy. I'll try to send something home, if I can. You know how proficient I am in the language you studied and I didn't [French]. You can imagine the bargaining that went on in the shops we went into. It's difficult in lots of places to make one understand. . . . It's started raining again; it's not an unpleasant sound. Shall see you again tomorrow night. Till then—

# 2 ITALY

## *June–September 1944*

In Italy, the 100th Battalion, a former National Guard unit from
Hawaii, joined the 442nd as its first battalion. The 100th had served
with distinction at the battles of Anzio and Salerno. Proud of its
service and its separate identity, it was allowed to keep its numerical
designation.—DIANNE BRIDGMAN

.........................................................................................................................................................

## MEDICAL DETACHMENT LOG

First sign of combat duty on 2 June 44 442d RCT was attached to
the Fifth Army and assigned a permanent APO number.

6 June 44 the Combat Team, less 2d Bn, left bivouac at Naples and
traveled via LST [Landing Ship Tank] to Anzio, Italy, arriving 7 June 44,
marching about five miles to our next bivouac area just outside of
town. Rather warm weather continued throughout the trip. During this
bivouac area the practice of using K and C rations was extensive.

6 June 44, our 2d Bn medics and others embarked from Mers El
Kebir, Algeria, aboard troopship HMT *Samaria*. Arriving at Naples,
Italy, entrained for Bagnoli, Italy just outside of Naples.

Bivouacked.

Air-raid occurred during the night of 9 June 44 on the town of Anzio.

Arrived Civitavecchia, Italy via truck convoy through Rome 11 June 44. 11 June found ourselves attached to 34th Division, the grand daddy of 'em all, of which our forerunners the one puka puka [100th Infantry Battalion] are part of.

SOMEWHERE IN ITALY
12 JUNE 1944

At last I'm getting to say something to you. As you can see by the top line I'm in the land of spaghetti. It's been about five days since last I wrote you. Well, in the meantime, I couldn't write for we were on our merry way here from North Africa where we'd first landed. They tell us now that we can mention our seeing Gibraltar—well, I've mentioned it—we saw it from some distance and believe me it was quite impressive. I'm rather glad we're rid of North Africa now—I didn't particularly care for it. On our way up we passed the Isle of Capri, famous in song, but not so glamorous as we went by it. The trip was uneventful and the passage quiet. I wish we had come on a Liberty ship. As it was we came on a larger ship and the food was terrible and we slept in hammocks. I slept on a table with a mattress under me. The quarters were certainly cramped. Made all of us sore. 'Nough said of that boat, the better. Well, we eased into the port and we can really see the marks of war that have left itself in the form of bombed buildings. The rubble and ruins are terrific. The populace seem to be just as poorly clothed and fed as those we saw in North Africa. But, somehow, in spite of that this place seems a lot nicer for there are greens here and trees and flowers, things we didn't see before. We've bivouacked in an orchard with the same kind of dust underfoot we first experienced in Minidoka—well, we have to sleep on it. Not so good. The dust gets on everything. There are camp followers all around and it's pitiful the way they hang around the kitchen garbage trying to dig their cans into it to take home and eat.

They certainly seem starved here. Incidentally I sent you yesterday a pair of small matched cameos. They're rather finely done. I thought they would make beautiful earrings for you. I hope you can put them to some use. All our money has been converted to lire now and I'm enclosing a small note to give you an idea of what they look like. The lire is equivalent to our penny, which makes things quite simple to figure out. . . . The first day we got here, we cooked up a mess of beans (string) and onions with our C ration for a darn good meal. It's a lot of fun haggling with the peasants for what they can offer in fruits, vegetables and trinkets. The cries of "Wash, Joe", "Laundry, Joe" wakes us up in the morning—and they're around us all day. They certainly harass the guards, for they can't come into the area. I haven't gone into town yet, but I'm expecting a pass soon to Pompeii (I can mention that historic place) to see the ruins there.

Kozuma and I bed together so you see that I'm in good hands or vice-versa. Golly, but the ground is hard. At least on maneuvers we could get leaves and grass, but below us now is good old terra firma and nothing else. And you know how bony I am, I [always] turn out where some protuberance hits the ground. I wake up each morning with a backache.

The first day we got here, mail was waiting for us and did we all hit the jackpot. I myself got seventeen letters (Kozuma got eighteen). Eight of them from you. . . . But from now as you must realize all correspondence will have to be of a spasmodic nature, dependent on circumstances, so if you don't hear from me for any interval of time, you can be sure that it is not of my doing. Please remember that. . . .

Although we've been here just a short while already the home touch is evident in the laundry hanging out between the rows of tents. It's amazing how one adjusts himself to the environment. Each succeeding post we come to becomes progressively worse, as far as physical comforts go—and we have yet the supreme test to face. That should be the worst of all. Well, we'll find that out, too.

You're doing a swell job of writing faithfully, darling. That helps out a lot. I'm trying to hold up this end, too, but as I said before, I'll write when and if I can.

A "hello" to Tama and Harry from me. And for you, all my love—

14 JUNE 1944

It's hello again from me to you. I've quite a bit to tell you. That's the reason I didn't write yesterday. I had [censored] to see what I could of Italy. . . .

Accordingly, Morimoto, Taira and I hied ourselves in our best khakis and boots to the station and off we clattered to the town. We get a big kick out of trying to carry on conversation with the Italians with what meager store of the language we have. All the gesticulations and inflections and constant referring to the small pamphlet must make for some second rate comedy scene. At any rate, I can say that the participants get a kick out of it. . . . Pompeii, that's where we were headed for—that famous town buried in 600 BC by the ashes and dust from the volcanic antics of Mt. Vesuvius. I'd looked forward to the trip and here we were on our merry way with a mess of Italians in a crowded tiny train with a responsible guide. Naturally the passengers were quite curious about us wondering as to our race and we told them in our beautiful Italian (don't forget the hand movements). They couldn't quite figure out how come we were speaking English, when we were Japanese. We had some good conversation all the way (or should I spell that confusion) . . . the tour was excellent and very worthwhile and we were in the ruins for three hours. After the hot walk, naturally, we had to go to an arbor where wine was sold and a bottle of the sparkling stuff was in order. There remained now, only the Basilica Cathedral to see to top it off. I'm enclosing two post cards of it. As you can see it's impressive from the outside, but once one gets inside, golly, it's gorgeous—words are inadequate to describe its beauties.

17 June 44 2d Bn Hq and Companies F,G and H finally showed up, erasing all ugly rumors. 15 June 44 they left port of Nisida, via LST arriving at Anzio. Leaving this one time famous battleground 16 June 44 and arrived Civitavecchia 17 June 44.

18 June 44, extensive use B rations, morale seems excellent, daily passes to Rome, swimming parties, special services; movies and PX were arranged for the anxious boys [the Allies had taken Rome only two weeks earlier, on June 4, 1944]. Daily training and conditioning continued. Such honors as an audience with Pope Pius XII in Vatican City was arranged for the boys. . . .

## 19 JUNE 1944

Busting in again via the APO to whisper sweet nothings into your delicate shell-like ears. (Now where in heck did I pick that up.) I don't think I'll be able to write tomorrow and although I haven't heard from you since the first two letters, I'm penning this to let you know how this old gent is. Incidentally, that pseudo-sophisticate brat sister of yours penitently took pen in hand and came forth with a thick letter so she's forgiven. Gave me some amusing moments, too. . . .

Since you came out with such a description of home, I must need tell you how I live. Our domicile is on the hill overlooking a meadow, dotted with haystacks. Our front porch is covered with green boughs and these are our mattresses, too. After this is over we can throw our Beautyrest away. . . .

We hied ourselves out to the beach yesterday, but it turned cold and I didn't go into the rolling surf. But, it was interesting to scan the evidences of recent German occupation in forms of barbed wires, dugouts and equipment lying around. They hadn't even gotten around to getting all the mines out—they must have taken off in a hurry, for there was a mess of ammunition lying around yet.

To get us into a little better physical condition, took a "mile run" today. Actually only four or five stretches of jogging with walks in between. Even then, we were puffing. Soon we should be able to run without stopping, I hope. After all, we haven't had much chance to be physically fit on our "vacation cruise."

Don't worry about any needs, for the Army takes very good care of us. Food is no consideration and we've had all types now—C ration, K and a new one that we had the other day. All are purely for expediency and all adequate substitutes when hot meals (B) aren't practical. And, boy, in these rations they have everything, even to gum, candies, cigarettes and toilet tissue—the latter is an important item, too, I can tell you. The thoroughness of our scientists is certainly amazing. Even with hot meals we get cigarettes and candy so that worry is eliminated. The PX somehow or other still functions— why we even had beer yesterday. Not like Rainier Special Export, but still beer and that helps a lot.

I've got two white circles painted on my helmet and soon I'll get a red cross painted on it. That's the Geneva Red Cross. Whether that will be a guarantee against small arms fire against us remains to be seen, but I know it's one swell target. However, reports here indicate that the Germans respect the conventions to a gratifying degree. My opinion is that it's better to indicate the medic; that's our job, anyway. I don't see bearing arms against the enemy—it's not my line. How can we expect them to respect us if we don't hold to the rule ourselves? I'll play it the straight way—I think it's the better course.

Hana, could you please send me some more air mail stationery, just the thin sheets. The envelopes are useless without stamps and the latter hard to get. Whereas I can get stamped air mail envelopes from the APO. The paper certainly seems to go fast. Wrap it up good, too—some of these packages are sure banged up.

My comfortable bed with the boughs awaits me. It's too bad I don't dream lately—I guess dreaming is a luxury now, too, but I'm thinking of you and missing you tonight.

MEDICAL DETACHMENT LOG

On 21 June 44, we moved by truck convoy to our new assembly
area, some four miles east of Grosseto.

Finding ourselves doing usual CP [Command Post] duties on 22 and
23 June 44. Leaving East Grosseto, Italia and arrived at Gavorrano,
Italia, by organic transportation arriving NW Gavorrano. Left this
assembly area. Arrived in vicinity of Montiom. Set up Regt'l Aid Station. EM told to well disperse and dig in deep.

## 22 June 1944

Kozuma's sleeping so peacefully beside me as I write this in the tent
that I'm tempted to do the same. Ah, but one must carry on, mustn't
one? Sorry I didn't write you any sooner, but unforeseen things happened and this is my first opportunity. You see, we moved again into
another home. We've had so many different ones now. This is like
the rest. On a hillside only this time we're in an olive grove. It's very
nice here—the cool breeze blows right through our tent and we fixed
it up so that we actually have a front porch overlooking the draw.
Someday when this war is over I'll show you all the places I've been
to in sunny Italy. This is beautiful country for landscape—gentle
rolling slopes and neat farms under a blue sky. Wonderful for honey-
mooners and leisure traveling.

One reason I didn't write sooner was that I had a chance to visit
Rome and I was off in a flash. The city is huge and impossible to
cover in the short time I had. But, as usual, I had a very full day.
With my aid kit full of my stuff, I sallied forth to do the town. Met
up with Vic, Abe, and Squeaky and off we went. The people here are
starving and they have the money. They swarm all over the GIs asking for chocolate, rations, cigarettes, etc, especially the first two.
A five cent Hershey bar will sell for fifty cents as will a pack of cigarettes. As for rations, both C and K, they'll part with $1.50. These
aren't beggars either—many very well dressed people ask to buy

food. The mothers are smart and bring their cute little bambinos and that works tremendously to their advantage, for most GIs are rather tenderhearted in that direction. I had six mashed and battered bars of candy that they grabbed from me for $1.80. You have to fight them off. It's rather pathetic. But, first we went shopping for stuff for the stores close early. You'll see evidences of that when you get the package that I've sent out. There's lots of good stuff here yet. . . . I put a map of Rome in, too; the dark line showing the route of travel. Start at the middle left hand side on the Piazza Pia, when we detrucked. We went to the better shops. They've set up two GI chow places already and the terrific line is discouraging. We'd had the foresight to bring our rations and ate in a grocery store that we temporarily took over. They had nothing to sell either. Then back we went to the Red Cross to take a look see. It's amazing how fast the ARC [American Red Cross] gets around—they were in Rome right after the armored trucks. And now they're going full blast in a beautiful place which formerly was a hotel—all glass, chromium, and marble. We were so tired after all the walking that we hopped into a horse buggy and he took us through some beautiful places as indicated.

Rome as you know is on the Tiber and its history is voluminous. As for its art, any little walk will tell you of that for wherever one goes statues, busts, and carvings are in evidence. One can see that history had some of its origins in Rome, "The Eternal City". I can't describe to you all its buildings and beauties—maybe the photographs I sent will help visualize them. Of course, the climax of all is the Saint Peters Cathedral, the home of Catholics, and the Vatican City where the Pope is head man. I won't describe the church for it defies that—its richness and vastness is enough to make one dizzy. The accumulation of centuries is in that hallowed place and one can see it. But, to us Westerners it's gorgeous and unbelievable. Although I liked the Basilica in Pompeii more as a religious sanctuary, this, Saint Peter's in Rome, is its splendor and vastness many more times. Someday, we'll see it together. There are quite a few students from Japan here studying and I happened on one and we chatted both in

English and Japanese. He'd been here nine years and his name was Asahi. He invited us over to his place and we went after we were through, but he was out. However, we met a few of the others and it was strange that we American Japanese should be conversing to a Japan Japanese in Japanese in Italy. One sees nationalities from all over the world at this capital of Catholicism. I know the Sakamotos and Otas would find more interesting things here than I could see with my Protestant eyes. Rome is a wonderfully historic place—I wished that I had time to really do the place. . . .

I shall be seeing you again soon darling. Keep thinking of me.


23 JUNE 1944

Here I've had dozens of your letters to date and all your letters I've had up till the 9th of June (the latest) say that you haven't received one from me yet from overseas. It makes me feel bad for that's not a fair exchange. But, I'm telling you that once it comes, you'll be deluged, for I've written quite a few myself. It just hasn't caught up with you. By the time you get this you should have received them all. I hope that all those I wrote in care of the Aloha USO were forwarded to you. I had four letters from you yesterday and two today, making six in two days. That's the way it goes, in batches. . . . I was a very good boy today. I wrote to Suzu, Roy and Jo, (I got one from her today) Mayme, (two from her in the past week) and one to Yoshiko. You know how I take time to write letters, so I'm flattering myself.

Your last letters were so chockful, I really enjoyed them immensely. Especially your description of our home. It makes me want to see it so badly. At last I've a place that is really home to come back to. It is a good feeling I can assure you. Heretofore we had no such anchor and now I've a place to hang my hat. Thanks to you for all the work you must have gone through. . . .

You speak of the Western front which opened on the 6th [D Day] I believe. Naturally, we wish them all the luck, but we're more concerned with our own battles and if you follow the papers, the army in Italy isn't doing bad at all, is it?

Speaking of Ethel reminds me of Chaplain Higuchi—he's with our battalion now and I see him often. We had services today, but I couldn't go. He's still the same Joe—one of the boys. . . . This afternoon we went to take a warm shower to a 2d Bn shower and clothes exchange unit. What a setup—it was so surprising to all of us. I've a new pair of fatigues on. And was the shower good—I can hope to tell you. And a damn good system, too. My hats are off to them. . . . Darling, thank them all for me, too, will you, all those people who were so kind to remember us on our fifth anniversary. I know you've done that, too, but I wanted to say it myself. In all our various moments, please remember that you are never far from my mind. A closing of the eyes conjures up your vision bustling around as you were wont to do. You're my dearest thing and remember that I shall love you always.

## 25 June 1944

Finally your letter of the 11th of June came with the good news that some of my letters had finally gotten to you. That makes me feel much better now, for up till now it had been all one sided with me the luckier. Now I don't feel so hoggish receiving all the time and not giving, although I did write. You certainly leave me in doubt as to your present location. For all I know, at this writing you may have gone off to Hunt to visit, you may be in Hunt packing or you may be in Minneapolis (no can't be, if I remember your reservation was for the 30th). At any rate, I'm writing to only one address—the one in Minny. By golly, my letters sure took their sweet time to get to you, didn't they? Maybe if you'd stay put, the mail call would be better. I heard from Rose yesterday, too. I must write her right after this.

They're showing us plenty of Italy and it's just as nice if not more so than when first I said so. As I write I'm sitting by a haystack in a paesano's yard, where we're bivouacked. Beautifully rustic here. You don't see anything like this in the states. Chaplain Higuchi just held services again, but I thought writing to you would be more profitable to both of us. Besides, religion is all in the heart and mind anyway. It's a beautiful valley here. On the far slope can be seen farm houses and on the top of one of the hills can be seen what looks like a monastery. One sees many of these buildings over the countryside. All the fruits are green yet, but there is a profusion of them. Figs, peaches, apricots, pears and apples all hanging so delectably green from the branches. But one taste is convincing enough.

We had a good time yesterday, cooking up chicken *hekka* [stew]. This poor farmer will find himself out of chickens 'ere long. Of course, we paid for two chickens, accidentally (?) killed. But, what we ate was actually four and in the pot went beans, carrots like tiny pencils, onions, green onions and spuds. A little job of foraging is all that was necessary. The farmer here was going nuts trying to keep his eyes on both his stock and garden at the same time. Our delicious *hekka* is good testament to his failure. You should have seen us about ten guys giving directions on cooking and preparing and arguing at the same time. That's natural with the facilities we had. The good chaplain joined forces with us last night and threw in his share a mess of onions that he'd gotten by his charm (?) from the female contingent of the house. That boy gets around as you are well aware. But, that *hekka* was really good—and did it hit the spot! Somehow or other three small rabbits have made their appearance here and Kozuma swears he's gonna carry his albino pet with him as a mascot in an empty shell casing. He thinks his fate lies in a mess of rabbit stew.

Don't speak so seriously of war—it's not as bad as all that. Over here we treat it lightly, but know its brutalities. Our sense of humor is always there even though the clouds of war are black and threatening. That is the one big way to morale. Once you let it get you down, you're not much good. In fact, from outward appearances, it seems hard to believe that there is a conflict going on from the horseplay and joking of the men. And thank God for that too. . . .

I'll say goodbye now until the next time. Take care of yourself, for I worry a little too about you. Here's a big kiss on its way to you. . . .

---

The 442nd fought twenty-eight days, from June 26 to July 24, 1944. They advanced fifty-five miles and were so successful that they liberated eleven towns and villages and two hills. Their progress allowed other elements of the Fifth Army to advance to the Arno River.
—DIANNE BRIDGMAN

---

MEDICAL DETACHMENT LOG

28 June 44, moved into Sassetto. Left to South of Castagneto, bivouacked here.

29 June 44, left vicinity of South Castagneto, Italia, and arrived in vicinity two miles North of Castagneto, Italia.

Left above area 29 June 44 and arrived at an assembly area, one mile South Bibbona, Italia, 30 June. Aid Station set up with usual activities surrounding each EM.

30 JUNE 1944

This must necessarily be short—time is very precious and this is a little God-sent time of rest for us battle-weary troops. Not that the war has stopped—but it's not here now. So it's been some time now since I last wrote—we've seen action now. It's very rugged—I won't bore you with the details. Unimportant, but warfare is tough and Sherman was right and more so. But, we're all okay and doing fine. Don't worry one whit about me. When I get back I'll tell you *all*

Second Battalion Medics, 1944. This was taken near Grosseto, Italy, on June 24, just before the 442nd went into action.

about it. By golly, I never did so much hiking in all my life and now I'm a candidate for a ditch digger.

Every once in awhile mail catches up with me, as now. But time is so dear. I'm just scribbling this now—they've hollered for outgoing mail already. Your last letter was dated the 13th.

Goddamn, gotta go now—be seeing you. I love you plenty. Will write soon as I can.

MEDICAL DETACHMENT LOG

Left vicinity 1 July 44 and arrived one mile NW Casale, Italia, as usual set up Aid Station in a deserted paesano's home.

2 July 44 left vicinity one mile NW Casale, Italia and arrived at assembly area in vicinity two and one half miles NE Cecina, Italia, left this area for NE Collemezzano, Italia 3 July 44.

## 3 JULY 1944

While waiting for orders here in this paesano's house where we have our aid station, I'm writing this to let you know how I'm doing. Just got through washing up, brushing my teeth, and shaving, a rare ritual, so I'm feeling pretty good. We're getting along fine. Of course, it has been a little tough. But we're going right along. We eat, sleep, and perform our functions whenever and wherever we can and when the time is available. We've had some casualties, naturally, and we've had business. That's not good, but in war it's no picnic. We get a certain amount of satisfaction in seeing dead Jerries or Tedeschi, as the Italians call them. As they go back, the Tedeschi ravage these homes by stealing their jewelry, killing livestock, wrecking houses. The paesanos here seem genuinely happy in seeing us move in—at least they help us out in many ways with water, vino, and material comforts. The Germans have themselves dug in pretty good as witness their deep slit trenches and dugouts and caves. (I'm a damn good digger myself now.)

There's plenty of vegetable gardens here as I told you before and in our movements we manage to pick up beans, onions, greens, potatoes, etc. and with the geese and chicken that somehow get into our hands we every once in a while manage darn good hekka and boy, does that help out. In fact, at the last place, the signora and signorinas of the household prepared the food under our careful supervision. Even Maj [Major] Buckley who happened to drop in ate his lion's share. But, at least, we give these Italians something for their goods and help. Not the Tedeschi, they just take.

As I sit here and write (bothered by the damn persistent flies) it seems hard to believe that there's a war going on, but I can assure you that there is. We all can vow on that.

Yesterday was Sunday (as if that made any difference) and the Chaplain is with us practically all the time, we had short services by him on the green grove where we happened to be at the time. I'm telling you that the saying "There are no atheists in foxholes" is the God's truth.

Some mail got to us yesterday with the rations jeep—none from you. One from Nay and one from Mariko. I hope I'll have the time to write them. In fact, I don't know how or when this letter is going out—but sooner or later it will get to you.

Darling, I'm gonna stop now, I'll write whenever I can. Don't worry too much about me—even though I know you will. My position is comparatively safe, you know.

MEDICAL DETACHMENT LOG

> 4 July 44, battle continued, no thought of a rest, five EM sent to 3d Bn Aid Station from Regtl [Regimental] Aid Station as litter bearers to vicinity of Molino A Ventoabbto. Moved into Molino A Ventoabbto, Italia and Regt'l Aid Station set up. Reports show casualties heavy in 2d and 3d Bns. Aid reserve litter bearers sent to evacuate wounded.

> 6, 7, 8 July 44, casualties passing thru 2d and 3d Bns rather heavy. Fighting taking place on Hill 140, also know as the "Suicide Hill". Aid Station taking care of PWs [prisoners of war] as well as allied casualties.

> 10 July 44, left Molino A Ventoabbto, (note—stayed at this locality longer than any other position) and arrived vicinity two miles SE Rosignano, Italia. Regtl Aid Station set up in an Italian home. Casualties going through 2d and 3d Bn Station rather light. 3d Bn Aid Station in reserve, usual activities performed.

10 JULY 1944
12:30 PM

Thought that I'd just drop in to say hello, since we found this hunk of stationery in this house into which we came just awhile ago. The going seems a trifle easier just at this moment and we've set up here temporarily. This house is pretty well beaten up from our shelling when the Tedeschi were cluttering the area. The padrone of the house just came crawling back from his cave where he'd hidden during the barrage and he's offered us vino and salami. These paesanos take a beating—houses torn, cattle killed, houses burned—all that kind of stuff. But, no matter how beat up, they always come back.

I wrote you last a couple of days ago while at a brief rest. Since then we've been hiking all over hell, so it seems. Up hill and down dale. Last night we shared a crowded rock cave in the side of a hill with twenty-two people all crowded out of their homes from war. I don't know how they ever got in the doggone place. Little ones and old ones, all in one tiny cave. They'd been in there thirteen days— four families. They won't be there too long now. Soon they'll be going home—that's more than I can say.

But it really was something for the books last night, staying in that crowded cave with all those Italians. We're getting pretty good at getting ourselves understood with vocal signs as well as motions. They're pretty darn glad to see us though. In fact, we even slept up in one of their beds outside under the trees—that was one luxury with a comforter over me, I can tell you. I slept like a log. Do you recall how we always used to say that who'd ever dream that we'd be doing this or that some certain time ago? Well, last night I had the same feeling.

Ah, but it's good to be relaxed for awhile. How I wish the lousy war was over so I could go back home to you. I try not to think much about it, but that's impossible, you know. But, if ever I wished and prayed it's for that—to be home again with you. Until the next time then, darling, all my love.

10 JULY 1944
4:30 PM

It's the same day as the blue sheets—dug this out somehow out of the paesano's cupboard—but later. The jeep finally caught up with us—the terrain is such that the jeep has to stay behind until the roads are more or less clear. Higgins (our driver—his real name is Higa—remember) was kind enough to hand me your letter of the 27th and gee, I was so happy to get it, so I thought that I'd write an addendum to the first.

We're still in the same house and on the pot now are two chickens and a mess of onions that always seem mysteriously to come into our awaiting hands. Naturally, being one of the cooks, I've tasted the fowl and it's darn good, and also welcome too. I hope there's enough, but I'm afraid not for somehow or other there always seems to be about a million people around when we cook something up.

Your letter had news of Mariko's baby—I had a thrill when I read of his coming. Golly, aren't you glad of it? Here we'd waited for what seemed such a long time and finally another newcomer. I'm so damn glad of it. They tacked on a good name, too, didn't they?

I know that you're in Minneapolis now. Hope that you aren't having too tough a time of it; I can imagine how tough it can be. Whenever the going gets rugged, darling, and you want to give up, remember that I'm over here going through something that's pretty rugged, something that's gotta be done so I can come back to you with the feeling that I've done something. When I got through reading your letter, I got so homesick my longing for you was overwhelming and I rather sat in a daze on the chair in that old Italian kitchen. But, good old Kuge (the other cook and butcher par excellence) restored me to reality with some facetious remark. Damn, but I miss you just the same.

By the way, did I ever tell you that I loved you darling? If not, consider that I have—never forget that even though I may still feel bashful about saying so.


12 JULY 1944

It was a beautiful day in Italy today, if only the war wouldn't intrude upon us in so forceful a manner. The more I see of Italy, the more I like it. But, it's another day another paesano's house. The last one I wrote to you had another house sandwiched between that house and this one. We just moved in bag and baggage on them this morning—if they didn't like it, it's just TS, but they are nice about the whole thing more or less terrified though they are from the harsh treatment given them by the Tedeschi. They just kicked these paesanos out where they had no food for three days while the Jerries used this house as an observation point—now two big (not big enough to suit me) red cross flags hang in front of the house and our station is set up. The Germans have been pretty good about respecting the medics—let's hope they preserve that respect.

MEDICAL DETACHMENT LOG

Left SE Rosignano, 13 July 44, arriving Pomaia.

14 July 44, left Pomaia, Italia, and arrived St Luce, Italia, set up Aid Station.

Left St Luce 15 July 44 and arrived at Pieve di St Luce, casualties clearing thru aid stations reported to be light.

15 JULY, 1944

I guess I've slighted you enough—two days now, I think. Time doesn't mean much out here, you know, we're constantly amazed at the date. Sunday is just like the rest—we don't even know what day of the week it is. The battle doesn't stop on the seventh day.

Hana, you don't know to what level I've fallen as far as scruples and hygiene is concerned. I know I must stink, and I know definitely that I'm dirty. I sleep practically anywhere, eat under any conditions, and live in a manner to make you shudder. I don't think you'd let me come to bed with my dirty feet. How you used to harp on my bath taking (or lack of it)—now a bath is something so far removed as to be ridiculous. At this stage, in fact, a Portuguese bath itself is a luxury. That reminds me, I must shave and brush my teeth today—no such thing as a daily habit. I eat with blood on my hands, flies buzzing around my food, and with vomit in my sight—it's a matter of getting used to it, I guess. In a war living is reduced to its essentials, though we try hard to hang on to whatever ideals we had before, at least what we call civilization.

Thank God, that the past two days since I last wrote have been comparatively peaceful. Of course, we're in a different casa again. We move practically daily—I'm glad we travel by jeeps, anyway, altho' if we hit the hills, it's back on our pedal extremities again and boy, that's not good. The paesanos were out in full force to greet us yesterday when we rolled in here—there's a mess of them here and yesterday evening we were like one big happy family when we brought up our coffee and bread and jam for a late snack. The things we have that are commonplace, to them are great novelties and although they want the stuff badly, they are well mannered enough not to ask, but we're pretty generous with our stuff, anyway. They gave us a couple of chickens, onions, and beans and did we cook up. We can't kick if we eat like that everyday—out in the open, in the cool of the evening, on plates, too. But, we get around. Usually, the medic station is the first one to hit the house, so we get the full force of their surprise and gratitude—when the later echelons come up, they're not so grateful and their gardens and orchards have been tampered with, not to mention the fowl and rabbits—so we're lucky on that score. Some of the boys slept upstairs, even, last night, on beds with mattresses. They cleared a couple of rooms for them and it must have been pretty good. I had to sleep on the aid station floor, as always in case of things happening.

MEDICAL DETACHMENT LOG

Leaving vicinity of Pieve di St Luce 17 July 44 and arrived one and one-half miles SW Lorenzana, Italia. 2d and 3d Bn Aid Station moved to vicinity St. Luciana, Italia.

## 17 JULY 1944

How are you today? Although it is a beautiful day here, I don't feel particularly happy for we had some—a few—casualties last night and this morning. You know how I'm always happiest when nobody comes here. I slept darn good last night, too—on a litter in the house. Didn't know a thing until they kicked me out of it at 6:30 this morning. For us, though, the past few days still are comparatively quiet although we've been pushing along in a persistent sort of way.

It seems that periodically I must tell you how beautiful the Italian countryside is. Gentle rolling hills and usually the houses sit on the tops of their ridges—just dotting this valley. Tiny towns and hamlets nestle along the higher hills, surrounded by greenery. It certainly presents a picturesque view.

I had a couple of letters from you yesterday. . . . It was so good to hear from you after the few days famine. I have no kick at all in your amazing regularity—something that I'd hoped for but didn't think was forthcoming. I don't know what I'd do without your words to help me. . . .

Saw Sammy yesterday for the first time in I don't know how long. Since his platoon isn't doing anything in their line, they've been drafted (as in our battalion) as litter bearers for the medics and he's traveling the countryside with the 3d Bn medics. He's fine and healthy, although his present job is tough physically, if and when they get busy. Same Sammy. Don's with the 2d Bn now, too. He's litter bearing, too, to make up shortage. It's rather tough on him with his bad back, but he seems to be alright. Dick is still way back with the Service Co [Company]—a nice job. Let's hope he stays there.

You know it's a revelation how during the stress of injury and front line tension, people's true character can show themselves. Lots of people with the big mouths have certainly proven despicable on occasions and some of the quiet boys have been marvels under fire. Too, when the injured come to the station for treatment, often as not it's the least injured that make the most noise, which makes us burned up at times. A man necessitating 500 cc of plasma will be uncomplaining while the man with diarrhea will moan and groan. Sometimes it's hard to see.

Chaplain Higuchi held a nice short service last evening in the house (a different house from where I wrote last—it'll be always this way, I guess). All of us crowded into the paesano's room and by dim lamplight we held worship. It helps—anything helps at times like these.

The 3d Bn boys were with us last night. Abe, Ogami and the rest. Had a nice talk with 'em for long time no see. They inquired about you and asked me to say hello to you. Our boys send hello, too. As does Munro Shintani, Haruo Kato, and the others I see at times.

Although you often wonder if I need anything, I can't think of a thing practical. It's wonderful how one manages to get along with a minimum of stuff, it's good, too.


MEDICAL DETACHMENT LOG

> Left Lorezana, Italia 18 July and arrived at St Regolo, set up aid station, ordered to move to a new location, leaving St Regolo and arrived Luciana, Italia. 2d and 3d Bns reports casualties light.

> Moved on to Nugola, Italia, 19 July 44 and arrived safely, setting up aid station and performing usual duties.


19 JULY 1944

It must be confusing to you the different modes of communication I send—one day V mail, the next Italian air mail, then some picked-up stationery. One has to do with whatever comes one's way. . . .

So far as the war goes—just a word. We've been pushing along steadily without letup. But there hasn't been much resistance. I don't like it—the quiet is a little too ominous, like the calm before the storm.

The days continue in their hot leisurely fashion. This Italian sun can get hot; now I know what they mean when they talk of sunny Italy. They can never say we didn't sweat through Italy.

We've run the gamut of houses since we embarked on our mission, from mansions to dinky shell-torn farmhouses. We've been jumping from place to place in such a fashion that we don't have too much of a chance to get really acquainted. Just a few hours ago we had supper cooked up by a paesano—previously, we'd stopped at a regal doctor's mansion atop a hill. The day before we lounged at a marquis' house—we had a swell setup there with a piano. Capt [Captain] Okonogi played the old tunes and I had a swell time singing them in the dark—reminiscent of the old days on picnics and at beaches. I sure wished we could have dragged it around with us, as if our trailer isn't loaded down as it is now. All filled with junk, just how we pick the stuff up is a mystery, but it seems to get more and more filled up daily. I guess we're all souvenir hunters at heart. The mess of stuff that's gonna be shipped back when we get our rest period should be terrific. I'm not doing too bad on that score either. Frankly, I don't know what you're going to do with some of the junk. But, I guess that's your worry. I'm still trying to get my hands on a Tedeschi helmet with SS or an eagle on it—getting particular now—there's all kinds of stuff lying around as the Jerries retreat, but I can't grab everything. We'll probably heave it all away sooner or later.

MEDICAL DETACHMENT LOG

20 July 44, nothing unusual happened.

20 JULY 1944

As any fool can plainly see, per Li'l Abner, this is being written with a different pen. It's one picked up by our driver, Higgins, from a Tedeschi. . . . You see, once in a while we have to treat German wounded and they're all so pitifully young looking, eighteen, nineteen, and twenty. We find Poles, Danes, etc, all mixed up with the

SS troops too, showing depletion of the elite soldiers. Most of them seem happy about being captured and we've taken many. No matter how much we may hate them, for they are the enemy and have killed our men, when they come in battered and pierced by our fire, I still feel that they should be treated and we do just as good a job as if on our own men, though naturally the latter must come first. These wounded Germans, some in gratitude for the care given them, readily give us their possessions and insignias. I only hope that the Tedeschi when they take our wounded and prisoners, do as humane a job as we. Some of these that were forced to become soldiers of the Reich, Poles, Danes, etc are very happy and quite talkative when taken. I suppose I would be happy, too, if I were in their shoes.

Just when I got through writing you yesterday, I received a letter of the 22d of June from you. Then a little later in the evening one came from you of the 2d and 3d of July. The latter letter was written from Minneapolis, the former while still in Hunt. Your letters of the time between have been received already. That shows how erratic the mail can be, as you commented on. This last one of the 3d finally bears the APO 464. I think that facilitates delivery, too. Of late, your letters have become better and better. Why, I don't know. Something a little more cheerful and uplifting seems to have crept in between the lines. You don't know just how much of a difference it can make. It warms my heart to visualize your doings as you depict them by pen. Last night in the quiet of the night, punctuated only by the boom of artillery, I could see the millions of stars and all the galaxies overhead, twinkling down on us as they must on you, thousands of miles away. It's a lonesome feeling. Golly, at times like those, I can sure get homesick. . . . So, finally those roses I sent from Oran got home. They certainly took their  time. . . .

I'm ashamed to say it, but I haven't written a single word to Franklin. But, Sammy says he wrote him and hasn't received an answer as yet. He's a lucky guy to have a furlough. And luckier yet that he isn't over here sweating it out on the line. I hope for his sake that he never has to come here to fight the Tedeschi. They're still good fighters, they know the terrain better, they're equipment is pretty good. Don't let the papers nor anyone else tell you different. It's just that we have more of everything to shove at them, the MAAF [Mediterranean Allied Air Forces] having done a darn good job of blasting their supply lines in the rear. I only wish at times that they'd come and help out the infantry directly by dive bombing and strafing. Gosh knows we see enough of them flying around. The Jerries seem to have no air resistance. The only planes we hear is at night when they throw one out for reconnaissance and we can hear it growling over head at night. But, it's nothing to even call a threat.

Although yesterday was not a rest period, it's been even better than that. We've been at this farmhouse now for two days. That's plenty good. The boys have just been holding the front line after all the travelling they did the two days before going through these small hills. The Tedeschi seem to have vanished temporarily, but only to entrench themselves more securely in some favorable position. That only makes it more difficult to dislodge them. But, at least, these last two days have been good. We've really rested. Chow came to us regularly and a rare casualty now and then. The paesanos here are just as starved as any place else. When the mess jeep and trailer pull up, they hang around for handouts. Since we're the last group in the Hqs Co to feed—the cooks give them all the leftovers and you should see the smiles on their faces when they bring their plates and pans up for filling. But, they work for it, too, cause we make 'em wash all our mess gear and cook pots and pans. But, that's small work enough to fill up their starved bellies. Then, too, we're always giving them something, candies, cigarettes, bread, coffee, sugar, etc. No wonder they're so glad to see us, after the months of slow starvation at the Nazis' hands.

Wonders of wonders, yesterday we got hold of some immature cantaloupes—but boy were they good. Knowing how crazy you were about them "a la mode", I couldn't help but think of you then. We try to get all the fruits we can, but everything is still green yet, but that doesn't stop us. Figs, peaches, pears, apples—all too green yet, but very welcome in their refreshing tartness. Someday, we're going to get someplace where all the fruits are ripe for the plucking. Will we be happy then!

End of the page already, darling; if only I could tell you these things myself and see and hear you again, then will I feel well and whole once more.

MEDICAL DETACHMENT LOG

21 July 44 Nugola, Italia.

2d Bn Aid Station moved to new position Colle Salvetti, Italia, 20 July 44. 3d Bn Aid Station remained in same area. Casualties clearing through Regtl Aid and Bn Aid Stations very light.

21 July 44 awaiting orders to proceed to Regimental Rest Area vicinity of Colle Salvetti, Italia.

22 July 44, pulled out of Nugola, Italia. Regtl and 3d Bn Aid Stations for the first time during this phase met up in the same building. Casualties clearing thru the aid stations very light, in fact none to speak of.

22 JULY 1944

I guess I wrote you a couple of days ago, I can't remember, time is such a fleeting thing. I'm happy to say that it seems the outfit is finally in a rest period, that is a rest period. For the first time since we moved in, the chance has come where we can have some sort of relaxation. We were relieved this morning and we've pulled back just a little ways, but far enough to ignore the battlefront for a little while anyway.

But let me give you more of the story in a chronological detail. After I wrote you we shoved ahead again a little further into a swell mansion. On the face of the hill looking toward the flat land we had more or less a grandstand view of the battle lines. As before it had been rather quiet, the Tedeschi having mined quite heavily the road and blown up all the bridges, making vehicular traffic a standstill. Our artillery certainly does a swell job, as we could see through our glasses. I guess it's a good thing we're on the right side.

We stayed there a couple of nights and this AM pulled out when all our companies had been relieved. All the time we'd been talking of relief, and rumors had been flying about this and that and now, it seems, we're finally getting a rest of sorts. Boy, it's a good feeling. (The shout that just went up was for the field movie we'll see tonight *Madame Curie*—golly, I wonder what it'll feel like to see a flicker again). So now, we're at this paesano's place and it's peaceful here except for some dumb clucks of artillery had to locate right behind us and let go a terrific crash every once in a great while. I hope they pull out soon. It's a nice place we're at—nice and green with fruit trees all around and vineyards on the sides of the hills. We've combed the near area for fruit already and robbed the trees of immature plums and pears. Kozuma and Iijima went across the road and brought back a load of corn and that went into the pot. It was good—and you know how I like corn. Not as good as home, but still corn.

There's a well here—the kind you throw a bucket into and haul up by hand. It's only for washing. Well, after we got through getting the jeep and trailer packed up properly and setting the station up, I stripped down to my birthday suit and took a long-awaited bath or a reasonable facsimile. The cold water was invigorating and though granting not as cleansing as a *Nihon furo*, [Japanese bath] at least, it was as satisfying as one. I'm sorry to say that your husband has lost all the modesty he ever had, performing his ablutions in plain view of the signora and signorina, as if they cared anyhow. I was going around here in just my towel while my underwear dried. Now if only I could get my ODs exchanged—rumor has it that we go to the mobile shower and exchange unit tomorrow. Hope that's true.

You'll find a mess of clippings from the *Stars and Stripes*—a GI daily that we get. It's a pretty good sheet. I've enclosed the cuts on the Fifth Army activities. If you'll follow the chronological order, you'll get a pretty fair overall idea of how we operated. The paper is very good and I'm sorry it can't be sent home—the Saturday copy can, but somehow today's was lousy—I guess all Saturday copies are, so I just clipped one column out. There are a few other articles, too, plus a cut from *Yank* that made us laugh. I'm going to try and keep a daily clipping and send it home. . . .

You don't mind if I go now? The show starts soon, the sun having gone down. I'll write tomorrow and tell you how good I slept or whether I dreamt of you. I hope so.

MEDICAL DETACHMENT LOG

24 July 44, finally moving into Divisional Rest Area, leaving E Colle Salvetti, Italia and arrived Vada, Italia. At the conclusion of this combat period the following communications are quoted.

Letter from Maj Gen Charles L. Bolte, Commanding General 34th Division, letter dated 25 July 44.

*Although your command has been attached to this division for only a short time it was during this period that your officers and enlisted men received their baptism of fire. Their enthusiasm and fighting spirit exceeded expectations; the Division has accepted them unreservedly and consider them an integral part of the Division. In token of this acceptance and the esteem in which your officers and men are held, there is presented to you the shoulder patch of the 34th Infantry Division for all of the officers and men of the 442d Infantry, 522d Field Artillery Battalion, 232d Engr [Engineer] Co and the 206th Army Band.*

Memorandum from Commanding Officer, 442d RCT dated 26 July 44.

*Upon completion of our first tour of combat duty, I believe it is appropriate to relate to all of you some of the accomplish-*

*ments of the unit. You have been of material assistance in driving the enemy back more than fifty miles. During this action you have never taken a backward step. You have stood firm under heavy shell and mortar fire and have beaten off enemy counter-attack. You have captured and killed many Germans, destroyed and captured much enemy material which, in reality, is our mission in war. On the last day of combat the division commander stated to me, "Your unit has done a splendid job" and yesterday we were privileged to wear the insignia of the division, a division whose long, successful combat record is surpassed by no other division. We have lost several of our comrades in combat, we mourn their loss and honor their memory. For the rest of us there is the work of tomorrow.*

*I am proud of you and am honored to be your commander.*

24 July 1944—Rest period begun. All personnel enjoyed hot showers and an exchange of clothing. Vehicles were cleaned and overhauled. Duffle bags came out of storage. Athletics and swimming and Special Service recreational program begun.

## 24 July 1944

Sorry I didn't write yesterday as I'd promised, but the lazybone attitude got me and I'm a day late, but I'm forgiven, aren't I? Right after I finished the letter, Kuge and I took off across the road and up the other hill toward the house against whose wall the screen had been set up. It was a rather horrible exhibition, all in all. We waited half an hour for night to fall (around ten) and then, they couldn't get the apparatus to function properly—no sound. So they had to horse around a good half hour before they could get it going. All in all, they had five reels and each time they put a new reel on it was the same thing all over again. With the night getting colder, the wind blowing dust in our faces, and us sitting on the gravelly ground, you can imagine that it can be quite a detraction from the enjoyment of a film such as *Madame Curie*—it must have been a good film in the theatre—to us out there, well, less than half were there at the end. Then, of course, the artillery had to start booming right behind us periodically, as if the sound system wasn't bad enough. Walter Pidgeon mouthing like a bullfrog and Greer Garson barely audible to our straining ears. Quite a disappointment, but the good intentions were there. Somehow, it all seemed queer to sit there watching a movie while just a few miles forward men killed and were being killed.

Yesterday, we just horsed around and did nothing but relax and get our stuff more or less in order. By the way, I've never told you of all the Italian signorinas we've met in our wanderings, have I? I can tell that we've seen all sizes and shapes, some beautiful; some ugly; some fat, some thin; some coarse and some refined—in words, all types. Knowing GIs as you must know by now, naturally, we make quite a hubbub of them and quite a fuss over them. Language is quite a barrier between us. Looking at them, they seem no different from our high school kids. On the main, they are reserved and wary, but some speak with surprising poise and at ease. We see both blondes and brunettes. I get a big kick at the way some of the boys make a play for the signorinas, as if they're gonna get anywhere. In the cities one may find looseness in the morals, I suppose, but these rurafied gals are another story. Some of them are very nice in every sense of the word. This last place I wrote from had one girl—Fedora—a very nice girl, she did our washing for us and wasn't non-communicative. Then, later on in the day when we were waiting to go to our new area, two of her girlfriends came over—forgot their names now, but they were friendly, too and sang songs and the guys gathered 'round for the usual bantering. I guess they get just as much a kick out of us as we do out of them.

Just exactly what is going on with us, I don't know, but we pulled out of the last area yesterday evening and came back some more miles to a place that's really safe and removed from the front, presumably for rest. At any rate, we're going on a schedule again starting tomorrow. Seems strange to have reveille again and a training schedule. I wonder how the boys will make out at this. But, I hear nobody is kicking although these "garrison" restraints can be quite irksome. Although the war is only about two weeks removed from actual combat, the attitudes of these people are radically different from those whom we have encountered. While those whom we saw previously were those who first saw American soldiers in us and were joyous in their liberation from the Tedeschi, these people now far behind have been so successively enveloped by echelons of Americans in a rather scourgelike manner that their attitude is one of "leave us alone." I guess we can't blame them, but to us when we pulled in last night, it made us sore, fresh from the front lines where we'd seen our boys die for the hunk of land and where we'd been used to cordiality, at least. So, in some respects, the front isn't so bad, where the people will greet us with wine and welcome and we don't have to take any dirt so far as rank goes. And, on top of that, the place here is in itself a lousy place for accommodations, compared to what we've been into. But, I don't think you'll find many who'd change even for all that. Just how long we'll be here nor what we'll do is speculation. In the meantime, I'm expecting to get relaxation and catch up on a lot of stuff. . . .

I just went to inspect my home for tonight and till as long as we stay here. The Germans have a swell three-man dugout in the courtyard here. Marvelous place—wooden bunks and shelves and even, miracles, an electric light socket. Momoda, Kuge and I should be snug during our stay. . . . Hana, did you ever eat fresh figs before? Well, all the Hawaiian lads can't believe me when I tell them of my first bite into that fruit. They grow in great abundance here and whenever I can, I eat my fill of them—they're delicious, soft and sweet, much better than the dried stuff that I'd only heretofore known. But, I suspect that I get just as much enjoyment out of climbing the trees and picking 'em as eating the blamed things. You can't stop once you start.

Say, I haven't heard from you for about five days now. Funny, I'm getting lonesome for a letter from you. How do you account for it?

MEDICAL DETACHMENT LOG

27 July 44 at an impressive ceremony, the 100th Infantry Battalion was presented with the Distinguished Unit Citation Streamers by Lt Gen Mark Clark, Commanding General Fifth Army. The General affixed the blue streamers to the colors and guidons of the 100th, and decorated the battalion commander and color bearers with the Distinguished Unit Citation Badge, which will be worn by all members of the 1st Bn.

The 442d was also commended by General Clark for its part in the recent fighting. Major General Bolte, Division Commander accompanied General Clark.

On 28 July 44—at another ceremony, the 2d Bn formed part of the Guard of Honor for King George VI of England at Cocina. The King personally felicitated the members of the battalion who had earned the purple heart and presented the Silver Star, for Gallantry in Action to four EM of this organization, out of the four, Medical Detachment had its representative, Pvt Yeichi Furuno.

27 JULY 1944

Here we sit, Momoda and I, in the flickering light of candles in the dugout, writing our respective letters. It's 10:10 PM now and chow is at 6:00 AM tomorrow. Since the morrow promises to be busy and I won't have much of a chance to write, I have to scribble tonight. . . .

Your speaking of the Sakais, reminds me that I see kid brother Sammy quite often. He's in E Co—2d Bn. He's fine. . . .

It has been a very nice day today, all told. At least the afternoon and evening were delightfully short. This morning Gen [censored] presented a citation to the 100th for achievement at Sasseto and

Belvedere and we were all in formation paying our respects. We got a faraway glimpse of him. He spoke over the mike while we sweated under the hot Italian sun in our ODs. He also welcomed the 442d and complimented us on our activities on the line. Then more stuff on how proud the division was of us. The Fifth Army and then America itself. But, it made us feel good, just the same. The long-lost band whom we hadn't seen in ages was up from somewhere and played their usual pieces. Saw Chip banging away on those silver bars. The 206th band's been playing in hospital behind the lines and entertaining in general. They've a good deal. They also passed out a mess of DFCs [Distinguished Flying Cross]. Tomorrow, there's a hullabaloo about [censored] visiting the front. The 2d Bn is going to be guard of honor. You know how I love that kind of stuff; I'm trying to get out on pass tomorrow. I think so; I can't see standing and waiting around for some Joe to review us even if it is the [censored]. Besides when one is in the ranks, you can't get to see anything anyway. It's much better to watch from the sidelines.

In the heat of the day, today, Capt Ushiro decided to go swimming so Mukai, he and I (we'd had a "dry run" on the review tomorrow in the noonday sun) went down to the beach for a swim. The water's warm and calm enough, the beach sandy. We swam out to some landing barges and played around there for awhile, came back and basked in the sun. Golly, it was a good feeling to have the warm rays hit the body and fill the tired muscles with their warmth and relax and know that we can relax. There'd been talk of a Red Cross here so off we went in the jeep and located it in a grove of cypress trees. But coffee and doughnuts weren't available, but on the way back I caught sight of a library and hauled out some "pocket books" so I don't lack for reading material either. And you know how I love to read. Of course, I'd take letters any day to read.

Then, today, too we had rice for dinner with our steak. Yes, actually *gohan* [rice]. Oh, it was so good. The kitchen crew was on the ball and dug it out of some paesano's place. It hit a sorely needed spot and I for one, was very appreciative. Some of the boys have been getting fish and lobsters from some of the fishermen around here. We're trying to get our hands on some. Golly, would that fit the bill. We're wondering whether to *shioyaki* [salt] it or fry it in flour. Anyway it's cooked, it'll be devoured, I know.

Capt Okonogi got chummy with the paesanos of our new house and he managed to arrange for them to cook us an Italian supper. We gave them a mess of our canned rations and the time was set for 8:oo tonight. By golly, they did darn good. We trooped upstairs to large tables covered with linen and we had silverware and plates, even. The first course was spaghetti (the first I've seen and good too). Then some chicken and finally meatballs. Of course, bread and wine was being eaten and drunk all through the meal. We were all surprised at the whole layout and were gratified that it had turned out so good. We'll have to treat them a little better now.

Out here money is more or less like paper. Since it is made only for the things that it can buy and we can't buy anything, it tends to depreciate in our eyes. . . .

They, [the Army] being very considerate of us, supply some form of entertainment every night. Tonight they had a movie *Her Primitive Man*—that thing seems to have followed us around from the states— 3d place they've shown it to us. Didn't go. Isaac Sijima, Kazu's brother-in-law, just came back from it—the projector was on the blink again. That being one healthy reason I don't care to go to the movies. The two previous nights they had a divisional swingfest (good, they tell me) then last night a stage production for [censored] *Eggs in Your Beer* that was really a killer. Missed both of them. The latter production was staged by wounded soldiers, all original music and acts. The boys were all in praise of their good [censored].

You must be in the throes of studying now at business college. [Hana briefly attended business college in Minneapolis.] Just don't bust a blood vessel, will you? I wish I could be there to help you in the tap-tap-tapping on the keyboard. In other words, I just wish I could be there, period.

MEDICAL DETACHMENT LOG

> 30 July 44 first Sunday since returning from the front lines, each
> battalion had a memorial service for our comrades, mourning their
> deaths and honoring their memory, dedicating ourselves to carry
> on their work here and forever.

## 30 JULY 1944

Today was Sunday, and the regiment held memorial services for those
that passed into the great beyond. I didn't go because I knew that
I'd be depressed, but I would hear our band playing and I was mind-
ful of the solemnity of the occasion. One cannot say that this outfit
hasn't seen action, if he sees the flag with the stars on it. . . .

Incidentally, the army's putting on a pretty good publicity drive
for us. We've seen clippings on activities and with anecdotes and stories. Have you seen any of them? They're getting nationwide release.
We're getting plenty of pictures taken, too, it seems. It makes me feel
good that we're getting credit for something.

It's 11 o'clock now and the boys are having a bull session on our
frontline experiences. We never seem to run out of those. Stories get
hashed and rehashed all the time, but they're all interesting—just
how accurate the stories are is problematical, but it's good listening
and talking about them. That's the least of our privilege. So, I'm
writing and throwing my two cents worth in at the same time. . . .

I miss you very much, darling, now that relaxation from battle tension has set in to give a guy time to dream and think of a few things,
my thoughts revert to you. The constant dream and hope of all of us
is to get this war over with and to go home to our loved ones.

MEDICAL DETACHMENT LOG

> 1 Aug 44 training resumed.

> 4 Aug 44 passes to Rome continued.

## 5 August 1944

As I wrote you yesterday—here we are in this new rest area. We pulled in yesterday morning. It's just a scant distance away, but what a difference. The air is freer, there's a sense of relaxation here in this cypress grove (beautiful trees, too) by the blue of the sparkling sea. Pyramidal tents are set up under the overhanging boughs and inside is strewn hay. We medics manage nicely on our litters. With a canopy of mosquito net, just as royalty have, over my bed, I feel that I can relax and dream here in a kingly fashion. And we're all doing that— I pulled CQ yesterday, so I won't draw that from now on, just pure relaxation and my sweet time stares at me dreamily in the face and that prospect is good, believe me. The uniform specified in this area is "anything decent!" That goes to show the spirit that rules this place. I wandered over the area with Ike Iijima, Mayme's brother, Kazu's brother-in-law, and found out all about facilities. Took some more books out of the library—pocket books they all are. Went to the ARC and had doughnuts and coffee—they've three live American Red Cross workers—female, I mean—it's good to see them. Somehow they're different—breezier, more unaffected, more natural— friendly, too, for they know how the men are. The men all respect them, too. But, the revelation was in the radio I saw in one of the rooms. I sat down and just listened in sheer ecstasy to the music over the ether from Count Basie to Rachmaninoff, Tommy Dorsey to Massinet—I absorbed it all, drenching myself into a reverie until past lunchtime. I thought of our radio—how I would love to listen to its beautiful tones again. To you the radio is a commonplace thing—to us, it's a wondrous thing that is rarely heard, and appreciated when heard. Music is a wondrous thing; its greatest thing is its universality. I got all sorts of radio stations—England, Algiers, US, even Axis Sally, somewhere we don't know—she has a darn good program of popular music, too. It was fun to twist the dials and have response at the flick of the fingers. I'm going back again and soon to get some more dosage.

9 Aug 44. Battle honors for participation in the Italian Campaign
were awarded to the 442d Infantry. This award entitles the regiment
to carry a battle streamer on the regimental colors and individuals to
wear a bronze star on the service ribbons for the European-African-
Middle Eastern Theater of Operations.

10 Aug 44—100th Infantry Bn (Sp) redesignated as the 100th
Infantry 442d Infantry Regiment, attaching 100th Battalion Medics,
increasing our strength by forty-two EMs and three officers.

## 11 AUGUST 1944

Before I forget, I'm sending you a booklet of Bill Mauldin's cartoons.
You recall that I sent you a couple of his works before. When Tsuka
went down to Rome he brought some back and I grabbed one. These
cartoons are really funny to us for they really strike home. These soldiers have their counterparts in the infantryman who's been on the
lines. Maybe, or I should say probably, a lot of these will have no
meaning, but we can recall in them our own experiences, so we can
easily see the humor of it. I hope you enjoy it.

I've disappointing news, too. I wrote you and told you once of
a ten dollars combat infantry pay raise. Well, the special order for us
medics, the chaplains, too, was rescinded and we won't be getting
either the badge or the pay. It seems some silly goddamned rule
involves our not carrying arms. It's griping to know that some of
these men who have not even seen the front lines will get the raise
and badge because they carry a rifle while us poor medics who have
been under combat fire are denied it. What irony that is when our
battalion section had so many casualties—our men in the hospital
is testimony to whether we know action or not. And to make things
even worse, guys back in the states get a raise and expect infantrymen's badge—imagine, back in the states—while we overseas and
who have seen action get absolutely nothing. We're all pretty damn

sore about it. The badge is an honor in itself, but when I think of what that extra ten dollars mean to you. I hope that something can be done about it to adjust this injustice, especially to the men some of whom may get decorations for gallantry under fire. What a laugh, but, unhappily the joke's on us and that's not so good.

The movie tonight is *The Song of Bernadette*. We've waited a heck of a long time for it and been disappointed a couple of times by substitution. I hope this is really it this time. The guys all left now for it—and I think I'll follow suit.

MEDICAL DETACHMENT LOG

15 Aug 44 442d Infantry detached from 34th Division.

17 Aug 44 442d RCT (less 100th Bn) attached to 88th Division effective 17 Aug 44.

17 AUGUST 1944

So the 442d is getting a lot of publicity—we'd been told that would be so. That's good, but at what cost. You wrote me of Bako, Bill, Nakamura, and George Sawada. These are only our friends—there are many more. About three days ago a special convoy took relations and friends to a bare new plot of ground where many of our boys lie. Just a little square hunk of ground enclosed by white barbed wire shining brown in the hot sun. There were rows and rows of mounds, seeming naked in their newness. But, a few months will see the green sod covering the graves and white crosses will dot that acre. It was with mingled feeling that we went out there and knelt and prayed for these men who had been our brothers, relations and friends. It's still hard to believe that these whom we had known so alive and eager now lie underneath that brown Italian soil never to see the sun again. Bako, Sawada, and Nakamura are there—I'm glad I went to see them; I know that their folks and wives will be glad that someone that knew them offered prayers for them. We came away depressed, but with a little more ease of mind. . . .

Just where you got the erroneous impression of the Yanagimachis I don't know; they're hale and hearty so far as I know, at least when you wrote that letter. You see, even if we know definitely of the death of friends we may not say anything about it, until the next of kin has been notified. Often these deaths are hard to ignore just like that. Brothers may not tell their fathers of the son's death until that cold telegram comes. "The War Deartment regrets. . . ." What a blow that must be to the receiver—just those words and nothing else of how, where, nor why. The chaplains write letters to the next of kin to soften the sorrow if that's possible.

I didn't mean to be so morbid in this letter—but you just can't ignore the casualties of war. Before this started I was making excuses about my not writing. It has been hot the last few days taking the starch out of all of us. But, the main reason I didn't write was because four of us took a little trip—overnight, in fact, to a town some miles distant. We started out as usual all loaded up and by prodigious use of our thumbs we wended our way on all sorts of vehicles from the lovely jeep to the huge two and a half ton truck. When we got to this famous town some three hours later (good time considering) we had a devil of a time finding a room to sleep and ended up being guests of the British MPs [Military Police] legitimately, of course. They gave us a room and blankets to spread on the floor. The English aren't overly friendly with the Americans. We wandered through the town and saw what there was to see. I've many cards, but for some strange reason I can't send them yet. If I could, then you'd know where I'd been and all the beautiful things I've seen.

## Medical Detachment Log

Lt Gen Mark W. Clark has brought to the attention of Fifth Army Personnel the address by Prime Minister Churchill quoted below. It was delivered during a visit by the Prime Minister to the 34th Infantry Division on 19 August 1944:

> General Mark Clark, General Rolte, officers and men of the 34th United States Infantry Division; officers and men of the Brazilian Expeditionary Force; Officers and men of the United States Negro troops; Americans of Japanese ancestry and your American officers;
>
> I greet you here this morning with feelings of pride that the honor should have fallen to me to inspect these units of the Fifth Army, one of the great armies of the United Nations, which are everywhere advancing victoriously upon the foe.
>
> The 34th US Division was first, or among the very first of all the United States troops to leave the new world and carry by their sacrifices and their valor the precious blessing of freedom and justice to the lands enslaved by Hitler's tyranny. That tyranny we shall break. We shall shatter the sources from which its evil powers are derived, which will be so obliterated and blasted that for many hundreds of years none will dare to do the like again. . . .
>
> I wish you—all of you—all the units represented here and the Brazilians—I wish all of you—all good fortune. I wish you God speed; may God bless you all.

...................................................................................................................................

Near Vada, Italy, the 442nd rested and trained. Then they were sent to the front, to an area along the Arno River. Three battalions were assigned to patrol the area and to protect night raiding parties. This activity gave the Germans the impression of great strength and screened major troop movements on the front. —DIANNE BRIDGMAN

...................................................................................................................................

## Medical Detachment Log

Left vicinity Giogoli, Italia, 21 Aug 44 and arriving vicinity of Scandicci, Italia concluding our first phase, and beginning of our second.

21 Aug 44—Scandicci, Italia, the Combat Team including the Medics moved up into the lines, relieving elements of the First British Division (8th Army) and took over the southern area of the Arno River.

Casualties cleared thru the battalion and regimental aid stations very light on 22 Aug 44. Harassing artillery throughout the day.

## 22 August 1944

We're in there again, moving up in the regular manner, but our positions aren't so hazardous. The cannons boom day and night, not constantly, but intermittently and they drop in the vicinity once in a while in retaliation, too. We've had some casualties, too, already. But the whole situation is very quiet. I hope we won't be moving around too much. The more we travel, the less comforts we can get. But, we're well situated in a house—pulled in at night. The paesanos are friendly enough here. Incidentally, the women in the area are noted for their beauty and such and there's a farmer's daughter here, too. Naturally, that doesn't bother me at all. But, all us GIs like to give the girls a whistle and holler at 'em along the road. We're right at home now—writing letters on the paesano's dinner table. . . .

This place is fertile and flat and there are orchards and gardens all around us. There have been complaints already of GIs walking off with fruits and vegetables. I just wonder now who could do such unholy acts. Incidentally, I had green peppers and onions for breakfast. Very good, too. Somehow, we must manage to get some eggplants we saw hanging on the bushes even if we have to barter or buy 'em. In fact, the law's been laid down about annexing things and the 442d loves to enhance their menu in their own little way. And we've already had plenty of peaches and pears.

Activity along the front line is quiet and it's more an artillery and mortar duel. That's okay with us. We've had more Italian patients than anything else—they come in for all kinds of treatment from sprained ankles to cuts on the head, falling from their ever-present bicycles. When the beautiful signorine come in everybody falls over each other to take care of 'em. What a kick that is. No fooling the uproar around a signorina is really something. That's about all we can do, anyway, raise a fuss over them.

## MEDICAL DETACHMENT LOG

An incident of note occurred on 23 Aug 44: Under the flag of truce, three aid men from the 3d Battalion Section advanced toward the enemy line, situated on the proximal bank of Arno River in the vicinity of Florence, Italia, to treat casualties of an M Company patrol which came under intense enemy fire consisting of machine gun and mortar barrage. About 150 yards from the enemy line they found two wounded soldiers to whom they rendered first aid, while they were being covered by our own and German riflemen. Following this the trio having been informed that a Lt was last seen with wounds on his leg, continued toward the enemy line in search of him. Under the protection of the Red Cross flag, these men encountered enemies in their slit trenches some forty yards from the front line. One of them waved a white handkerchief and as the trio went forward, three German soldiers came out to meet them. Under the truce these six shook hands and exchanged souvenirs. From these German soldiers they learned that the Lt was a prisoner and had been taken back to the enemy's aid station for treatment. After seeing that our wounded men were evacuated by litter squads, our three aid men returned safely to our lines.

On the following day, 24 Aug 44, a Staff Sergeant led a group of twelve men and returned to the previous day's scene of action, to retrieve two fatally wounded soldiers and again met a German party under the Geneva Flag. Once again handshakes, cigarettes and words were exchanged. One of the Germans spoke a little of our language. Under the truce which lasted about ten minutes the S/Sgt and his group safely returned with the two dead soldiers. Exchange of rifle, machine gun, mortar and artillery shell continued immediately afterwards.

## 23 AUGUST 1944

Life here goes so smoothly and on the quiet side, so much so that it can be boring at times. Although we do get shelled at intervals and sometimes they can get close enough to disturb our slumber as they did last night. It's a static sort of situation with both sides sending out feelers and throwing artillery and mortars. Casualties have been few and far between, but the way Italian paesanos flock in here for treatment is really something—I know I was CQ yesterday and had to take care of a mess of 'em. We're glad at any rate that it's not our men that we have to treat. There are paesanos all over this place, trying to keep up their way of life in these hectic times—no wonder so many of them get hurt carrying on as usual. Traffic is heavy around here, too, because so many folks from the town come out to this area for food—they're more or less starving there, it seems. Plenty of them come around here begging for our food and rations. You see in this situation we have been chowing in "10 in 1" style—cooking the stuff ourselves, aided and abetted of course with vegetables here and there. We get ourselves pretty good meals, too. You recall I told you last time of the succulent eggplants I saw. Well, I bartered for some yesterday and *tsukerued* [pickled] it. The manner was rather doubtful, but the product we had for lunch today wasn't bad at all. If only we had some rice for that—the Capt got himself a padre for a friend and he's promised to get us some rice—oh, happy day! We sure miss our rice. You see, besides our regular aid station group we now have two litter bearer squads from the collecting co attached to us and we all eat and cook together, making a sizeable group. We all pitch in and have a hand in the preparing. As for the aftermath, the young Italians of this house take care of the KP [kitchen police] in very good fashion in return for the food we've left over. For both it's a good deal all the way around.

The paesanos have become more friendly and even now one signorina (age sixteen) is singing to us some songs and we carry on conversation in our inadequate way with all of them. In our travels we find out more and more of these Italians. They're as human as any of us and fun loving and love to sing, too. To them, I guess us Americans must seem a screwball lot—can't blame them, too. We joke with them in all sorts of outrageous manners—but, it's all in good fun. I'm going to try and learn one Tedeschi song, "Lili Marlene" that these romantic Jerries have been singing probably to these signorinas. It has a nice lilting tune. If we get those three bottles of cognac we're gonna get from a paesano tomorrow AM then we really will sing up. The Chaplain (yep, he's still with us) borrowed a ukelele and we're trying to get a guitar from the collecting company. We could stand some singing.

I haven't had mail from you for quite a while now. They're accumulating somewhere and probably catch up with us soon.

MEDICAL DETACHMENT LOG

> 25 Aug 44—the Regtl Aid Station and its surrounding area were heavily shelled by enemy artillery. Shelling continued throughout the day. Casualties clearing thru aid stations very light, usual duties performed.

25 AUGUST 1944

The Tedeschi are still throwing them all around, but we're giving them back fivefold so that's a lot better. The best feature of all is the lack of casualties—both sides are pretty well dug in and even though when dusk comes on, the heavier barrage begins, the chances of getting hit aren't too great. As for us, we can hear the thunder of both artilleries and the shells whistling overhead—sometimes going and some coming. At nights, the flashes from our guns illuminate the clear night like lightning. After the flash comes the report and then finally, the explosion of the shell landing. While seated out by the road one day, we counted fifty-seven Jerry shells land one right after the other in one area, and not too far away either from the sounds. And they're not mere 88s [88-millimeter artillery] they're heaving nowadays, it's 170s [170-millimeter mortars] and 270s [270-millimeter mortars] and these babies ain't midgets. They can certainly make a loud crack. The people around here are adjusted to it now and go about their daily tasks, but with the ears open, just as we do. So although we are all under more or less of a tension, still life here is practically normal, if we choose to ignore the shells. The trouble is that sometimes they forcibly impress themselves upon us. Remember that the last time I told you about the songfest scheduled that night. Well, we had a nice sing and so we did again last night. We got hold of some wine last night, one bottle that was gone in fifteen minutes, but it helped things along. The wine was quite vile. I wonder where they hide the good stuff. Whenever you ask them they always say "Tedeschi, tutte portale via" meaning the Jerries took it all away. It's so that it's almost a song with the paesanos when you ask them for anything. We even parody it in a song—very funny.

The guy showed up with a bottle of Marsala and one of Chianti (both wines) yesterday AM but when we tried to bargain, he wanted some butter, milk and six packs of cigarettes. He said the others would give him as much; we laughed at him and sent him on his way. These Italians, give them an inch and they want a foot. Sometimes, you feel sorry for them in their genuine plight, but more often they're too damn smart for their own good.

I suppose you've been reading about the progress of our forces in France, both in the north and south. It does our heart good to read of our advances and how Paris itself is in our hands. I only hope it doesn't lull us, both here and back at home, into a false confidence as to the quick end of this war. I think there's a lot of fight left in the Tedeschi, although I fervently hope that's not so.

I've been trying to strum the ukulele. I think I can play along to "Manuela Boy" and "May Day is Lei Day in Hawaii", but somehow or other when I play, the chords don't seem to fit. You know how big and clumsy my hands are—can't hit the strings and strum just so.

At nights, often, as I lie on my litter, I can see the stars (between the flashes). I wonder where you are, what you are doing. Even though I don't know, I always imagine that you're studying now, you're washing dishes now, and now you're lying on your bed, too, possibly thinking of me. At times like these I'm glad that even war can never take that away from me.

## 26 AUGUST 1944

And now dear Hana is learning about business. Don't be too naive about deals—it's essentially a crooked world and may the best man win. Not compatible, I know, with your ideas and mine, but it can certainly give one a broader viewpoint on human nature.

Took a nice shower yesterday—a Portuguese bath, I should say. Higgins, Mukai, and I hauled water up the well behind the house in five gallon cans and behind the truck washed up. It wasn't my innate modesty, but rather that I wanted to spare the signorine a view of my manly physique. Yes, yes! But the bath was very good and I've on a clean change of underwear. And, of course, Loretta insisted on washing my dirty ones—oh, didn't I mention her before, I don't see how I could have forgotten. Well, there's she, Silvana, and Antoinetta here. Pretty names, aren't they? We get a lot of fun with them anyway. Very friendly and voluble, too, in their own inimitable way. Too bad that there's no cause for worry, just the prerogative of the male eye wandering.

The status quo of the situation is unaltered as yet. The same shelling goes on either way, the paesanos still stream in for treatment, and time lies heavy, but not unpleasantly, on our hands.

The old Red Bull Division, 34th, has a quaint craze for wearing silk neckerchiefs. Everybody from the Colonel down to the lowly private sport them and we've taken the fad on wholeheartedly. All of the colors of the rainbow are represented—all either silk or rayon. The GIs just go around finding them and they do. I got myself a black silk crepe with dotted white flowerwork on it. Momoda and I are having the signorine stitch their names on ours and we're gonna connive to do so in our wanderings. We should have a scarf full, don't you think?

I think that I've spilled enough beans for today. I just wrote your mother in my hopeless Japanese—there's a remote possibility that she may get the drift; I wrote it on that strength. Maybe I'll see you again tomorrow.


Medical Detachment Log

27 Aug 44—No casualties; usual front line duties.

All is well on the 29th.


29 August 1944

We had a lecture this AM on the evils of liquor up here and consequently we won't be having any vino, cognac, etc passing down our throats while we're in the lines. You see, we'd gotten a trifle too boisterous last night and made a lot of noise singing and talking. The CP, none too far away, heard us and gave the captain and Hayashi reprimands and this edict. I don't think that most of us mind too much, even tho' this does not happen often. He had every right to forbid drinking, for we were too rowdy. It's a good thing that I was in CQ else I would have been worse. As it was, I was in very good condition and had to help take care of a couple. There's some sorry looking boys this morning. If the major hadn't heard us there would not have been this repercussion, but we would have to sing loudly and that was the cause. Capt Ushiro doesn't mind the boys kicking up their heels every so often, but when the higher ups dictate, there is nothing he can do but comply. Now, we'll have to sing more softly at night or in the house. But, somehow, that doesn't quite seem to have the appeal when one sings under the stars in the cloak of night.

I had a good day yesterday in the way of mail. Received four of them—one from you, Shigeko, Glo and Setsu. . . .

All of them do mention that they've been reading and hearing of the work of the 100th and the 442d and express their gratitude for their achievements. I'm afraid that they eulogize us a bit too much, although the units have paid a big price, but so have the others. But, we're all glad over here that what we're fighting for is being realized, although often we read of the California race baiters—that makes us boiling mad.


30 AUGUST 1944

It was a good day yesterday—two of your letters. The snap of you taken by Nobi was in one of these. I was so very glad to get it. Still the same Hana—the living room looks nice. The picture is tucked away safely in my wallet now. I showed it to Chaplain Higuchi and he told me to write hello to you.

Your account of an item in the *Irrigator* about my treating Mike Hagiwara gave me a chuckle, as if the whole thing was something to write about.

Incidentally, did you read the account in *Time* of 31 July on page fifteen? It's a good writing on us and has a group picture, probably of some of the 100th boys. That kind of publicity really hits us right in the proper spot. But, that was offset just now, when the Capt showed us some clippings from the *Fresno Bee*. They were from Letters to the Editor, and were in reply to a request for fair play to the Nisei. I've seen some samples of misguided ignorance, but one of these actually had the gall to accuse us of foreknowledge of the attack on Pearl Harbor. Oh well, I suppose that sort of thing will always be coming up. We all read them and felt both amusement and anger, with the proper amount of bull session among us seated around this table. I'm sure and glad that this sort of thing must come only from a minority.

The routine here is unchanged; the same leisurely tempo with all the time in the world. But, we have been getting some work at night, last night being the third in succession we've been awakened. Sight of the wounded, their blood and broken tissues is still not a pleasant thing, although we are pretty well immune to these things.

That picture of you brings back a nostalgia—a homesickness, if only for the moment, for all that a home can represent. To be able to sit down to a meal, with a tablecloth on the table, to come home from work in the evening, then to go for a ride wherever our desires dictated and to go to bed, an honest to goodness bed again, between white sheets—it's all these and many other things I can see when I gaze at your picture.

Medical Detachment Log

31 Aug 44—Regtl and Bn Aid Stations caring for Italian civilian patients

1 Sept 44—Scandicci, Italia, casualties clearing thru Regtl and Bn Aid Stations light. Usual duties performed.

1 September 1944

Life here has assumed such a boring time-heavy routine that I have a difficult time even writing to you, which problem I did not have before. There doesn't seem to be anything of interest to talk about. . . .

So far as the war situation goes, it remains unchanged. I'd just as soon be on the move, but when I realize that the more we push, the greater the casualties, then we can't say very much about that. . . .

Had to leave just now to treat a casualty that was brought in. It seems that he stepped on the mine when in reconnaissance. The Jerries just love to leave these mementos around. His foot had been blown off, but he was in pretty good condition. We redressed it and gave him plasma and sent him on in. That's how wily these Tedeschi are. We have to be careful whether they're around or not. He's the second one since yesterday afternoon. . . .

---

After September 1, the entire front suddenly exploded into action. The 442nd crossed the Arno River in two places. —DIANNE BRIDGMAN

---

2 SEPTEMBER 1944

The station has finally moved; they went out last night. I think that everyone was glad to be on the move again, slight though the move may be, for even a few days at one place can become boring. I recall one time previously when in one day we stopped at three different places. You can see the contrast. Although they've all moved out in their respective aid station groups, I've been left behind only because the telephone is here and someone has to man it. It seems that wire is unavailable at present and soon as we can get the wire through to the new location, I can move up, too. The chaplain's driver is with me, in case of any emergency at all. So now I'm still here, left all alone, more or less, but I don't lack for company. The paesanos just got through threshing a mess of wheat and now they are going to sit down to eat. . . .

I'm writing this now at the new location. The surroundings are so much nicer and cleaner. We've more room here, it seems, the people of a better class and well, it's just nicer that's all. Flowers such as dahlias, asters, and geraniums grow along the side, there are peach, persimmon and fig trees in abundance and wonders of wonders, we've an actual concrete square tub and you can bet I'm gonna try that baby out. Kuge already has. I can feel the cold water already.

After all the guys had left last night, the place was strangely quiet, especially since the bright full moonlight made the courtyard almost like day. The family misses the noisy bunch and I had a nice chat with them. They told me all kinds of things—among others that there are plenty of Fascists left here, that we're just driving them northward with the Tedeschis, and that the northern section is more Fascist than any other part. They told me to be careful when we hit Milano. That's still a long ways off—who knows, we may not even see that place. All we do is bypass towns and cities, anyway.

### 4 SEPTEMBER 1944

I was kind of lazy yesterday and so I didn't write, but today I feel good. Besides I have your letter of the 15th, which came in last night. I've a lot of things to tell you this trip.

You mentioned the newsreel that showed the 100th receiving its citation. I think that I wrote you an account, didn't I? Maybe, if you'll look hard, you can see me. As is the wont of the medics, we were in the rear again and to tell you the truth, though we were in ranks, most of the time I was either sitting or standing on my helmet. It may look good on the screen; we never saw it. And so to see, the whole thing was "waste time", although we were glad that the 100th received recognition. . . .

Minneapolis seems a fine place—we've enough of our friends around there to come and visit us, so we can keep the memories alive. Aya and Sam, Joe and Nobi make for pretty good company. It was with a sigh of relief when I heard of Joe and Mary—my comment: "It's about time." [Joe and Mary had just married.] We'll have one good get-together when I get back.

I think that I'll be seeing Franklin soon. Various latrine rumors scurrying around says so at various places at various times, but I think that there is a basis for these and that it won't be long now. Wonder how the old boy is. I'll have to tell him a few tales. . . .

From the last house we brought over a tiny pup just a few weeks old from her mother's teats. The man of the house had promised her to us. Being filthy with fleas, it was washed the first thing and now it's a white, cute, little, rascally thing that drinks its milk from a dropper, sleeps most of the time and tumbles and bumbles along in its learning the art of walking. Higgins and Kozuma are more or less her, yes, it's a she, foster mother and take care of "Bambina" as we call her. Even at this tender age, she growls and tries to bite as if she were something older than the baby that she is. . . .

This is positively the end, darling. It was another gorgeous full moon last night. Need I say more.

MEDICAL DETACHMENT LOG

6 September 44 all sections left Scandicci, Italia and arrived in new area, Castiglioncello, Italia, and set up aid stations. Usual duties performed. No changes in personnel.

7, 8, and 9 Sept remained in same bivouac area, no casualties thru aid stations.

10 September 44 left Castiglioncello, Italia, by truck and arrived at Piombino Port leaving Piobino Port on board Liberty Ship *Ambrose E. Burnside*. . . .

The following letter from Mark Clark, Commanding General Fifth Army, dated 7 Sept 44, addressed to Commanding Officer, 442d Infantry, Combat Team, we quote:

*I desire to commend you on the occasion of your departure from Fifth Army for the superior job you and your troops have done while assigned to Fifth Army. Assigned to Fifth Army in the latter part of May, your men took an active part in the*

*capture of Leghorn. American Troops of Japanese ancestry*
*are well known to the Fifth Army from the splendid showing*
*which had previously been made by the 100th Infantry Battal-*
*ion during the course of the past year. The conduct of your*
*troops was exemplary both on the battlefield and in rest areas.*
*Your men have demonstrated an eagerness for combat and*
*have proven themselves to be better than anything the enemy*
*has been able to put against them.*

## 14 SEPTEMBER 1944

I'm writing again after a too long lapse. It wasn't entirely my doing, for I've been busy running around and we've been doing some traveling, too. So let me tell you the whole story from the time I last wrote till the present moment. . . .

The Capt was nice enough to allow Kuge, Iijima, Kozuma and I to visit Florence on an overnight pass. It took us about five hours by the good old hitchhike method. Florence, having been declared an open city by the Germans, is teeming with people, the influx of people from the surrounding countryside swelling the population to about half a million. It is a clean, neat town as Italian cities go and the people are in marked contrast to the southern Italians, being of a higher class and dress. We sought out a girl, Mary, whom we'd met at the aid station and she greeted us kindly and found an empty apartment for us across the street. She plays the piano beautifully and she played Beethoven, Chopin, Gershwin's "Rhapsody in Blue" for us at her grand. She speaks English quite well and the next day she showed us around the shops with her fiance who's a medical student. He's a nice guy, too. I'm afraid I didn't see too much of Florence so far as artworks go nor the church because of all the time we spent in shopping. I don't think that my time was lost, though. I just got through packing the stuff I bought there and it'll go out today. . . .

For good measure I've thrown in the 34th Div shoulder patch, the

"Red Bull" Div. to which we'd been attached and which we'd fought for . . . there will be a Saturday issue of the *Stars and Stripes*, the anniversary edition of the Salerno landing; it makes for interesting reading and also gives us recognition, too. . . .

So we thumbed our way back the long dusty road and came back tired, but happy, for we'd had a pretty good time all told. We're lucky to have seen both Pisa and Florence—not many in the 442d can say that. We had dinner at a GI restaurant, newly opened, and I must say that food was never more welcome for we hadn't eaten solidly since we'd left. We were served by waiters, at a table, on plates, with silverware and napkins. Boy, we ate in class. Whether to our credit or not, I don't know, but all of us ate two plates of everything. That chow was plenty good. After that we were content to go home. Glad to say that we had good connections all the way, coming and going. When we got back that night, we found that we were pulling out the next AM and with our aid station. I with a couple of others are shooting the bull around. I'm trying to get this letter written, but extremely interesting stories of various natures are getting thrown around. . . .

It took us two days to get here—a none too interesting trip although we did get to relax and meet some of our old friends that we hadn't seen in quite awhile, for the 522d was with us.

So now here we are and I wish I could tell you where, but we are near a town. The Captain was on the ball and we've occupied an unfinished house and we've very nice accommodations, while all the others have to pitch their tents on this extremely dusty ground.

Incidentally, little Bambina our pooch is doing just fine and now scrambles all over the place with so much friskiness that she's the darling of the place. And she helps keep the dust down on the floor with frequent wettings that drives the CQs mad. I wish you could see her, she's damn cute. . . .

Our replacements are supposed to be here, around someplace, but we've yet to see them. But, we'll meet up with 'em soon. Can't help but do that since we're in the same neighborhood.

Incidentally, giving you a hint of things happening, our APO has changed from the 464 to 758. Don't forget because those three numbers can make a big difference in the delivery.

Au revoir—

MEDICAL DETACHMENT LOG

Pianodiquarto, Italia. Various inoculation shots administered to the officers and enlisted men. 17, 18, and 19 Sept 44, usual rest area activities throughout the day.

17 SEPTEMBER 1944

Franklin was over day before yesterday. Up till then the replacements' presence was only to me a rumor, but he told me they'd been here for over a week already. He looks fit and fine and is the same Joe as ever. They're quite a ways away from us in another direction and he had to hitchhike to see us. There are quite a few of them—I probably know a great many of them—mostly mainland boys and a few from Hawaii. They were fortunate, coming over with a USO troupe and some WACs, or was it nurses, at any rate on a liner and not a Liberty Ship. They were fourteen days afloat and now are undergoing the usual mild sort of training and conditioning. They should join up with us soon. I hope Franklin gets into his old M Co as he wanted. It's heavy weapons and mortars and the casualty rate is lower there. He was kind enough to bring me a Ronson lighter that he'd bought in Seattle on his furlough. I was glad to see that. . . .

He happened to come in when we were busy for the first time in a long time. The dreaded time for the GIs was at hand again and for the last two mornings we've been giving shots. Typhus, typhoid, and smallpox were the three. As usual, there were the usual moans and groans and the threats to the medics and the expected bitching. . . .

There isn't too much to do in town. I went in yesterday for no particular reason and just wandered around both on foot and on the jeep that I went in on. One of these days I'll see an opera. *Tosca* played yesterday and today is *Madame Butterfly*. These are at the original San Carlo Opera Co. Yesterday, Lt Kanaya and Lt Futamata had to drag out of the stockade a fella (medic) that was thrown in there by a lousy Limey MP who happened to catch him selling some PX rations. He'd been missing three days and Kanaya finally located him through the Hqtrs. It's just that he was unlucky—everybody sells or trades stuff. He just happened to get caught at it. I never told you of the narrow escape we had at Pisa when an AMG [Allied Military Government] officer saw us selling cigarettes and told us to quit or ten years in the brig would stare us in the face. We took his advice that time and took off, but that kind of thing is always going on. We're always short of money, more or less; the guy who said we'd have no use for dough overseas sure sold us a bunch of horse collars. . . .

Tsukayama is trying his hand at the new portable organ the chaplain got today. Sounds good. Incidentally, Cpl Kozuma has left us for the 3d Bn Medics—he replaces Kanaya who got his commission. So it's now S/Sgt Kozuma. Hated to see him go, but he's the logical man for the job. But, with Tsukayama here to take his corporal's job, we've a spark plug to take a lot of the beef that goes out as supply man, etc. . . .

Do you know Yoshito Mizuta; he was with us at Puyallup and Hunt and I'd gone to school and played ball with him on the same Taiyo teams. He received the Hunt annual, *Minidoka Interlude*, and I got to cast my peepers through it. Brought back many memories— I hope you have a copy.

Little Bambina is getting more and more dear to us as the days pass. She frisks around on those wobbly legs and growls and tries to bite with her newly formed teeth in ridiculously adult fashion. She eats meat now and other solids and still wets the floor to our exasperation. The other morning when she banged into a litter handle at full speed I almost died laughing. She does the damndest things.

MEDICAL DETACHMENT LOG

> 20 Sept 44. Replacements attached to Medical Detachment from
> 24th Replacement Depot.

## 20 SEPTEMBER 1944

It started raining early this morning and the wind and rain blew in through the opposite window much to some's discomfiture. It is still raining and everybody's inside the house, getting caught up on correspondence, singing and playing the guitar and uke and others just fooling around. On a normal day, this place should be deserted now, all taking off on passes. I'd probably be out myself. We'd planned to go swimming at the pool, shower and go to see the opera. *Madame Butterfly*'s on the menu and should be good fare. I bought four tickets yesterday and I'm gonna go rain or shine. I hope it lets up though. Momoda, Kuge, Iijima and I were expecting to go.

Yesterday I saw *Barber of Seville* and the day before, *Faust*. Both were excellent, being of higher caliber than our San Carlo troupe. I think we all enjoyed the former operas more although Rossini's rippling violin strains strike a responsive chord within me. This was the first time that Ike, Momoda and Kuge had heard G. [Grand] Opera and they were impressed, whether favorably or not, I don't know. At least, they're willing for a repeat today. The theatre is shaped in a horseshoe with boxes rising all the way up to the ceiling. In normal times in good repair, the place must have been gorgeous, you can see the beauty through the grime and misuse. The British authorities run the theatre and us GIs only pay forty cents and that's a godsend to this pocketbook. I've been saving the programs and stubs as is my wont, and I'll send them home soon. I only wish you could be with me to enjoy the music as we used to. Operas are scheduled every day and I'll try to see all that I can.

Tsuka and the Capt are manning the guitar and ukulele now making with the music and it's nice, practicing and all. The guitar belongs to Higgins. We bought it for him in town yesterday at the Red Cross. A GI left it there to be sold and when Momoda and I were browsing around the joint we inspected it. Why we don't know because we know nothing about the thing anyway. When we came back that night we told Higgins about it and he asked us to buy it for him. They wanted fifteen dollars at first, but I got it for twelve dollars. The ARC gal was very nice—they all are though. But, Higgins is satisfied and we all benefit from his playing as we did last night, just Higgins, Tsuka, Morimoto and I singing softly after all had gone to sleep and talking about all the old songs. I enjoyed that. . . .

Darling if I know you, you're racking your brains for a Xmas gift for me. Please, believe me, I don't need anything. In fact, I'd feel bad if you sent me something. I'd much rather you used the dough yourself. . . .

Just tried my hand at strumming the ukelele; the thing just infuriates me. I think it's hopeless.

I hope I see a letter from you today. It seems like such a long time now.

PS Saw Franklin yesterday and he's attached at least temporarily in E Co. The replacements have been distributed through the companies.

MEDICAL DETACHMENT LOG

> 21 Sept 44, left vicinity of Pianodiquarto, Italia in the rain via truck convoy and arrived at Staging Area #1, Bagnoli, Italia billeted in Building 1 at the College of Naples.

21 SEPTEMBER 1944

Yesterday, I wrote you that rain or shine I was gonna see *Madame Butterfly* in town. The continuing rain certainly discouraged me, but with a letup, Kuwayama dragged me out and so I went almost reluctantly. We had good rides in and made it just right as the orchestra struck up with the "Marseilles", "Star Spangled Banner" and "God Save The King". It was very stirring and as we stood at attention, I was quite proud when they played our anthem. Did you ever stop to think how beautiful it can be?

It was certainly an effort well paid when we saw *Madame Butterfly*. I enjoyed it very much. Hearing the opera again only intensifies one's enjoyment and the soprano was so very good that "One Fine Day" was encored. I'm certainly glad they dragged me out.

Not being content with the opera, we bought tickets for the night performance of *La Boheme* and ballet. They played the first act only of the opera. That was all I wanted to hear anyway. . . .

I think that I told you once of the fad of the 34th in wearing neckerchiefs of all shades and colors. I wear one of ancient design in red and I hold it with a mystical ring that I bought in Florence. It has arabic figures in some weird hieroglyphics on it. . . . I think it'll bring me luck.


23 SEPTEMBER 1944

This life of inactivity can be quite boring although we are pretty free to do as we please. Just why, I don't know. Maybe it's just simply that we're all so homesick for our homes and countries. I for one, would trade all Italy for a hunk of the United States especially around 1417 Third Street NE in Minneapolis.

I'm sending all my opera and concert programs home today. You will be getting a couple of copies of *Yank*, too. It has an article on the Battle of Belvedere. Before the issue came out, they told us that the 442d was gonna have a feature in the *Yank* and for us to order souvenir copies. So we all upped and paid for a mess of 'em. It was with great chagrin that we learned it was all about the 100th and put us in a very poor light. We were pretty well sore about it. But, I'm sending mine out (a lot of guys burned theirs) because the article is interesting and anyway, we're all in the same boat. According to this, it seems the

100th saved the 442d from annihilation and disaster. I don't think that it was that way at all, but it makes for pretty good reading. . . .

MEDICAL DETACHMENT LOG

26 Sept 44—left staging Area #1 by truck convoy, arriving at Port of Naples. Boarded USS *Samuel Chase* along with 100th Bn.

27 Sept 44—on board USS *Samuel Chase*—left Naples Harbor.

28 Sept 44—still on board ship, trip so far calm and pleasant.

# 3 FRANCE

## *October–November 1944*

In October 1944, the 442nd was sent to France to join the Thirty-sixth Division of the Seventh Army. The Seventh Army had successfully invaded southern France and liberated eastern and southern France. Their progress was stopped, however, in the Vosges Mountains in northeastern France. The Germans had been ordered to defend this territory with all their resources. —DIANNE BRIDGMAN

MEDICAL DETACHMENT LOG

29 Sep 44—arrived Marseilles Harbor and disembarked via assault boat.

30 Sept 44—left Marseilles, France by railway, 29 Sept 44 and arrived vicinity of Septemes, France. Aid station set up, routine rest area activities. Weather windy, rainy and cold. The Combat Team improvised their shelter for the nite, near Septemes, France, 30 Sept 44 Training schedule was resumed. Half day passes to Marseilles and Aix-en-Provence authorized.

SOMEWHERE IN SOUTHERN FRANCE
1 OCTOBER 1944

As you can see from the above you can understand why I haven't written to you. There's always the hustle and bustle of packing and the attending myriad of things that go with it and one can't very well send out mail on a boat, for that's the way we came. Now you know why the change of APO we'd guessed for some time back just where we were going, but, of course, I couldn't tell you. And now we can finally say "Lafayette, we are here."

The boat trip over was the best of all that we'd taken. We were rather looking forward to seeing France, being somewhat bored with all that Italy could offer. Had a brief ride on a Higgins boat, you've seen those things plowing about the water in all the movies and I can tell you that those things aren't pleasure craft, by any means. We were on an American, good old American, ship this time as compared to the horrible trip on the British transport from Oran to Naples, we had plenty of room this time and the food was good. We'd movies every day, a library to browse around in, and best of all, the boat was clean as they come. We took care of the usual routine sick call and the trip was comparatively calm until the last night which did me no good. I retired early that night. As we neared and moved along the coastline, we could see that the terrain, what little we could see was pretty rugged. Just as any tourist at destination, we were all curious to see what we could see. We finally anchored and the Higgins boats took us ashore; we waited around in the town till an interminable time which had us all cursing, but we had ample time to size up the place and get acquainted and you can probably guess what I mean by the latter. We were all disappointed at the French Mam'selles. We didn't see one good looking one, but the people are very friendly and clean looking. We're having a terrific time with the language. I realized French was difficult, but now that we've actually come to grips with it, I can see why it's a tough nut to crack. We have to unlearn what little Italian we know and fumble around with the meager French we've read in our language book, courtesy US Army.

From sunny Italy, we've landed into chilly France. Although the sun shines brightly, there's always a nippy breeze blowing, and the nights and mornings are terrific. I've my woolens on now as I write this by candlelight in my pup tent which Ike and I have put up together. (He and Sakamoto are shooting craps in what little cramped space and I have to contend with "Joes" and "boxcars" all the while writing.) We buttoned up the front of the tent with our raincoats, but the chill wind still sneaks in somehow. It looks like a cold winter. Most of the guys have caught cold to some degree and I'm not immune either. Your wool knit sox and helmet I've used to good advantage already and I can see they're going to be pretty well worn before the war's over. We can build fires, and we do, but wood is so scarce around here. I've been out foraging for wood around the vicinity and we've done all right. Speaking of countryside, it is reminiscent of Algiers, not a particularly scenic place, Italy being much more appealing. But, we haven't seen the more fertile valleys as yet and I may change my mind about that, but right here, it ain't so good.

I can't tell you too much about the French people, for we have as yet to know them well, but they, at least, are cordial in their smiles and greetings. I wonder what they think of us? . . .

I've seen Marseilles and I sent you another of my periodic packages. . . .

Oh yes, I'm enclosing, too, a snap that the chaplain took of Momoda, Ike, and I in the vineyard behind the half-finished house that was our station.

Little Bambina has grown considerably now and amuses us no end in her actions. But, she can be a nuisance, too, doing bad things on peoples' beds and clothes. We certainly got a kick out of her last night, harassing a big dog with her picayune barks and growls and messing around with its tail, legs and head. She's a kick.

1 and 3 Oct 44—Usual procedures and passes continued according to plans.

4 Oct 44—Slightly cloudy day.

## 5 OCTOBER 1944

I'm sorry I didn't write you for a couple of days but I was too busy fooling around and so I've a lot to tell you just to make up for the absence. I was CQ on the 3d and I was pretty busy all day as the cold weather has brought most of the boys down with colds in some form or another. Thus, in the morning we have a tremendous sick call and we're busy stuffing pills in one guy and giving nosedrops to the next. It must have been the sudden change. Happily, I'm over my slight attack.

When I got back I found three letters for me from you and my morale went up way over par. . . . It was a relief to know that the alabaster and stuff got there safely in one piece. . . .

Speaking of souvenirs, I just sent some more stuff this morning, and more will be on the way tomorrow. . . . I sent you another bottle of cologne in a rather cute bottle. Frankly, I don't know how it smells even, but I hope you like it. . . .

I visited Marseilles yesterday. . . . I just walked around the downtown and it's a pretty big place. People just crowd the streets, trains clang and vehicles, both military and civilian crawl along. It's an extremely busy place.

Got to talking about medication and personalities with Ike last night and so bed felt heavenly after all that walking about I did. It began raining around 2:00 AM and it's still continuing. Everything outside is all wet and the ground is a churned up mess of mud. And there doesn't seem to be any prospect of a let up. Thank God that we have new shelter halves we put up a couple of days ago. It's shedding the heavenly water very nicely. Breakfast was a soggy mess and sick call (we were excused from it) hasn't materialized due to the rain. I guess the training program will have to be forgotten today. This rain certainly can make life miserable. Both Ike and I have our raincoats protecting the front of the tent so we can't use them. A long day inside the small tent confronts us today, just listening to the rain pattering on the canvas and the occasional thunder that rolls down from the gray leaden skies.

But, to get to where I left off last night before our erudite discussions, Marseilles is again that curious mixture of the new and the old, something we don't see back home. We just don't have anything that old and historical. I spent the whole day just walking the streets gawking as the proverbial hayseed, just trying to absorb all that I could, I found it all interesting, the myriads of shops selling everything from soup to nuts, the street vendors, the wide streets and the narrow alley-like passages both teeming with people. As in Italy, the food situation is bad. All the food shops are bare of goods and I mean really bare, absolutely bare and the people are out hunting for food. It's very pathetic and naturally, black market flourishes. In contrast to the musty, tiny shops there are beautiful specialty stores and huge glittering department stores that put some of ours to shame. . . . Marseilles has not been hit so badly by bombs and shells; certain sections show some damage and a glance upwards shows evidence of shrapnel and bombs, but not very much. They were quite fortunate in that. It's very easy to get lost because the narrow streets go every which way and I wouldn't trust the streets at night, for there have been cases of soldiers getting shot at night, although I can't imagine Germans still lingering here. . . .

On the way back home we picked up a hitchhiking couple who lived just about five miles from our camp. We took them right up to their door and in their gratitude they invited us in for a short while. We came out about two hours later. We met the mother and grandparents. The couple were Juliette and Rene LeGuen and they were very nice—just married last year. They gave us wine and cut up a melon for us and we in turn gave them chocolate, cigarettes and a cigar that I happened to have. The conversation was very delightful, the Chaplain delivering more or less of a monologue in the extremely scant French he knew, delving for every word in the dictionary. They taught us a French regional song and we showed our pictures around and they showed us theirs and we had all in all a very enjoyable evening. . . .

I guess that Tama's having a bad time, thank goodness, I'll never know that. Anyway, tell him that I said a special cheery "hello" to her and to Harry. He started it all. And as for you, Hana, all my love and extra special kisses.

Au revoir

## Medical Detachment Log

No change in personnel, 6 or 7 Oct 44, with continued rain all day.

Waiting for movement order. Only five mile radius passes author-ized, cancelling passes to Marseilles area. Cloudy day, no rain, usual routine duties performed on 8 Oct 44.

9 Oct 44—The Combat Team less Anti-Tank and 3d Bn began move-ment to our new assembly area. Route followed first day—Highway 7, thru Aix, Avignon, Valence, arrived vicinity Vienne, France, ate hot meal and bivouacked for the night.

On the 10th, continued journey north, departing Vienne, France thru Bourg Lons le Saunier, Besancon. Second night of the trip bedded down in the vicinity of Vesoul, France. Third day, the motor convoy closed in at destination, arriving vicinity of Charmois Devant—Bruy-eres. Aid stations set up. Usual duties performed. Two casualties from other unit treated, wounded while riding jeep neighborhood 522d Field Artillery area, when a mine went off. The entire move-ment covered 450 to 500 miles, traveling under trying conditions, accompanied by rain, mud and slippery roads.

12 Oct 44—Charmois, France. Cold rainy day, no casualties. General bivouac duties. Waiting orders for final commitment. Enlisted men

enjoying much needed shower privileges. Killing time under cover from rain and cold. Usual pre-movement routing.

## 12 October 1944

We've been kind of busy the past few days, moving around, so I didn't get a chance to write to you. I think you understand. . . .

I rode with the Chaplain and his driver and we had a lot of fun. You know how the former is, and passing through the towns and villages, we'd make all kinds of noises at the ma'mselles. So we've traveled quite a distance now and seen France from a jeep.

I'm happy to say that the French countryside has made me change my opinion of it. Even seen through the mist and grayness of the inclement weather, it has unfolded its greenness, and its characteristic beauty. This somehow, I can't exactly place it, is different from the Italian vistas we knew so well. The rocky barrenness of the view has changed to rolling hills and green valleys with many rivers and streams. The villages, though of the same order, seem cleaner as do the inhabitants. My French is coming right along with the good help of my GI French book, but these pronunciations really get me. The way they twist their "r's" and blow "n's" out through their nose while making coy sounds is still tricky to grasp. We should be pretty good linguists before the army is through with us. We may have to learn German before long, too.

As it is now, we can hear the boom of big guns and I think action stares us in the face. That was expected anyway and we'll be going through the same kind of hell again. The trouble is that the coming of winter complicates things as if we didn't have troubles of our own. You remember, darling, that wool sox and helmet you knit for me. I'm certainly glad that I brought it along. I've been thinking that if you could knit Franklin one, he could certainly use it and I could use another pair of sox, too. And this is only the beginning of winter. I hate to think of the months coming up.

Miracles of miracles, I got some mail yesterday. I don't know where it came from, but the main thing is that I got it. . . .

I've been dreaming and thinking a lot more than usual these "bad time" days and some of the thoughts I think can be too sweet to bear for the longing that comes over me. I guess I can't help it if I love you so very much.

MEDICAL DETACHMENT LOG

The 3d Bn Section arrived at Vesoul, France, 13 Oct 44, detrained and traveled by truck to Charmois bivouac area.

14 Oct 44, inspiring worship service conducted by Chaplains. Regiment alerted for movement. Men in area busily working on last minute preparations. Left Charmois, France by truck convoy and arrived vicinity of Le Void de La Borde, France.

15 Oct 44—Vicinity of Le Void de La Borde, France. Warm sunny day. ENTERED COMBAT. Bn area muddy and very difficult to walk. Full of snipers and heavy enemy concentration of tanks, "Beaucoup" tree bursts, causing heavy casualties, company aid men, litter bearers, technicians laboring overtime.

15 OCTOBER 1944

It seems that we're in it again. We've moved up into this house and it starts all over. The shells whistle overhead and land heavily on the enemy before us. Today has dawned sunny and we're in this farmhouse some distance behind the lines because of the scarcity of houses. The aid station is set up nicely in the front bedroom and I slept comfortably on the floor in my bedroll while lucky Capt and Momoda enjoyed themselves on a fluffy, mattressed bed. There are only two women living in this house; one a white haired lady and the other a woman about forty or forty-five. They rattle off very confusingly in French and luckily, we have a fellow from the Collecting Co who can savvy it and get us around. Yesterday, I was asking this lady in my very best French (?) for a pot to make coffee and after I'd gone through my act, she said "Yes, the water's cold." That got me. Do you think it's my ignorance of the tongue? They've been very accommodating to us and they had some of our chow last night.

As soon as we moved into this place we were hunting for food and we bought ourselves a chicken and three rabbits which we cooked up with potatoes and carrots last night—a real rabbit stew and it wasn't bad at all. . . .

The nights are still terribly dark and dusk falls very rapidly and last evening caught us flat-footed when we were cooking outside and we had to put up a blanket to screen the flame of the burner from the enemy eyes. The stars were out last night—where in the hell's the moon at? Maybe, it's in its new phase, but it's still awfully dark outside, but in this house we're warm and cozy in the gleam of candlelight. We play cards and I'm really practicing up on the strum-box. I can play quite a few songs now and learning new chords every day. But, my fingers just won't go where they want to on the strings—too big and clumsy. But, I can feel myself getting in the swing of it and that's an agreeable feeling. Just like that day in skiing when one has a feeling that he had a good day. I may surprise you when I come back.

Things are still the same in our personnel, except we have one buck Sgt, a Kibei [A Japanese American who had been educated in Japan] replacement. Kuge and Morimoto have gone forward to a more handy position to render aid, if necessary, but the station is back here. Bambina is still the frisky, pesky canine and still cute with her ears standing up now, but today she is rather out of sorts because a water can was dropped on her forepaw—she's always getting underfoot anyway.

Nary any mail from anyone and we all know that there must be a mess of them for us hanging around somewhere. So we're just waiting for that glad day. Haven't seen Franklin, but I don't think that they're in action as yet.

MEDICAL DETACHMENT LOG

16 Oct 44. Enemy shelling near Regimental area.

16 OCTOBER 1944

We're still here and in the letup and spare time I've sat myself down at the round table in our aid station to write a little something to you. It blew last night and this AM began to rain in the perverse French manner and it's still coming down. It's miserable weather and yet our boys are out there in these woods trying to clean them of Jerries. Momoda, Ike and Wachi replaced Kuge, Morimoto and Onodera forward with the infantry men. The terrain is not a very good one for fighting, at least for us, but I guess that holds for the Boche too. It's pretty rugged up forward what with the weather and all. The casualties are coming in now as was to be expected, not too heavily, but bad enough to keep us worried. Being some distance back here in this house with its accompanying comforts makes one feel rather inadequate, but the situation is such that we have to remain here with just the two technicians and driver forward. We've been throwing a heck of a lot of shells and mortars, so the Jerries are having a bad time, too, but they've the advantage of prepared protection. It may take a little time, but we'll drive them out yet.

Back here, it's a world set apart from the front lines even though the distance is not a factor, for we've protection from the elements and we've not the worry about shells and gunfire. We've hot meals and sleep cozily—all this just a few kilometers away—what peculiar circumstances war can bring. This kind of situation is not particularly to be relished by us, at least it makes me feel funny and as if I'm not doing anything. But, I guess there's nothing we can do about it.

18 Oct 44—Cold day, rain continued to fall for the fifteenth consecutive day. Casualties very heavy, extra litter bearers from 886th Collecting Co and Regtl Aid Station sent to 2d Bn Aid Station.

19 Oct 44—Left vicinity of le Void de la Borde, France, by motor convoy. Convoy held up due to enemy artillery being "zeroed in" on highway near Bruyeres, France. Arrived Bruyeres, France. Description of Bruyeres all "busted" up and inhabitants liberated. Blue Aid Station located in bank building in same town. [Beginning in this entry, the 3d Bn is sometimes referred to as the Blue, the 2d as the White, the 1st (100th) as the Red.] The Germans shelled the town continuously during the day and night.

20 Oct 44—Sunny day. Casualties passing thru BN aid station heavy. Captain Kawaoka's Aid Station moved out into a civilian hospital in the outskirts of Bruyeres. Continued enemy shelling, town of Bruyeres. Mortar shell landed on the doorstep of aid station, wounding a S/Sgt. He was evacuated.

21 Oct 44. Casualties passing through bn aid light. Left city of Bruyeres France, 22 Oct 44 and arrived vicinity of Bruyeres, France. Regtl Aid Station established in French sanitorium. During the morning of 22 Oct 44 an attempt was made to evacuate the wounded from the advance troops of the 100th battalion, which was temporarily out of direct contact in the vicinity of Biffontaine, France. The two litter squads left moved here with their respective aid stations. The litter train also consisted of some PW who were used as litter bearers, as all available men were needed to evacuate the wounded speedily. Aid men contacted the wounded men of Company A. After proceeding a short distance the litter train was beset by a large enemy combat patrol, following our battalion supply route. One of the officers, tho' seriously wounded . . . and a couple other

riflemen managed to escape and made their way back. One of the riflemen was sent back to contact and inform the rest of the troops, but they were gone and have not been found since. It is believed that the wounded and the Medics were captured.

22 OCT 1944

It's been so long since I wrote you last that I find it difficult to pick up where I left off. Even with an envelope back of items to write you about, it's hard to plunge into this letter. But, it was such a good day today—this afternoon, our long-awaited mail finally caught up with us. As expected I received fifteen in all. Seven from you. . . .

Mariko sent me a snapshot of her holding one-month old Dennis. Although she says that people say he looks like Jun more, I can't tell it from the picture. . . .

You asked me to send Helen something in one of these letters. By now you should have those bottles of perfume I sent from Florence. I told you this before, I think. I hope she likes it. . . .

I'm sorry that Tama's having such a bad time and to have the complications of appendicitis. But, I know she'll pull through the appendectomy okay. Remind me never to become a mother, will you? Suzu wrote me the usual refreshing letter and her anticipation of University of Minnesota and its subsequent college life and curriculum was something that I could feel myself, too, having once gone through the same sensations of registration and all. I think she'll have a darn good time there and find things a bit different from Guilford, that cloistered hearth.

As I sit on my haunches writing this letter we're in a farmhouse room—a whole mess of us with our beds on the floor. Candles are lit here and there—the stove burns cozily in the corner—Tsuka is strumming softly in the semi-darkness and crooning with a guitar. The kitchen is noisy with pinochle and the French farm folk. If what I heard tonight about the regiment being relieved is true, we could all see a little rest and recuperation. This is the first chance we've had to write since the other farmhouse of Marie's and we welcome it. But, there's been a lot of things happening in the comparatively few hours that have elapsed since then.

The day after I wrote you, Hayashi, Tsuka and I relieved Momoda, Ike and Wachi up in the rain-drenched woods where we'd set up a crude stopover in the evacuation to patch up the casualties because our forward progress was stymied by German road blocks of felled trees. It was drizzling when we went up and during our stay there, it was miserable from the fitful rain and wind. They'd set up the station in the woods by the sea of mud called a road, where vehicles, jeeps, trucks and trailers splashed noisily by or got stuck up to their axles. There was no shelter for the station—it was just there under the trees and we waited for the telephone to ring to bring the casualties in and they weren't long in coming and it was no picnic, treating them in the pouring rain—we were soaked, the patients all wet, the bandages all wet—everything was wet. I never felt so damn mad at weather than at that time, because there was nothing we could do about it. The rain just made everything impossible to do, but worst of all the casualties had rain in their faces, we couldn't strip them to take care of their wounds adequately and it beat down on their faces and added to their cold and misery. And they came in too steadily to suit us. It didn't rain constantly all day, but gave us plenty of trouble in gusts. In between times we'd huddle in our dugout and a slit trench widened for two and with a protective layer of logs over it, against tree bursts and a mound of earth on top. Tsuka and I took over Ike and Momoda's dugout, over which entrance they'd pitched a tent and they'd slept comfortably that night. But, when we slept in the blankets, the rain had soaked through everything and it dripped down onto us. We started out well enough, but by 3:30 AM the moisture had crept up so insidiously feet upwards that by that time we were all curled up to escape it, our feet all wet and cold. I woke with a leg cramp and we got up cussingly struck matches and rearranged everything but with not much success and dozed fitfully till daylight. When I look back on it the whole thing is amusing and laughable as hell, but it really was something that night. And oh, the helluva time we had putting our shoes on—our socks were all wet and ditto the shoes. Some fun, eh kid? Just like putting on a wet bathing suit and you know how that feels. From this rain exposure and tramping in the mud and drenched earth all the GIs have wet feet constantly and some have come in with trench feet—a sad condition. And to top it off, the Medical Department comes out with some crappy memo about GIs must not sleep with wet shoes and socks. How the hell is the infantry man gonna do that when he's out there day and night in the rain fighting the Jerries and takes his shoes off when he goes to sleep. He has no blanket—he's all soaked anyway—even the socks that he carries are probably all wet and he can't carry an extra pair of shoes around. Some of these guys higher up should come around once in awhile instead of sitting in some soft chair giving good advice. But, that gave us all some sort of amusement, ironic as all hell.

By noon the next day the engineers had cleared out the mines and blocks and we moved into the town that we'd been assaulting. The place has certainly been broken up—first from our artillery and now that we're in it, the Jerries, of course, had to open up on it. So the town took it coming and going. But strangely enough there were quite a few people left in town and all sorts of GIs busy dashing hither and yon. We set up house in a doctor's establishment, first cleaning out all the rubble and making haste to light the two stoves in the rooms we occupied, and dry out slowly both ourselves and our equipment. Business is too good for us nowadays—don't care for that at all.

There are some amusing incidents that happened in town, but one that I want to relate is about certain females that carried on with the Jerries. Well, the FFI [French Forces of the Interior (partisans)] rounded them up, headed them to the barber and cropped off all their hair and as they walked through the town, shamelessly it seemed to me, people made big noises and the GIs just stared. They really looked funny and rather forlorn to me. You'll probably see pictures

Dugout in the Vosges Mountains, France, 1944. The entrance was protected by sandbags. The snow indicates how cold it was in October and November.

of many cases like this from time to time. I know that they did that in Italy, but this is the first I've actually seen.

After a couple of nights on the kitchen floor our boys had pushed ahead slowly enough for us to move ahead to our next station, a big hospital where they were kind enough to let us use a ward. There were spring beds all lined up and I got one with a mattress on it and I slept comfortably that night. The room was big and high and we were set up handsomely and for the first time it seemed for a long time we'd some leisure.

And then this AM we moved up a little further to this farmhouse regretfully leaving the hospital where the Regimental Aid had set up shop after us. This area around the house certainly shows the scars of battle, but the stations are in the adjoining barn and here we are cozy for the night at least in this farmhouse parlor. Everyone's gone to sleep now, but I must finish what I have to say when I have time to say it.

I've been practicing the ukulele quite diligently and have added more songs to my repertoire in the manila colored book that Tsuka requisitioned for me. But, where Higgins, Tsuka, and Morimoto can make the uke sing, I still make the thing unmelodious and flat because of my big fingers and clumsiness. You'll be surprised when I come home with that little brown book full of songs and chords. And there'll be plenty more in it when this war's over.

By airmail I'm sending you also, some clippings from the *Stars and Stripes* which we have not been getting regularly, but have read more or less on the sly, borrowing from someone else. I thought they might be interesting to you. . . .

I guess that back home all must be in a frenzy about Xmas shopping and millions of dollars worth of laughable stuff will cross the seas to GIs who will snort in pity that the donor's been taken in by the stores. Setsu, Aya and Glo wrote me that they've sent me something and all the others always ask me to make a request, but I'm darned if I can. You remember once I asked you to send me some *nihon mono* [Japanese food] for Xmas. That's the only Xmas request I'll make and that's the best for all of us can enjoy it. I know that it will be appreciated. Of course, over here there isn't too much of the Xmas spirit, and you know why. We're all too busy doing a dirty job and one doesn't have the beatific attitude for these moments. But we often do wonder just where and what Xmas day finds us. In the last war there have been cases of times at the Yuletide with fraternization of enemy forces, and then the day after killing each other again when the night before they were singing "Silent Night, Holy Night" together. There's something wrong in that picture somewhere. . . .

And I would like for you to be a Y hostess if you want to and have the time. Don't let that interfere with your studies and work.

Because I want to have you go out and meet new people and have some fun. If I begrudged you that I'm not any kind of a man. And I think that it would do you a lot of good, too.

I did get a lot off my mind tonight. I only wish that I would get a chance to write every day so that I can tell you my impressions while fresh in my mind. Oh, but I was happy when mail call came around today. It had been such a helluva long time. Now I feel so much better having heard from you and having written to you. And next to dreaming, I guess there's nothing better is there, darling?

MEDICAL DETACHMENT LOG

> 23 Oct 44 left vicinity of Bruyeres and arrived near Belmont, France. Cold foggy morning, slightly warmer in the afternoon. Casualties passing thru aid station very light.

> 25 Oct 44—vicinity of Belmont, France. Cold foggy day. The Bns are on momentary and much needed rest, sheltered in farm houses around Belmont. By order of the Division Commander, shuttled back to Laval, France for a hot shower. Hot food served to all. Weather: Cold and rainy. Extensive shelling by enemy village and vicinity during the afternoon and night.

24 OCTOBER 1944

We're still at the farmhouse resting up. Things have become more or less peaceful for us in this rest period, the war having moved on ahead. The only reminder we have is the heavy stuff the Jerries throw in the vicinity, not too close nor not too far, just enough to let us know that they're throwing 'em. But, it's purely harassing fire and at random. But a couple of nights ago around midnight when we could feel the house shake a couple of times from the shell explosions, you should have seen the household take off for the cellar, while most of us slept through it all blissfully. . . .

So far as I know, Sammy's still in Italy—he's probably at some replacement depot sweating out an assignment. I hope he never comes back here, but stays in some PBS [Peninsula Base Section] or CBS job. Haven't seen Franklin nor Augie, but I'm sure that they're both okay. I'll bet that lazy brother of yours is neglecting correspondence again.

On clear days when visibility is halfway decent the usual quartet of Thunderbolts—P47s—cavort in the skies above looking for targets and it does our hearts good especially when they bank in succession and go into a dive and start strafing at some sad Jerry object that's their target. We've seen them lay their bombs in, too. We can see them go into their steep dive and then the puffs of smoke from their eight 50 cal. Mgs [Machine guns] and then seconds later we can hear the staccato report floating to us. That certainly is a lift to our morale.

Momoda and I've been talking about the French Alps and if and when we ever get a chance we'll see what the skiing's like over here. That seems a very remote possibility, but we can at least dream about it. I don't think we're too far from the mountains. . . .

It's good to know that Tama's recuperating now without too much ill effects. And how's Harry nowadays? I hear no mention of him at all. Tell them both that I sent a big "hello."


25 OCTOBER 1944

The status quo so far as we're concerned, remains unchanged and we're still ensconced in this French farmhouse where we clutter up the parlor and kitchen like one big happy family. The language constitutes a big bar to more friendly relations with the folks here, but we get along very well exchanging services and goods. The other day they had a whole mess of meat and it made our mouths water to smell the aroma, that fragrant odor of a frying steak. Whenever we talk about food it's always with the great longing for *nihonshoka* [Japanese food] of rice with *sashimi* [raw fish], fish, *tsukemono* [pickled vegetable], *tempura* [batter-fried food, usually fish or vegetables] and *china meshi* [chinese food]. Just why we do like to torture ourselves with these gastronomic thoughts and talk is beyond me, but it never fails whenever we begin to get hungry. It must be awfully confusing to the haole litter bearers with us when they hear us talking about *nizakana* [poached fish] and *buta dofu* [pork tofu—i.e., bean curd], etc. Poor guys, all they can talk about is steak and chops and roasts. How limited their capacity as gourmets!

Five of us hopped on a jeep this morning in search of a shower unit somewhere in the vicinity, but rambled for nothing. We couldn't find any bath units and so I'm afraid I'll have to remain dirty for awhile yet. I haven't changed my longies since I put them on when we got to France—they're just like another skin on me—I guess I'll have to change them when they rot off.

The ukulele lessons still come right along—just making more additions to the music book and the fingers are getting more facile in their choice of strings. I've been playing pinochle with the fellas and that helps occupy the time too.

I'm signing off for tonight, darling, there isn't too much to talk about. Dusk is falling now—the time goes pretty fast. It's a pity that man can't think of anything better to do with his time than to wage war.

......................................................................................................................

On October 23, the First Battalion of 141st Infantry Regiment was cut off by the Germans. After only two days of much-needed rest from combat, the 442nd was ordered to rescue this "lost battalion." They met intense resistance. —DIANNE BRIDGMAN

......................................................................................................................

MEDICAL DETACHMENT LOG

26 Oct 44. Weather: Warm, sunny in the morning and cloudy and colder in the afternoon. Battalions enjoying their second day as

reserve, had their rest abruptly alerted and were ordered to pull up the following morning.

27 Oct 44—Belmont, France. Blue Bn and Aid Station moved into the forest near Biffontaine with the important mission of breaking through the reinforced German line of resistance and relieving the "LOST BATTALION" [the first Bn of the 141st Infantry Regiment]. Aid station set up in a dugout, jointly with White Aid Station. Enlisted men in respective battalion paid, under fire and shelling. Heavy enemy shelling of vicinity during the night.

## 27 OCTOBER 1944

We've moved up again after the cozy four days at the other farm-house. We're kind of chiseled in with the Regtl boys in occupying a couple of houses by the side of the road. The forward elements of our group have set up some distance forward much closer to the boys while we in the rear sit on our fannies and wait for I don't know what. I slept quite nicely last night by the stove although the inconsiderate Jerries threw in a few last night to disturb our slumbers. They tell me that this is a regular procedure. I don't doubt it. Even our guns firing make a heck of a lot of noise, shaking the house and causing distinct pulsations that we can easily feel, not to mention the rattling of the windows. It's funny how one gets used to this noise, though, doing what we were before the firing, but the Jerries throwing it our way can certainly be a harassing factor.

## MEDICAL DETACHMENT LOG

28 Oct 44—The Ammunition and Pioneer Platoon of the BN section sent up forward to construct additional dugouts for the litter patients at the forward aid stations. Heavy casualties throughout the day and

night. Wounded were taken care of in dugouts with candle light and flashlight power, due to blackout conditions. The dugout could accommodate two litter cases at a time.

Both White and Blue Aid stations worked all night and finally evacuated their last casualty about 2:00 AM 29 Oct 44—vicinity of Belmont, France. Colonel Pence injured in action, evacuated to the rear hospital. Casualties passing through aid stations heavy. Sent extra litter bearers from Anti-Tank Company to 2d and 3d Bn Aid station 28 Oct and 29 Oct 44. Continued freezing weather and cases of trench foot were becoming more numerous daily.

30 Oct 44—First report, about two o'clock in the afternoon, that the advanced patrols of the 3d Bn broke through to the "LOST BATTALION". Five days of hard fighting on the line, aid men working tirelessly trying to evacuate the wounded under continued fire and in foggy wet and freezing weather.

...........................................................................................................................

The Third Battalion of the 442nd finally broke through to the "lost battalion" on October 30, 1944. The rescued men leaped out of their foxholes and hugged their rescuers. The 442nd had sustained 814 battle casualties. They saved 211 men.

More than any of their awards, the 442nd valued a walnut-and-silver plaque given to them by the "lost battalion" The inscription reads: "To the 442nd Infantry Regiment with deep sincerity and utmost appreciation for the gallant fight to effect our rescue after we had been isolated for seven days, First Battalion, 141st Infantry Regiment, Biffontaine, France from 24 to 30 October, 1944."
—DIANNE BRIDGMAN

...........................................................................................................................

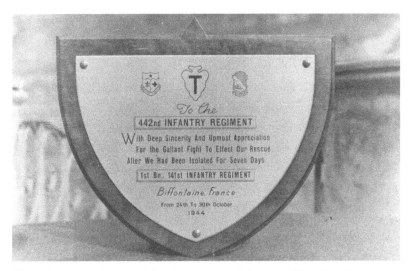

Plaque honoring the 442nd for their rescue of the 141st First Battalion. The 442nd sustained 814 casualties to save 211 men.

## 31 OCTOBER 1944

If you hadn't noticed before these lines are being written on German paper. It's of pretty good quality, isn't it? The watermark says Argentina, but this was picked up from some German stuff left behind, so naturally, I have to use it. It's better than our onion skin—smoother.

Don't be angry because I haven't written you for some time now. I'd been up into the woods at the forward aid station for a couple of days and just got back last night. In my last letter I told you that we'd edged in with Regtl. A couple of days ago Momoda, Ike, Higgins, Hayashi and I went up to relieve the others at the advance station high up in the woods. It's a long terrible haul up to there from the main road—the road all mucky and the engineers are hard at work on it—when we came back we noticed quite an improvement, but it's still bad from the standpoint of the casualties who have to suffer each jolt in the slow moving ambulance. No houses being available in those pine woods on that ridge, they'd dug a dugout about eight by fifteen over which they'd placed hewn logs and branches to obstruct any shrapnel that happened to come along. And being only about three feet high, you can see that it wasn't made for comfort. The 3d Bn had consolidated forces with us up there and that was rather fortunate for them because we gave them quite a hand. At the time it was made, we could not have gone forward much more than that and still be prudent. They shelled quite often and inconsiderately enough, usually around mealtimes when the kitchen jeep (good boys and hardworking) pulled up with hot chow. At nights we'd throw shelter halves over the front end and work inside (only two litters' space) with flashlights. Under conditions as that the work can be extremely trying and especially with a dearth of flashlights. That last night I hacked out a couple of reflectors for candles so that we would get some control on the light and that was a help. It was quite cold in the woods and at night in that dugout where about twelve of us slept on the ground it wasn't too bad because of our proximity and at least, I slept cozily, wedged (how true that word is) between Futamata and the bank. I'm sorry to say that we were quite busy and although I'd taken my stationery up there, I didn't get a chance to write you. That one day we worked till 1:00 AM steadily and that's not good. We treated quite a few Jerries and I'm sending home some stuff that I acquired off them—but that'll be later. I saw Eiji up there, looking just like GI Joe and he wanted to volunteer as an aid man, since they were short. He'll probably get his wish. He worked with Abe and Ogami and the rest of the 3d Bn crew and Abe told me that Franklin has been sent in for an arthritic knee, so he's been missing some of the fireworks on these hills, thank God for that. Incidentally, Kozuma sustained a slight shoulder wound about a week ago and he's gone, too. When we were relieved yesterday, the 3d Bn station had moved up the road further and we were contemplating it. But, we came on back here to this house anyway and we're expecting a call (I hope not today) to go forward to a better position for treating and evacuation of casualties. One other thing we're thankful for is that it didn't rain while we were there, otherwise it would have been that same misery all over again for everybody.

Mail came to us up there with the chow wagon and now I have to start writing all over again to catch up and here I'd thought that I was through for awhile. . . . You've been such a good correspondent that I've seven letters of yours to answer with this one—seems as if you're getting gypped in the exchange. . . .

I'm glad that you had an opportunity to meet Ted Matsuo who must have given you some good stories about what's going on over here. He was hit on the 2d day of our going into the lines, but his F Co had a hard enough time the first day for him to know the rigors of war.

The weather here is just as cold as ever—today the sun has condescended to show its face and that's good, not only from the angle of heat and light, but because that gives our planes a chance to go out and bomb and strafe the Jerries and that's a terrific help to the ground troops. It does our heart good to see them wheeling and banking in the sky. Even though the sun does come out there is always a threatening cloud bank to mar the sky. Even as I write this now, it has become overcast.

We set up our own GI stove last night in this room of ours in pretty quick time and it's a very big help. The fuel is derived from the woodbin of this unsuspecting French farmer. But, it was pretty cold last night after the fire burned out—I slept more comfortably in the dugout night before last.

I've a lousy headache today and I'm in no mood for letter writing so I think I'll close for now. I'll write better on some better day.

MEDICAL DETACHMENT LOG

New month began with cold, frosty wet weather. Forward aid stations established in dugouts, with heavy logs for protection against small arm fire, artillery and mortar barrages. Regtl Aid

Station left vicinity of Belmont, France, and arrived vicinity of Grebe-fosse, France, and set up aid station in the same farmhouse with 2d Bn rear aid station.

Casualties passing through aid station 2 Nov 44 very light.

## 2 NOVEMBER 1944

I feel much better this morning—I've changed all my underwear, longies and all, the first change since about a month ago. It was just like peeling the skin off me. And now they're hanging up in the room by our GI stove drying. Even though I hadn't bathed before putting the clean changes on, it still feels good next to my skin.

At the present time our aid station group that was relieved and sent back here are still here enjoying a very good rest. That's what we were told to do and we're not kicking it one bit. Back here one wouldn't know that there's a war on. The forward group has moved a couple of times into houses from the hectic days in the dugout, but as yet we're still awaiting orders to move up. And in the meanwhile, we're taking it oh, so easy and catching up with stuff and things.

I spent practically all day yesterday making myself a bedroll in anticipation of a cold winter. What a job that was, too. I've four blankets and a comforter (picked up somewhere) all sewed up in an ingenious manner and wrapped up by a couple of shelter halves. I tried it out on the floor last night and it was very satisfactory. It certainly saves one a lot of time and trouble in going to sleep at nights and packing up. All I have to do is unroll it, pile in, and in the AM pile out and roll it up. For me who loves that extra wink, you can imagine what a time saver that is. . . .

Xmas packages have begun to come in and naturally, everybody shares everybody elses. When Futamata got one up in the hill the other day, the poor guy didn't have chance to even dip his mitts into it. If the sender could ever see the way the stuff is grabbed at, I'm sure that she or he would feel that the money and trouble were well worth it.

## Medical Detachment Log

3d Nov 44—Vicinity of Grebefosse, France. Cold rainy day. Casualties light.

4 Nov 44—Usual duties. Weather: Cold rainy day. Casualties passing through aid stations very light. Winter clothing issued to personnel, consisting of the new-type field jacket, wool sweater, shoe pacs, and heavy socks.

5, 6, 7 Nov 44, vicinity of Grebefosse, France. Cold weather continued and a steady rain impeded operations and filled the slit trenches. The cold rain and hot shell fell steadily and turned the litter train route into a mudhole. Jeep evacuation was over narrow and very rough terrain under persistent enemy shelling, causing our jeeps and the Chaplain's to be riddled with shell fragments. At one occasion in order to evacuate casualties, the litter train had to station jeeps on both sides of the bog and trans-ship the wounded.

## 6 November 1944

It's hard for me to begin writing even though there is so much to say to you. It gets like this whenever we have too much rest and such. Back in Italy with our constant moving I could dash off letters easily, but this situation now makes it different. . . .

You recall that when I last wrote, we were more or less rear echelon and considered ourselves at some CBS rest camp, while we were burdened with an acute case of boredom. The next day a call came down for a technician to come up so I gathered my junk and made my way up past scores of rear echelon outfits (we were quite a ways back, I saw) up to this middle echelon house, where most of the guys and officers were. Kuge, Wachi, and Onodera had gone up further to a forward station and Morimoto, Tsuka and I jeeped up to replace them. After the five days of fanny beating, the activity was welcome. The road up (we're still on the same horrible ridge) was muddy and all chewed up, as was expected. Although the forward dugout is only about five miles up this road, it's still a long and slow haul.

The 3d Bn Aid Station had set up housekeeping on this spur of the hill, by a point so they say—(I never took the trouble to explore) and us three and the two technicians and jeep driver just kind of moved in on them. So we were working together again as we had a week previously—this dugout wasn't so very big and so we set about enlarging it with an extension. The hard working engineers were hard at it fixing a road close by and they were minus a few of their planks before we got through. But, needing more protection Morimoto and I girded ourselves and labeling our efforts as lumberjacking, chopped down towering pine trees with expert precision. It was the first hard labor for a long time and I was plenty corked, but the extension was a huge aid and with the tent flap over it both waterproof and a psychological comfort against treebursts. I broke my blister again, too. I'm very glad that business wasn't too rushing. It was darker than the ace of spades that night and we three decided to sleep together 'neath the slanting logs on our tent blankets. Unfortunately the terrain was such that Morimoto on the lower end just rolled down slowly dragging the blankets and Tsuka and I'd follow suit periodically when we found ourselves stripped of cover and that was too frequent that night. We ended up the next morning in positions far distant from where we laid our weary bodies that previous night.

At that we were rather steadily busy, but we were relieved by the previous crew and we came back to this house. But, at this writing Kuge, Wachi and Onodera have come back and the CBS having moved up—Momoda, Ike and Higgins have gone up with the two officers and they're hashing over the situation with the usual bitching and tales going around. If this damn outfit doesn't get relieved pretty soon, there's gonna be nothing left of it. All that we're waiting for is relief. The usual latrine talk permeates the atmosphere about that.

The rear station also had the Regtl in the same house in a rear room—we have the front living and bedroom. The only bad thing about this place is that there are cannons and artillery about and one 155 [155-millimeter artillery piece] is only fifteen yards from the house and when that thing goes off, and it does unexpectedly, we all jump. Dust comes down and the blanket covering the window just concaves in from the blast. It can be quite nerve-racking—luckily it doesn't fire too often but when it does what a helluva noise.

It's good to be back here safe and comfortable under a roof and with the stove burning cheerily in the corner. Last night the ukuleles and guitar were in noisy evidence and Capts Okonogi and Ushiro, Morimoto and I had a good time singing and playing the old songs. That's what I like best. Incidentally, Higgins wrote home to his brother for a couple of ukes and one of them is gonna be mine. Isn't that swell of him? It should be showing up in about three months. Jitchaku's a swell player and I had fun trying to follow his too nimble fingers. Can you picture my fumbling hands?—but I can still holler loud enough to drown the discord my digits make.

It's drizzling outside, the same as when it began this morning. That means just that much more misery for the front line. What a horrible place this is for weather. The jeeps go clanking by on chains and even for them it's a difficult thing to plow through some of the mess of gumbo the roads are. In sharp contrast to this I've read of the fine weather some of the past days have seen back home—in Minneapolis, too. There the leaves must be falling and with the coming of fall comes King Football. How I miss those sharp autumn days of sunlight—the roaring stadium cheering twenty-two specks of men on the green turf. Minnesota's Gophers aren't doing too good, are they? And the terrific [loss] UW took from Southern Cal was very discouraging and a crushing blow to my Washington pride.

It did my heart good to hear that you had dinner together with Joe and Mary and Sam and Aya. That must have been a festive occasion. I certainly wished that I could have been there. I'm so darn glad that some of our old friends are about that can bring back such good memories by their actual presence. . . .

Remember that I asked you for a sweater? The supply just issued us the GI sleeved kind and it's a big help so if you want to, you can forget that request. Also the socks since we're gonna get thick woolen ones with our Arctic shoes of rubber bottoms and leather tops. It keeps the water out and is a very big help. I've one on now that came off some haole infantry man and since I had the only feet big enough to fill 'em I got 'em. The army tries pretty hard to get us outfitted properly, but the distribution is still pretty slow. If I could get winter coveralls now and a new field jacket I'd be happy. Let's hope that by the time you read this I have them.

What a kind forethought to stamp some of these envelopes, but that's just like you as was the cute little "Dammit" card. I and others got a huge kick out of that. Thanks again, darling, and now having said my say I'll break off this overlong missive with a very forlorn

So long

## MEDICAL DETACHMENT LOG

7 Nov 44—During the day, relief of the 442d Infantry by the 142d Infantry was begun. The 100th Bn Section returned to Bruyeres during the morning, while 2d Bn Aid Section displaced rearward to Fays in the afternoon.

8 Nov 44—Vicinity of Grebefosse, France, cold misty day, rained steadily and late in the evening changed over to our first SNOWFALL.

9 Nov 44—Cold cloudy day with slight snowfall, causing much discomfort on the wounded and likewise was causing numerous cases of trenchfoot among the front line troops.

10 Nov. Casualties passing through aid stations light. Left vicinity of Grebefosse, France and arrived Femenil, France. Aid station set up in a farmhouse. 3d Bn set up their aid station at Le Panges, France, upon being relieved by 1st Bn, 142nd Infantry Aid Station. 1st Bn Aid Station moved along with 100th Bn and left the Bruyeres area in the morning of the 9th to Army rest center at Bains Le Bains.

## 10 NOVEMBER 1944

Hello darling—It's about time that we got together again. Possibly you can detect a little more cheerful note to the greeting. And there's a darn good reason for that. We've pulled back!—and that's no rumor. We'd sweated it out for days and it's actually come to pass. Just how long it'll be and where we're going is the subject in many a latrine, but I have no concern about that. The point is that right now we're in rest and I intend to put it to the best use. If you can only comprehend what that means—to pull back out of the lines. Away from all the things that make war the nightmare that it can be. But now that that's in the past, we may as well enjoy the present to the full and be optimistic about the future.

When we finally dragged our fannies out from the hills in the fast deepening dusk of that last afternoon, the rain was coming down and the trucks and jeeps jammed the road but we were plenty happy. For a warm room with a crackling stove awaited us. And then there were packages waiting and mail, too. One package was from you for the boys—they'd held up opening it until I could get back to break the cord. That was certainly an inspiration and the boys were very happy about it—they asked me to thank you for the kindness. Natcherly, it's all gone now. Mayme sent me a package of stuff, too. Had *foonyu* [a Chinese egg dish with vegetables], rice, *ebi-no-tsukadani* [pickled shrimp] and *ika-no shiokaru* [salted squid] in it. It was certainly relished today when we had rice this noon. I'm enclosing the card she sent with the package.

Now that we've pulled back out of the lines and back to this little town, everything is so nice. Even the weather doesn't touch us. The last night in the dugout it began showering and has sprinkled sporadically. A thin layer of white blankets the trees and fields. It is a pretty night, but I'm more concerned about the cold. It's begun falling again and I can see it slanting down, driven by the wind, but in here it's cozy and warm, crowded though the room is.

That last night in the dugout was really one bitch of a night. It had rained continuously and the dugout leaked like a sieve and there was a regular stream running through it and where the stream wasn't was just a mess of mud. If one could see the scene in retrospect, it must have been an amusing one—all soaked to the skin and trying to keep warm, a physical impossibility by the way. The day wasn't so bad, but how in hell were we to sleep? Only five slept in the protected part of the dugout that night—the rest piled into the warm ambulance and sat all night trying to sleep and not succeeding while spending tortuous hours with aching cramped limbs. We were all glad for the daybreak. And casualties—trench feet and all came in steadily—even though we were pulling out that day. We could see our boys moving out but we couldn't wait until our Bn had gone out. We cussed and sweated that out—all packed and ready to go. When the signal finally came in the late afternoon twilight, we were afraid we may have to sleep there again that night because once the night sets in about 7 it's impossible to move because one can't see one's hand in front of one's face. But we took off amid jammed traffic and got home thankfully. We sang up that night, I can tell you.

And then we moved over here yesterday and occupied this house, at least the one room. It's a pretty nice room, but we had a devil of a time getting the room. The madame here objected, but we moved in anyway, with the Colonel's permission, but I think they're happy about it now because they've got so much in return in the form of chow, candies, tobacco, etc. In fact, she's doing my washing now. There are two small girls here, Jeannine and Simone, that are the most rascally girls, but we have a lot of fun—they call us Japanese 'Boche and heave snowballs at us and generally give us a bad time.

Yesterday morning we took a shower at a well ventilated, steamy shower unit and though we near froze to death, we came out feeling clean and refreshed and our RSO [Regimental Supply Officer] was on the ball and dished out clean underwear and ODs so we were clean the first time in weeks and it was a darn good feeling.

I had a letter from Kozuma yesterday and the doggone guy outlines all the fun he's having back in the hospital. He's recuperating nicely and tells me to get hurt and come back and have a good time and chow. We should be seeing him soon—he didn't give any return address. . . .

I'm sending out by another air mail along with this some clippings which all should be self explanatory. . . .

I'm sending a small can home filled with all kinds of junk. You can sort them out. The separate book came off a Jerry as you can see by the picture in the front. He's wearing the combat badge and an Iron Cross decoration. Inside the can you'll find—two plastic (one red and one black) containers of water purifying tabs, I think. Then a couple of Jerry ribbons—one (the red with black stripes) for the Russian campaign and the other (the red, white, and navy) for the Iron Cross. The flower arm patch is the Edelweiss and identifies that certain outfit. You'll notice the gray green patch with it—that's the Nazi uniform color. And then the T patch of the 36 Div which we were issued. The German eagle over the target was cut off a Jerry cap and the other eagle was cut out over the pocket flap. Interestingly, I found an evangelical field book showing that just as us they have belief in God, too, although they put the Reich first. To fill the can you'll find an Italian and German-aid packet of small bandages. Oh, and then there's the epaulet of the 109th—some outfit that ran up against us. I don't know what it stands for. I got some other junk too I'll be sending off soon, if you can stand it.

I have said enough, haven't I? I guess everything at home's going smoothly—I wish I could say the same. No matter what, I still miss you very much.

10 and 11 Nov 44. Cold cloudy day with slight snowfall. Memorial Services were held for those who had died in battle. Bns taking it easy with usual rest area activities. At a Regimental formation in the vicinity of Le Panges, France on a cold and cloudy day with heavy snow falling, a special tribute was paid to the fighting qualities of the officers and men of the unit by Major General John E. Dahlquist, Commanding Officer of the 36th Division. General Dahlquist told the assembled, we quote: "We have only the utmost admiration for you and what you have accomplished. No fighting nor finer soldierly qualities have ever been witnessed by the US Army in its long history."

12 Nov 44—Femenil, France. Cold cloudy day, moderate snowfall during the night. Casualties treated at aid stations and evacuated including trench foot, battle fatigue. Disease and carded for record cases in the battle just finished in the Vosges Mountains sector were well in the neighborhood of 2000. Men enjoying Special Service recreation, movies and the Combat Team Band furnished well prepared musical entertainment. Later a ration of beer distributed to all sections. Men given special attention to instructions in the prevention of trenchfoot.

13 Nov 44—Battalion section making preparation to move into line. Movement began to forward area, relieving 2d bn, 142d Infantry, in a defensive position. 3d Bn followed up in the afternoon.

## 13 NOVEMBER 1944

I guess you can tell by the fine point that I'm writing this with the pen that you sent me. It's just what I wanted—thanks very much. The package arrived in very good shape and has now departed into various mouths. Just now Ike. . . . cooked up the soup. He didn't realize that a cupful isn't anywhere near one canteen cupful so it was kind of dilute. But with rice on the menu the past three days for lunch we've been eating like kings what with our collective accumulation of *foonyu-zuke* [pickled tofu] etc. Boy, do we consume the rice? I think you know the answer already. Was it good, too! Yesterday we had fried chicken and we just sat around and picked on it to our hearts content up to our elbows in the delectable fowl, our first for a long time. Incidentally, the cookies you sent Hayashi came the same day as mine and he was both surprised and happy. It really doesn't make too much difference who receives a food or candy package because once it's opened it's community property anyway. It works swell that way—share and share alike. That's one way we have a variety of delicacies. It looks as if we feast on rice again tonight. Having just got some from the kitchen and we've some of that stuff left. . . .

It seems that our days of rest (sweet days) are come to an end. The outfit has moved up into the lines again this morning. We moved up bag and baggage, too, but found no houses available yet so had to drag our fannies all the way back again to this same house. They were surprised to see us again after we'd bid them "au revoir" this AM. We'll move up tomorrow again though. Decimated though we are we still have to go into the lines. Sometimes I wonder if they know what they're doing.

If you could be over here you'd wonder just how we could wage any type of warfare. Snow has fallen and now blankets the whole countryside in its mantle of white and we have its accompanying cold. Yet under this beautiful snow-covered vista there still lurks death and destruction. And this is still the beginning of winter. The snow is just about a two inch coat, how is this war going to be conducted when the snow lies so many feet deep and when the cold becomes more intense? Well, we'll find out soon enough, I guess. But the few days that we've had here have been ones of good relaxation and companionship. The poker players huddle around the makeshift table and rattle chips to their hearts' content (but only till ten because the whole floor becomes occupied with sleepers), the ukulele and guitar con-

Package from home, 1944. Packages of Japanese food were anticipated and shared.

verts make with the noise, others write letters, but the best fun we have is after we're bedded down and the lights are out. Then we have all sorts of arguments and discussions over women, radio, music, sports, women, food, war, politics, women, etc. These last nights we've gone to sleep with belly pains from laughing so hard at these arguments.

On Saturday (11th) memorial services were held on a newly swept mine field. I didn't go. You know how I feel about funerals and services. We've had more stars put on our flag now— more than what we had the first engagement in Italy. That's depressing enough for anyone, and for those who are waiting for these to come home, how crushed they must be.

Yesterday saw a parade formation held to present individual citations for those whose applications came through. There must have been quite a few—Bronze Stars, Silver Stars and such. These were for the Italian campaign just come through.

I'm sending you some clippings that will be of very much interest to you—at least they were to me. This one issue devoted solely its Sunday supplement to the 442d and it's the best we've seen yet. The other gives you an idea of the hell the infantry has to go through. The other clipping will give you an idea of some of the troops we've run up against.

I've yielded to temptation again and tried growing a mustache again. It seems to be going better than it ever did before. The previous time I just took one look and whacked it off. This one promises to have greater longevity. Wish I had a camera. I've had some very critical and promising suggestions on its proper growth and care so don't worry about it.

Thanks again, honey—gonna stop now. The guys are all bedding down now.

## Medical Detachment Log

Nov 14, 44—Marmonfosse, France—Cold cloudy day with light snowfall. Regtl Section left Femenil, France, and arrived vicinity of Marmonfosse, France. Aid station set up in a farmhouse. Casualties passing through aid stations light. Usual combat duties performed.

15 and 16 Nov 44—Marmonfosse, France. Cold and foggy, light snowfall. Casualties light. Sometime back on 22 Oct 44, we sent a letter to Dr. Ernie Pyle of the Scripps-Howard Newspaper Alliance, 1013 Thirteenth St., NW Washington, D.C. We quote his letter:

*Dear Folks:*

*Ernie Pyle has asked me to thank you for your letter of October 22d, in which you wished to enlist his aid in behalf of the Medics for an infantry medics badge and the ten dollar raise which the combat infantrymen have been awarded. As you can see by the enclosed copy of Ernie's column of September 4, he has already tried to 'go to bat' for you all.*

*IN FRANCE—The last time I was with the front-line medics—a battalion detachment in the Fourth Division—they showed me a piece in the Stars and Stripes about Congress passing the new ten dollars-a-month pay increase for soldiers holding the combat infantrymen's badge. This Combat infantry badge is a proud thing, a mark of great distinction, a sign on a man's chest to show that he has been through the mill. The medical aid men were feeling badly because the piece said they are not eligible for the badge. Their captain asked me what I thought, and so did some of the enlisted aid men and I could tell them truthfully that my feelings agreed with theirs. They should have it. And I'm sure any combat infantryman would tell you the same thing.*

*Praise for the medics has been unanimous ever since this war started. And just as proof of what they go through, take this one detachment of battalion medics that I was with. They were thirty-one men and two officers. And in one seven-week period of combat in Normandy this summer they lost nine men killed and ten wounded. A total of nineteen out of thirty-one men— a casualty ration of nearly 60 per cent in seven weeks. As one aid man said, probably they have been excluded because they are technically noncombatants and don't carry arms. But he suggested that if this was true they could still be given a badge with some distinctive medical marking on it, to set them off from medical aid men who don't work right in the lines.*

*So I would like to propose to Congress or the War Department or whoever handles such things that the ruling be altered to include medical aid men in battalion detachments and on forward.*

*They are the ones who work under fire. Medics attached to regiments and to hospitals farther back do wonderful work too, of course, and are sometimes under shellfire. But they are seldom right out on the battlefield. So I think it would be fair to include only the medics who work from battalion on forward.*

*I have an idea the original ruling was made merely through a misunderstanding, and that there would be no objection to correcting it.*

## 15 November 1944

Now that the outfit's up in the lines again and we're settled in this house, there's time to write so this is it. We moved into this house yesterday after the usual snafu situation. It never fails and makes us bitch no end. Not that it could have been helped, but it helps to release tension and steam by vocal emesis.

The house is the usual farmhouse, but the people have moved to safer localities and we've the house to ourselves. It's a good thing that there's plenty of rooms because we've a couple of extra litter squads to take care of. The situation is more or less static for which we are very thankful. After all what with all the snows and rain and cold, one can't do too much. It's been snowing every day, but not constantly—one day, sleet; the next big flakes wafting down slowly (a beautiful sight) and then today it swirled down in tiny particles. Snow is particularly bad for all because one can't see the wires that trip off mines—we had one case this morning while at breakfast.

Speaking of breakfast, we don't have the kitchen bringing up hot chow now—we're reduced to the 10 in 1 rations, but Kotoku from the kitchen has come up to keep coffee for the casualties and he's good enough to take charge of our meals, too. Good thing that. But, the fellas all pool their talents and manual labors to help out. What a helluva time I had preparing and cooking the fried potatoes. There's a cow here and to relieve the poor beast of any complications, Pat the litter bearer, did a little work on the faucets and we had fresh milk with our cereals. Unpasteurized, un-tuberculin tested though it may be, it was very welcome. Who knows, we may expect to make our own ice cream soon. Yesterday, the boys got their mitts on some cabbage from the French garden and we had corned beef and cabbage—very good, it was, too. . . .

The fact that we're so close to the actual front lines stymies our nightly ukulele and guitar sessions, but we play it in the daytime. When we've our rolls on the floor all stretched out in the night and the candles burn low, the usual bull session starts up over the myriads of subjects that these usual conferences bring up. This is one good part of the day, and I enjoy it very much, this interchange and argument of ideas and events.

MEDICAL DETACHMENT LOG

17 Nov 44—movement to rear area for new assignment begun. 2d and 3d Bns sections left Marmonfosse sector and set up aid stations in Docelles, France, some thirty miles rearward. Regtl section closed in the same vicinity.

18 Nov 44—Docelles, France. Warm sunny day. Regiment in rest and enjoying a much needed cleanup and rest. Permanently attached Red Cross Field representative, Mr. Larry Collins, brought two Red Cross girls to help distribute coffee and doughnuts to the enlisted men in the various battalion sections. Photographers took pictures of EM to make the "Home Town Edition." Fourteen new replacements assigned to detachment.

18 NOVEMBER 1944

I don't even know whether the above is the correct day nor even what day of the week it is, time is that elusive a thing here. But, it doesn't make too much difference; time for us will begin again when the war is over and we can begin to live again instead of just existing.

Since I wrote you last, we've pulled out of the line again. We'd heard the usual smokehouse talk, but when we scrammed, we scrammed fast. We didn't sweat anything out—one morning the relief outfit came, we packed and out we went just like that. Since that period (quite short) was not at all trying, there was not that overwhelming desire for relief. It was practically the same as a rest period, just eat, sleep and pass the time away. But, we're not gonna stay if they don't want us, so here we are now, quite some distance back from the lines in a French farmhouse that is quite adequate. We've much more room here than in previous billets and the bulk of us sleep upstairs. . . .

It's a sunny clear day today—a rare occasion and as I look out through the window the French countryside is clean and green, basking in the sun. And though the chill is in the air the sunlight has its illusions of warmth. The drone of P47s out to do their deadly work brings back the war again even as one enjoys the pastoral scene.

Just where we go from here still remains a conjecture, but you know that I'll keep you posted. My best to the whole house and until the next time, darling, my very best extra special twenty-four carat love—

MEDICAL DETACHMENT LOG

The following "Commendation" letter received by our Commanding Officer from Maj Gen John E. Dahlquist, Commanding General of the Texas Division, dated 18 Nov 44. We quote:

> The 36th Division regrèts that the 442d Combat Team must be detached and sent on other duties. The period during which you have served, 14 Oct to 18 Nov 44 was one of hard intense fighting through terrain as difficult as any army has

*ever encountered. The courage, steadfastness, and willing-*
*ness of your officers and men were equal to any ever displayed*
*by United States Troops. Every officer and man of the division*
*joins me in sending our best personal regards and good*
*wishes to every member of your command and we hope that*
*we may be honored again by having you as a member of our*
*Division.*

# 4 FRANCE

*November 1944–March 1945*

In November 1944, the 442nd journeyed by truck to an assembly area near Nice, France. Here they were attached to the Forty-fourth Antiaircraft Artillery Brigade and sent to guard the French-Italian border. Their zone of action extended from the French riviera on the Mediterranean to the mountains. Although this proved to be a quiet sector, it was an important one—the Germans could have chosen to attempt to cross the border into France. Combat was limited to sporadic artillery fire. The 442nd stayed here four months. They enjoyed passes to Nice, where they stayed in hotels and shopped in stores formerly frequented only by the very rich. —DIANNE BRIDGMAN

....................................................................................................................

MEDICAL DETACHMENT LOG

19 Nov 44—All sections left bivouac area. The convoy headed south trekking 137 miles arriving at Dijon, France. Remained overnight. 30 percent of the strength allowed to visit the town of Dijon.

20 Nov 44—Left Dijon, France, by truck convoy, arriving vicinity of Macon, France, for dinner, continued southeast arriving North East of Valence, France. Bivouacked for the night. 2d day traveled 190 miles.

21 Nov 44—Left bivouac area by motor, passing thru Aix, Cannes, France and arrived at the rear assembly area South St. Jeannet. Aid stations set up. Usual rest area procedures.

22 Nov 44—Sunny blue sky, rest area activities. Usual reorganizational activities and preparation for further movement.

23 Nov 44—3d Bn Aid Section displaced forward defensive positions at Sospel, relieving 19th Armored Infantry Battalion on a very mountainous and rugged terrain, "beaucoup" hairpin turns made evacuation somewhat hazardous. White Battalion Aid Station Section remained in reserve, vicinity St. Jeannet.

Thanksgiving Day services held by all battalions, and the traditional turkey dinner enjoyed by all. Casualties very light. Colonel C. H. Pence rejoined the regiment from hospital and resumed command.

24 Nov 44—As of 18 Nov 44, 442d Regimental Combat Team (Less 100th Bn Section) relieved from all attachment to VI Corps and reverts to Army control as of 21 Nov 44, 442d RCT attached to 44th AAA [Antiaircraft Artillery] Brigade for administration, supply and operations, assignment to 7th Army remains unchanged. Sunny warm day. Casualties through 3d Bn very light. Delayed turkey dinner for 3d Section.

## 26 November 1944

It's been such a long time now since I've written to you that it's hard as hell to start. Here it's evening now and the kerosene lamps are lit in the aid tent and it's taken me all day to write this. . . .

First of all, the main reason I couldn't write was that we'd been on the move as is our usual wont. I can't tell you yet, at any rate, we've done some traveling. . . . At one town that we bivouacked close to, Kozuma (incidentally he's back now and in good shape) and I went to the standard carnival in this town. . . .

Kozuma went crazy on the Skooter (remember in Playland) where everybody goes around bumping each other's tiny cars. We had great fun bumping the gals brave enough to ride, as everybody else was. The carnival was just like the ones at home—there were so many cute children riding their miniature rides, all dressed up, just like dolls; very pretty these French infants.

But, all trips come to an end and this one wasn't monotonous in the least, in fact very interesting. But we were glad to get on solid ground again and stay put for awhile when we finally got here. . . . The weather here has been wonderful—the sun making its rounds daily and after the cussable weather we'd been incurring, what a welcome change.

I've a chance to see Cannes and visit Nice and I must say that this strip is beautiful. The place is really something to see. A gentle curving sandy beach with the blue Mediterranean gently lapping the shores where once the elite of the continent frolicked was now bare, but the beauty still remains, but possibly more accentuated by its solitude. Being the resort of the idle rich you can imagine the setting and the atmosphere of the city. There are gorgeous buildings and hotels—apartment houses galore. The promenade along the beach is wide and flanked by the most beautiful. No wonder they call this the California of France. There are beautiful stores of the luxury type selling the luxury type of commodities—jewelries and perfumes are everywhere. It is about the prettiest city we've seen to date. But, words can't do justice so I shall be sending you postcards of this place as soon as they lift this apparently aimless restriction on postcards.

There are many English-speaking people in Nice and that's a great boon and a relief to us who up till now, more or less relied on the sign language. But when I went into a shop and said "Ave-vou-" and she said, "what was it you wanted?" I felt very foolish indeed. After that I used English practically all the time. The people dress here in their accustomed swell clothing and now that I've seen the female population here, my opinions of French mademoiselles

Min in Nice, France, 1945. He enjoyed sitting at a sidewalk cafe, sipping drinks and watching the "passing parade."

have made a complete turnabout. They are dressed nicely, painted adequately and when they go by on their ubiquitous bicycles I can testify that they have shapely gams, too. . . .

   We discovered one restaurant on a hungry night and it was a revelation to us (the superior attitude of Americanism again). It was one of those cozy type of places that has an air of refinement. It's reflected in the old but shiny clean furnishings and walls and in the clientele. They were all dressed in the ultra and there was only the subdued hum of voices and the lamps burned cozily in the corners. Best of all it was clean, the waiter very courteous and the food excellent. We'd a salad (these French make very tasty salads) and then a steak cooked just right with watercress and mashed potatoes and rice of all things. These we washed down with wine and topped it off with fresh grapes. The silverware and plates and servings were of the best and I enjoyed the meal. For me it was the first time that I felt as if I'd eaten someplace back home, since arriving on Europe's shores. I hope I can get back to that place again.

I must say that in Nice money meant nothing—nothing at all. Everything is priced ridiculously, but the GIs are buying the place out. We got much more for our money in Italy, so actually we're not getting paid as much I guess. For example, the above meal in American money cost me $4.50 or 225 francs. It was worth it really to me, but can I picture myself eating at home $4.50 worth—but of course, that's America.

You know what I did in Nice, don't you. Doing the town over and shopping. I don't know where in hell I get the money but it goes faster than snow in June. You'll see what I mean when you get the packages I sent out. One is Revillon's Carnet du Bal perfume that struck my fancy. . . .

Mail started catching up to us again today and I'm answering your letters. I hope mail will be coming to us regularly. We're resting now but I can't, naturally, tell you just what we're up to. . . .

We've been here some days now so natcherly the "garrison" life setup has begun again— "tents in a row," "saluting", "training schedule" and all that stuff again. But, nobody can squawk too much—a lot better than freezing up at the front and dodging shells. We had our Thanksgiving dinner here—it's a good thing that we weren't in the lines then—a feast of roast turkey, spuds, vegetables, and fruits. But, oh, to be back home on that comfortable day. I guess one can't have everything though, can one. . . .

You mentioned the passing of Yosh Kato. That was a quick job of notification and that's good. When I found out some days afterwards, it was a great shock and somehow there was something unreal to the words. Somehow, I always feel this way when I hear of one of my dear friends going. There are more, too, but like Yosh's I can't mention them at all. Many have been wounded, too. But, they at least will return, while nothing can bring these other fine boys back to the life that they struggled so hard for. Yosh was hit in the early days of our initial engagement (Abe told me this later) when a tree burst caught his squad and it just so happened that he was the unlucky one, the only one, that got hit by the spraying shrapnel. I'm glad that he died instantly, since he had to go. Maybe you might write his mother and tell her of that—it may relieve her if she knew of the circumstances. He was a good soldier and had all his comrades respect—there can be no higher tribute. But, that's still no consolation to the sorrowing heart. . . .

We've a radio set (GI) that communications has put up and the music that emanates from the speaker is appreciated by all. Today I heard the "Hour of Charm" and Albert Spalding and Alec Templeton. Other nights has been Bing Crosby and Jimmy Durante on the air. We're grateful that we can hear some of these things that were everyday with us back in the dim days. This is the first time that we'd a radio like this to listen to practically all day and boy, it's swell.

MEDICAL DETACHMENT LOG

27 Nov 44—Warm "tropical" day. Regtl section left vicinity of St. Jeannet, France and arrived Nice, France. Aid Station set up in Hotel Angleterre. Usual duties.

28 Nov 44—2d Bn Aid Station moved from bivouac area vicinity St. Jeannet, by motor convoy arrived L'Escarene at distance eighteen miles. The 100th Bn rejoined the Regiment and entered combat line in the outskirts of Menton, France. Red Bn committed on the right of the 3d Bn, the Regtl frontage reached from the Mediterranean coast at Menton to Moulinet, through extremely rugged, hilly and rocky terrain.

29 Nov 44—Enemy artillery increased in intensity throughout the day.

30 Nov 44—White Section discontinued training schedule, making preparation to displace forward, duffle bags went back into storage. New month began with first PX rations being distributed since landing in France. 2d Bn Aid group left its position as Regimental reserve at L'Escarene and moved up by motor convoy to Peira Cava, France. Shower unit started, men enjoying shower facilities, getting haircuts, shave and general physical clean-up. Artillery exchange continued.

## 1 DECEMBER 1944

With the fire crackling merrily in the corner fireplace, the chandelier blazing overhead and the bull session in progress (they're haranguing about orchids—of all subjects) I can get down to business and write to you. I'd a minor jackpot today with three letters from you. . . . The days just seem to go by on wings. It seems unreal that Christmas is almost upon us and yet we can ignore it so blithely.

I received a package yesterday from Setz—dear Setz. It was nice of her. And then today a surprise package from the Federated Christian Church of Hunt who was very thoughtful with a package of candy and dried shrimp.

We have moved again but as you must have guessed by the above we are very comfortably settled in this two story house in these hills. . . .

I'm glad to know that the perfume I sent from Marseilles got home safely. Frankly, I don't know why I send so much home— must be a passion with me. Don't scold me but I've sent another home—Dorsay's de Belle Jour. I've also sent small bottles of Weil's to Rose, Glo, and Jo. . . .

I didn't tell you much about the house, did I? Well, it's two storied and we've plenty of room both upstairs and downstairs. It's a mountain villa and the forest surrounds it. The town is close by. . . . All the men sleep upstairs and the bars sleep below. The station is all set up for business, but we're not asking for any, I can tell you.

With so much room here, this one room has been set aside as a sort of a dayroom where we may sit and read, or write letters or do anything we want. Electricity is running and we've two toilets, so it's altogether a very good setup.

There is a war going on—one could very easily forget except that once in awhile we can hear some of our 155s going off. But, that's not very often. War hasn't touched this place very much. Another reminder and a rather humorous one at that is the file of pack mules that wind their way up the road led by our GIs in a somewhat novel role as mule skinners. They'll probably cuss at their stubbornness in *nihongo* [Japanese].

3 DECEMBER 1944

The radio's going full blast down here in the Capt's room. He got it yesterday from somewhere for about $100, I think. It's a small five tube job, but it does a pretty darn good job. Right now we've a German program and a soprano's hitting it up in an operatic solo. Just awhile ago we all crowded in to listen to Berlin Sally give us the news in her silken-voiced best propaganda manner. She's got a pretty good program with American music. The commentator—"George" gave a news summary of the Western Front with emphasis on Allied losses and setbacks. Then there was a period in which they tolled off some names of Allied dead that died in German hospitals. Although calculated to undermine the morale, I don't think that it is too effective and we do get a kick out of listening to it.

This afternoon (I was CQ) I listened to the "Hour of Charm"— if this radio gets a chance it's gonna be one good source of morale boost. To hear a good orchestra beating out hot and sweet swing or a symphony rolling majestically along, or a good voice come floating over the waves does our hearts plenty of good. By the way, this German program is damn good—and coming in very clear, too. The singer—a tenor—and the soprano have very good voices. . . .

I'd the most wonderful experience yesterday. I just feel happy thinking about it. I took a hot bath yesterday—actually a hot bath! What an utterly delicious sensation. What's the difference that Higgins and I shared the tub squatting and grinning at each other in a few inches of water. We reveled in the hot tub and scrubbed each other's backs and were just as happy as two kids. And you should have seen the hue of the water after we'd washed ourselves off (and with fragrant Camay, too—Higgin's contribution)—you couldn't see the immersed portions of the anatomy at all in the murky gray water. But we rinsed ourselves off in more of the fresh hot water and just poured it over ourselves still squatting like grinning Buddhas, with a canteen cup. I don't know when I've felt better, but when I got out, I just up and shaved off my mustache that I'd nursed along the past two weeks. It had been coming along nicely (that's my opinion) but it involved too much worry and time, so I sacrificed it to the altar of neatness and now I'm a shorn lamb, but I feel much better about it. Oh, but that bath, pure heaven it was.

As you can guess, we're still here at this villa that I described to you a couple of days ago. It is very peaceful here, albeit we are in the front lines, and for that we are all very thankful. The longer I stay here more appealing does this place become. We are expecting snow here soon. It had snowed in October—about three feet deep—but with the return of the sun that had melted off. Now Momoda and I are anxiously waiting for the white flakes to fall again so that we can try out our ski legs. What a thrill that'll be again!

To prepare for the coming of snow and cold, we've been busy putting away wood. We've a mess chopped up now and there are plenty of logs by the side of the house that need working on. Today being Sunday, we'll start again the assault on the logs tomorrow.

Darling, please dig up my camera—my ski camera—and box it up good and send it to me tout de suite, will you? I've been thinking about it for some time now and just now made up my mind. I don't know why I didn't ask for it before. Try and get the 620 film for me, too, will you? Any kind, but Verichrome preferred. I've been told that a request from a soldier helps in getting the films. If

so, consider this an urgent one and the more I can get the merrier. . . .
If I can get the camera and film, the record of my meanderings is
set down in black and white. I think you'd like that better, too,
wouldn't you?

MEDICAL DETACHMENT LOG

6 Dec 44—Day and night quiet except for spasmodic firing of our TD
[Tank Destroyer] into enemy's position.

7 Dec 44—Seventeen more Christmas shopping days left. Harassing
enemy fire landed in Sospel area.

8 Dec 44—A Rest Center for enlisted men of the 44th AAA Brigade
was opened at the Hotel Continental, Nice, France. Rest Center for
the officers was already in operation at Hotel Angleterre at de la
Grande Bretagno, Nice, France.

9–10 Dec 44—Enemy artillery occasionally.

9 DECEMBER 1944

I've got all my Xmas shopping done (just like home) because I was
fortunate in being able to go in with the chaplain one day. I've sent
pipes off to Roy, Yone, Sat and Dr. Rising. Also small bottles of perfume are on their way to Setsu, Ruth and Skigeko. I sent Mom a
print neckerchief or scarf. I didn't forget you, either. One flat package has all the postcards I've been accumulating once they prohibited
the mailing, but now they've lifted it. . . .

Christmas packages are still coming in and mail has been held up
because of them. That is why I haven't heard from you for some time
now. But they get here eventually. Mayme had another package for
me (the third one, incidentally) and she'd sent me hoarded packs of
cigarettes, pocket-books and candy. How like her to be generous. A
surprise package from the residents of Block 10 came too, with some

nice contributions. I sent them a thank you note yesterday. Packages are nice, but I wish those letters would get here in a hurry. . . .

I don't think I told you, but we had movies the other night at a hotel annex down the road a ways. They even showed a double feature. We trooped down there early enough to get front row seats and eagerly anticipated the films, *Janie* and *Princess O'Rourke* were on the menu and they were both tasty dishes. Did you see either or both of them? The films were a welcome break to give us an evening's entertainment. We're supposed to get more, but as yet that rumor's been unfulfilled.

## MEDICAL DETACHMENT LOG

11 Dec 44—Casualties passing through Aid Station light. Left Nice, France, by motor convoy and arrived Berre le Alpes, France. Set up aid station. 2d Bn Aid Section, Peira Cava, France—No casualties. Concert by 206 AGF [American Ground Forces] Band at the recreation hall. Weather cloudy and snowing throughout the day. 3d Bn— Heavy snowfall in mountain area, rain in valley of Sospel, activity almost nil. Twelve more shopping days before Christmas—2d Bn— Enemy shell active. Section in preparation to move back as Regimental reserve. Elements of the 3d Bn Aid Section, 65th Infantry Regiment, bivouacking vicinity Sospel to relieve 2d Bn Peira Cava.

13 Dec 44—2d Bn relieved today by the 65th Infantry, relief completed. Left Peira Cava by motor convoy and located in vicinity L'Escarene and billeted in buildings

14 Dec 44—Berre les Alpes—Sunny quiet day. Menton, France— Delegate Jospeh R. Farrington, Congressional Delegate from Hawaii, spoke to the boys yesterday afternoon at 100th Bn Rest Center, Hotel Imperial, Menton, France. Red Cross girls passed out doughnuts during lunch period and helped cooks serve. Morale superior, no activity during the night. Enlisted men enjoying passes to Nice. Show at recreation hall, usual rest area activities by 2d Bn Aid Section.

Sospel, France—Few shells landed near aid station, while throughout the night thirty-five rounds of artillery shells thrown into this sector.

## 14 December 1944

We've been on the move again and we're in this little town that I wrote you about previously, the town that was nestled in the hills. We've taken over the same house so we feel right at home here. . . .

You recall when I went on that little vacation to town. At that time I had some photos taken and yesterday I got them back. They're going out with this letter. . . .

By the way, I received the *Star Tribune* and enjoyed it very much. A couple of copies of the *Irrigator* also came and in one the casualty list from Hunt was printed. It also had pictures. Yohei was killed on the 17th—I found out today, he was the first KIA [killed in action] in his company. And he just a brand new replacement, too. That casualty list made me acquainted with some facts I hadn't known of some friends that I hadn't known were injured. It's funny, isn't it, that we're in the same outfit and we have to hear from the home paper about some of our own injuries.

Kuge bought himself some films in town and he's been having a field day snapping the camera at everybody. Onodera'd bought a camera using 116 and this beat-up thing really got a workout. Some (I should say most) came out very nicely and I'll be sending them home as soon as we can get the reprints which have already been ordered. You should be getting another set of prints (did I tell you this already?) from Kuge's gal friend to whom he sent some negatives. . . .

The Collecting Company drivers were good enough to squeeze some rice for us out of their kitchen and so it's gonna be eats tonight. Everything's prepared and we're only waiting for the others to come back. The *funyu shoga* [Japanese ginger], *umeboshi* [plums], *nori* [seaweed], and *ebi* [shrimp] are sitting patiently on the floor just waiting to be consumed. What heaven that'll be—eating funyu on hot rice!

15–19 Dec 44—Usual combat duties, weather cold with intermittent rain and poor visibility. German one-man submarine was sighted off-shore about 150 yards, headed for the beach—50 yards from the shore the submarine got stuck on a sandbar. The submarine was captured.

## 18 December 1944

The other night we got our beer rations and we drank it up in comradely fashion with the proper amount of noise and singing. Tsuka and I wielded the guitar and uke respectively and we went through the whole repertoire in boisterous fashion. It still amazes me the number of songs I know now. And then after that we had one terrific time, while I tried to teach Kuge and Momoda the jitterbug, polka, schottische, conga, rhumba, one step, two step, three step, lindy hop and waltz. You can imagine in this small crowded room. We went to sleep tired and happy that night.

For tonight, the chaplain has arranged a Xmas party for the children of this and the surrounding area. After seeing the beaucoup and beaucoup of candies stacked up in our kitchen for distribution, I can see that there'll be plenty of happy kids tonight. There'll probably be a program, too, and I'm gonna help dish out the candies. I like that job.

This morning while at sick call and taking care of a patient, I noticed Momoda making a card out for a GI who said he was from Washington. I looked at him with a healthy Washingtonian curiosity and glanced at his card. It read "Sagami, Waka." He turned out to be Yohei's brother. We had quite a chat. It's too bad when brothers have to be in the same outfit and worry up about one another. . . .

## Medical Detachment Log

20–21 Dec 44—1st Bn men not on duty went to 602 FA Battalion area to hear piano concert. Men alerted to be careful suspicious character or civilian on the street. 2d and 3d Bn Aid Stations exchanged places.

22–23 Dec 44—Menton, France—Men alerted, due to possible enemy paratroop activities. Information was received from higher headquarters that German intelligence was engaged in a major effort behind the American lines. The activity of enemy saboteurs and agents dressed in American uniform and carrying American weapons was reported. Accordingly the whole Regiment was alerted. Passes to Nice were cancelled except for "Continental" Brigade Rest Center.


## December 1944

It's only three more days till Xmas as I write this. It hardly seems possible that tempus can fugit so fast. Back home, everything must be in an uproar what with all the shopping and feasting to be done. The QM [Quartermaster] has promised us turkey with all the trimmings, but like Thanksgiving it just won't have the heart and spirit behind it to be called a feast. We'll eat out of our mess gears and everything will be more or less mixed up and we'll eat in a cold room. Nope, Xmas does not promise us too much.

Sorry I didn't write sooner, but there was a little matter of movement that we had to make. We're in another spot now and when we moved in Abe, Ogami and Co. moved to where we'd been. Just a little switch and with not much choice either way. Here, we've occupied two two-storied houses and we've plenty of room, although these are pretty well battered, probably from our shelling prior to taking it. Morimoto and I have one corner room that we've fixed up pretty cozily—and it has a fireplace that is at this moment crackling with burning logs that we chopped up this morning. I forgot to mention the 3d occupant of our suite—Morimoto's daughter, Bambina, who has a permanent bed in Jimmy's bedroll. She's quite a problem child though, sleeping when we're awake and frisky as a dog can be when we're sleepy, in the morning or at night. But, we all have a lot of fun with her; it's still a mystery why we can't teach her anything and Jimmy backs her up to the limit. I slept in the ambulance all the way up here so I don't really know what this place looks like yet. If I should ever walk around the town here, I'll try and get post cards. . . .

I told Morimoto about your decision to settle in the New England states, narrowed down to Connecticut and we had ourselves a talk. You see he comes from there. Must be a beautiful place. I don't mind going there at all. However, I can't seem to get crystallized on anything involving future plans. So, I guess we'll cross the bridge when we come to it.

The news from the other front has not been so good of late, as you probably know. The Jerries have taken an offensive plunge which might lead to anything. Naturally, we're quite anxious about it, but we're confident that they'll stop 'em soon, if they haven't already. I hope we don't have any repercussions of that offensive in our sector. [The Battle of the Bulge, an offensive in the Belgium-Luxembourg sector, was a serious threat to the Allies. It was stopped mainly by the American Third Army.]

MEDICAL DETACHMENT LOG

CHRISTMAS EVE—CHRISTMAS DAY—Cold "White Christmas" day. Men at Hotel Imperial entertained with Hawaiian renditions by 206 AGF Band. 2d Bn Section tending to their usual combat duties, while Blue section enjoying holiday as Regtl reserve.


24 DECEMBER 1944

I'm expecting to go to town again tomorrow—hence this third letter in three days. Frankly I don't exactly know what I'm going to do in

Jimmy Morimoto and Bambina, 1944. Jimmy fed, bathed, and slept with Bambina, the 2nd Battalion Medics mascot.

town except for a little shopping, but it'll mean a couple of days away from this place with my time my own and that peace of mind is something worth having. . . .

I'm enclosing another batch of reprints which should make the album more complete. If you want to you can begin an album. I've written comments on the back that you can use as titles. . . .

Since this is the day before Xmas day—Lt Futamata has promised us a bottle and we may drink up and sing up to our heart's content. Then I'll have to go to town to rest up. It'll be nice singing Christmas carols. How we used to love to sing them together.

There'll be other days in better times. So tonight I'll wish you the merriest of Christmases and send you the love in my heart.

MEDICAL DETACHMENT LOG

> 26–29 Dec 44—All aid stations remained in the same location. Weather clear and ice on trails. Unidentified plane circled overhead, then flying toward friendly naval ship approximately five miles SE of Menton and dropped bombs—no damage. Routine duty throughout the day, with preparation for IG [Inspector General] inspection. Men enjoying PX rations.
>
> 30–31 Dec 44—No changes in location of Bn Aid Stations. Regtl Aid left Berre les Alpes and arrived vicinity 4 km West Berre les Alpes, France. New Years Eve spent listening to artillery duel. Men ordered to carry gas mask at all times.

31 DECEMBER 1944

In a few hours from now, the old year will pass into the new. If ever there is a time when a man can get sentimental, maybe it is now. I don't know why this should be, for time has no special significance and tomorrow, the first day of 1945 holds no promise of a better day. But, because I love you and tonight you are so much closer in my heart, an inner compulsion makes me write to you while the seconds tick away and God begins to wind up the clock for another year.

1944 was not too kind to us—maybe 1945 will be more benevolent. As I write this in the coziness of my room, lit only by the dancing reflections from the fireplace, I am wondering what you are doing, so far away at home, and gazing into the glowing embers only serves to accentuate the grip of nostalgia. We shall try to welcome the new year with an attempt at gaiety, abetted alcoholically, but for me, the only true "Happy New Year" can be when we can sing "Auld Lang Syne" together at the stroke of twelve and I can look into your eyes, hold you close, and know that you are mine. And then and only then, can I say "Happy New Year" and know that it is sincerely said.

All my love and goodnight.

## MEDICAL DETACHMENT LOG

> New Year began with all sections in defensive positions, enjoying New Years' dinner with plenty of turkey and food for all. Enemy artillery barrage in 2d Bn Sector, causing one KIA and two WIA [Wounded in Action]. Weather throughout the day below freezing.

### 1 JANUARY 1945

Hello, darling—I may as well start off the New Year sprightly and cheerfully; there's no better way. I wrote you last night in a somewhat somber mood, but that doesn't happen too often.

Under the circumstances, I've had a very nice New Year. The last day of December dawned bright and clear and so Tsuka, Higgins, Onodera and I went on a log-gathering detail so that we wouldn't have to be bothered over New Year's Day. We found our way up the road to a point high on the mountainside where we could see the town far far below, nestled in the valley and the snow covered peaks way beyond. We could see our houses and all the surounding terrain unfolded in a beautiful fashion. We had our camera so we took some pictures. After climbing up the hillside we found some felled logs and sawed them in leisurely fashion. While browsing around on that slope we found two equipment piles of Jerry stuff that they must have left behind when wounded, because we could see plenty of mortar holes and fragments. In one pile we found some canned fish which we opened and had for lunch. Not bad at all, but it may make us smell like the Jerries who certainly smell oily and fishy. It was quite a job rolling that mess of logs down the hill to the road where the truck was. I was pretty well tired out when I got back. Wanting to be right for the New Year, I trotted off to the showers they've set up by the schoolhouse and though the water was hot enough, undressing and dressing again in the cold barnlike place was not so good. But, it was good to feel clean and have washed clothes on—a complete change all the way. You see, we've laundry service once a week now—ten pieces and that helps a lot.

In the evening, after I'd composed a letter to you, we got hold of another quart of rye and we passed it around, but we went into Higgin's and Tsuka's room and just a few of us drank it up and we played the instruments all night and sang. And then we had toast and the fish we'd gotten from the Jerry packs. We were mellowed but not drunk and it was nice. We sang "Auld Lang Syne" at midnight and had another drink all around. At twelve, I sang "I Love You Truly" for you and Higgins sang one for his Florence, too. I got to bed late, but it was a sane New Year. I got up this AM late again and thankfully without a hangover.

I just got up in time to eat the turkey dinner the kitchen had prepared for us. We had all the requisites for a dinner, too. We should be thankful that we can eat like this on holidays even though it holds no candle to being home and the food is rather messed up in our gears.

And then this evening there was a movie which they showed in shifts. I just now got back from it. Jean Arthur and Lee Bowman in *The Impatient Years* was the picture. I can't make up my mind whether I liked it or not.

From all the above, don't you think that I had a nice New Year? . . .

To help us celebrate the coming of the New Year, the Jerries have been acting up of late throwing shells with gay abandon and being a great nuisance. Evidently they must have been bolstered by the German thrust up north. None has come close to us, though we watch where the shells land some few hundred yards away. Our house is in a nicely sheltered spot. But even then, it is irksome to be awakened by the falling shells and to have to be careful more or less. We have had a few casualties from them and a couple of them were civilians. By golly, you'd think they wanted to hurt some of us by their harassing fire.

3–5 Jan 45—3d Bn Section moved into Peille, France and immediately moved into defensive operation.

## 3 January 1945

You mentioned in your letter about seeing the newsreel on the rescue of the trapped battalion. Didn't you notice the 2d Bn station flash across the screen? They're showing some shots down here in town and some of the boys have seen it. Higgins, Harry, Abe and Capt Kawaoka were recognizable. Maybe, they cut out the aid station shots in your newsreel—that's too bad, because in one they showed the actual administration of plasma to a casualty. The only reason I'm telling you this is that the hand that held the plasma bottle was mine. The guys tell me that the hand holding the bottle is shown. But, evidently, they must have cut out the aid station scenes, because you made no mention whatever of it or are you just lazy to tell me. The Signal Corps cameramen were up there by our dugout all day and snapped and shot film left and right. But, anyway, you must have known the hellish kind of terrain our boys had to fight through and the more hellish kind of weather. Thank God we're out of that—for awhile anyway.

I must have skipped writing to you yesterday—nothing to write about anyway. Things are just the same as a couple of days ago. Jerries have been quiet so far as shelling is concerned. Last night I went to see another show—*And The Angels Sing* with Betty Hutton and a mess of others. What a blonde bombshell that Hutton gal is!

## 5 January 1945

As for the war, and its progress here, one would still not know that there is such a thing. The same indolent life goes on, thank goodness. . . .

6–9 Jan 45—Misty, cold weather with heavy snowfall, knee deep at places seasoned with intermittent hostile artillery barrage. Casualty at White sector—due to mountainous terrain it was necessary to take three hours by nine litter bearers to evacuate the injured, who were wounded by an accidental grenade explosion.

11–14 January 1945—Regtl Aid left vicinity of Berre les Alpes, France, arrived at L'Escarene, France. Aid station set up with usual defensive duties. Battalion Aid Stations unchanged, weather cloudy, snow with sporadic enemy shelling in surrounding vicinity. American Red Cross girls distributed doughnuts to forward CP. PX rations of beer and candy were distributed to all. Allied military currency notes in the denominations of 500 and 1000 Francs were recalled and exchanged for Banque de France notes, due to active counterfeiting.

15–20 Jan 45—Bns in defensive with usual combat duties. Casualties in White battalion, officer and EM killed while being sent out to evacuate wounded lieutenant, ran into friendly mine field. Evacuation started for the wounded and completed 16 Jan 45, after much difficulty, due to mountainous terrain, snow and ice on trails.

## 20 JANUARY 1945

Tis a happy man that's writing this tonight, because the mailman brought me (finally!) two of your letters after what seemed a seven-year famine. And yet it was only about seven days, I guess, but nobody's been getting any mail around here. The situations becoming desperate. The *Stars and Stripes* gave an explanation for mail being stopped up; the trucks are being used to haul needed supplies and to allow movements in other fronts. If that's so, I think we can wait, but it's damn hard waiting for all of us. . . .

Nay wrote me a couple of days ago and it warmed my heart when she told me of Mom and Pop getting your Xmas gifts. They were so happy and proud to get them—they must have been wonderful gifts to see. She told me that Pop cried because he was so overjoyed. I'm sure that this news will make you just as happy as it made me. Yessir—you're right on the ball there. I'm beginning to suspect that my Mom and Pop love you almost as much as I love you, especially Pop—gee, but I wish I could see them both again. I never was good enough to them, especially Pop, and I've been sorry about it ever since.

Life is becoming very boring here, broken only by the passes into town which even at best is still only a temporary sedative. It's still very quiet here, and we have nothing to do but amuse ourselves all day and you know how dull that can be. The musical instruments that we've gathered help out some. Now the mandolin captures some interest for me and it doesn't seem too difficult to play. And now that I'm trying to play in the key of G on the uke instead of F, I'm starting all over again. . . .

Increasing your perfume collection by two more specimens. I'm sending home a package containing Lentheric's Gardenia de Tahiti and very nice looking bottle of prewar perfume called Point Rose. Couldn't resist the bargain. Also in the package is a silk parachute that was used when they sent up a flare in the night fight. These flares are beautiful to watch—they're shot from special pistols and then break open and the flare lights up (all sorts of colors) and float very slowly down, lighting up the terrain for some coverage. I also found this on one wood-gathering excursion.

## Medical Detachment Log

21–26 Jan 45—Enemy artillery increased in intensity throughout the sectors, causing casualties.

## 21 January 1945

Today is a beautiful day with a blue, blue sky above and the sun shining for all its worth, trying to eliminate the chill from the air. You know that it began snowing late yesterday afternoon and it was quite cold with the wind and all. I thought that by this morning we would have a new carpet of white, but it was just sparkling and now the sun is attacking that. I'm certainly glad that we can be in such sunny weather instead of the blizzards and snow drifts up North where the heavy fighting is raging.

Morimoto's just given Bambina, his adopted daughter, one of her weekly baths and now she dozes sleek and white by the warm fireplace. As soon as she saw Jimmy bringing in the bucket and pouring the hot water, she knew what she was in for and looked for egress, but fat chance. In a trice she was in and getting her deserved scrubbing. How she can get so dirty is beyond me. She's still our loveable pet and yet bothersome mascot, especially when she feels frisky in the morning or late at night and we're cozy in our bedrolls. Does she love to trample over us then! Ah, but she can be very appealing at times, too, as only dogs can be. Jimmy says he's gonna take her home when the time comes. You know Morimoto would make a good wife—every morning he starts the fire and breakfast going and we just get up and cook what we like. Oh, but we eat swell. No wonder none of us ever go to breakfast—at least the occupants of our room. This AM we had ourselves bacon with a couple of eggs, any way we wanted to cook 'em and good hot toast and the best of coffee. What a luxurious life we're living. Did anybody mention war? That's an alien subject around here.


22 JANUARY 1945

I'm sorry, darling, that I can't mention anything about Yohei, altho I do know the circumstances. I made it a point to see the aid man who treated him and was present. There was no suffering and the end was quick—maybe there'll be some consolation in that.

The life of leisure still goes on and this is really leisure. Last night, Jimmy and I stayed up late, playing the guitar, uke and mandolin and educated Tsuka on all the old songs and boy, they came crowding in a rush of memories. Isn't it amazing how one remembers all the old ones? It was certainly a night for reminiscence—of "Lets Fall in Love" and "There Goes My Heart" and "Smoke Gets in Your Eyes." How can we forget those, too? You know, Japanese songs sound very nice on the mandolin—sounds as if the *shamisen* [Japanese stringed instrument] is plinking out the melody.

## 24 JANUARY 1945

I'm starting to write a little late this evening because Jimmy Morimoto finally got his *New York Times*. We'd both been sweating it out ever since he sent his ten bucks in way back in November sometime. You know how I love that paper and Jimmy shares the same opinion. That's why I'm so late tonight—because I had such a field day scanning the papers. And today's was the Sunday issue, too. Oh, happy day. I read all the wonderful advertisements, the news, editorials, stage section—everything. I even read the stock quotation on Am Tel and Tel [American Telephone and Telegraph]. Now that the papers have started coming—that'll mean good reading from now on. That's one of the best darn papers in the world. To add to the enjoyment, one of Nay's *Irrigators* showed up and that's always good.

Of late, chow has been inadequate. Why this is, I don't know although the thing smells of skullduggery. It's not so much the quality, but the quantity and that's no mean factor. After today's scanty lunch, I got hold of some meat scraps that were castoffs from the supper. We brought it back and boy it was good the way we cooked it up with bouillon juice and sugar. Just like home cooking it was and we went for it—but, maybe hunger had something to do with it although it really was good.

## 26 JANUARY 1945

I read your enclosed clippings. We're hoping that this Bolton Bill passes Congress—it entitles us to a Medic Valor badge and the extra ten dollars. There's a companion bill which authorizes only the extra dough. The latter seems rather silly, but it's still better than nothing. That medic badge should be a caduceus, it'll look smarter than the old musket rifle on the infantryman's badge. . . .

You can recall my always moaning about being so close to the Alps and yet not being able to go skiing on this famous terrain. It got me so much that I did something about it. Mr. Collins, our ARC director, got some facts for me and I'm expecting to go skiing up to a resort the next weekend (right after I get paid—a very necessary factor). The bus leaves Saturday morning at 7 and gets there in some three hours—it returns the same evening but we're expecting to stay over night. By we, I mean Momoda, Osozawa (aid man) and myself. We'll rent our equipment, but we'll have to struggle along without shoes but in the wonderful anticipation of going skiing again, that drawback seems minor. . . .

Every letter to me of late mentions the lifting of the West Coast ban and the rescinding of the Army order. Everyone seems to be more or less waiting and watching before they make a move and I don't blame them. I don't care to go back to the coast. It's congested already, the economic situation won't better itself and for my own self, the field for my work, such as it is, is not available. I haven't given any location too much thought because I'll have to see for myself, but I'm sure that I wouldn't care to go back to Seattle, although I can't think of a more wonderful place to live. I'm afraid that for me it's all a beautiful memory. But, these are my opinions and let me hear more of yours. It'll never be definite until I get back anyway. How is Tama coming along in her approaching motherhood? . . .

MEDICAL DETACHMENT LOG

31 January 1945—Cold clear day. Officers and Enlisted Men paid. Usual garrisoning duties.

A Presidential Unit Citation was awarded to the attached Medics of Companys "F" and "L" of the 442d Infantry for outstanding performance of duty in action, near Bruyeres, France. These attached medics had comprised a Task Force which on 21 October 1944 turned the flank of German MIR [Mechanized Infantry Regiment], attacking from the rear, encircled the enemy and disorganized the enemy resistance causing "beaucoup" casualties, thus contributing to the cause of advancement on all fronts.

## 31 JANUARY 1945

It is almost eleven now and only Tsuka, Jimmy and I are up. The fireplace sputters with a newly thrown log and we've been talking up till now on post-war plans and daydreaming. Onodera has curled up on floor in his bedroll already and now sleeps peacefully. It's the quiet hour and the time I like best to write, the time is right, the mood appears magically and you are most in my thoughts then.

I have just finished reading one of the most beautiful pieces of writing that I have ever come across. There is a chapter—short chapter—on pages twenty-eight to thirty in Louis Adanics' *My Native Land* entitled "A Dying Guerillas Last Statement." It is about a Yugoslav patriot who in final agonies of death for his country, pens this masterpiece of writing to his unborn child. It is wonderfully written, so pure and simply to the point that I just felt overpowered when I read it. I cannot recall when I have been more moved by words so masterfully put. Please get your hands on the book, just borrow it, any old way get it and read it by all means. It will bring tears to your eyes and hit you with the impact of emotion as powerful as a sledgehammer and yet as tender as a father's caress. If this doesn't make you feel richer within you, then, I think that there's something amiss. So please don't forget to read it—I don't think it should be missed. . . .

Momoda, Ike, Osozawa and I are going skiing for the weekend up in the hills. Everything seems to be set, more or less, and the Captain's okayed it. Tomorrow we'll have to prepare for it in packing. We'll take along a stove and coffee rations to brew up at night. Our hotel will be 250+ a day with meals per person and we're going into town early as possible to see if we can scare up some shoes, though I doubt that, and we're expecting to use our G.I.'s. I'm rather thrilled over the prospect. We'll stay at least overnight depending on the situation. The resort is only about 60 miles away and we'll catch the 7:30 bus and be up there in a matter of hours. When we get to town we'll phone again and find out more about it.

MEDICAL DETACHMENT LOG

1 Feb 45—Month began with 100th Bn Section and 2d Bn Aid Stations covering casualties of the forward elements, while Blue continued to remain as Regtl reserve, with aid station located in a civilian hospital in Peille, France. Today marked the second anniversary of the activation of the 442d Combat Team.

2–7 Feb 45—Enemy activity in immediate area negative.

6 FEBRUARY 1945

The ski trip—oh, I had a wonderful time. Time just flew by and our stay now seems more like a dream. Everything was as good as it could be and if only you had been there to share the golden moments together, then I could not have asked for anything more. All throughout the trip I couldn't help but feel a twinge of sadness because you weren't there beside me to make the happiness complete.

MEDICAL DETACHMENT LOG

8–12 Feb 45—Cold clear day, with men about their usual duties. Men "sweating out" scattered enemy shells throughout the day. The Red Cross girls were up in forward areas, entertaining the boys with Hawaiian melodies and "do-nuts".

Ski trip, 1945. Min and his friends took an overnight ski trip to the Alps, sixty miles from Nice.

## 10 FEBRUARY 1945

Every letter I get from you now mentions the hectic romance that seems to be going on between Suzu and the Capt. Evidently it's reached serious and alarming proportions. What is this, the real McCoy? I wrote Suzu a short letter, giving her razz; I'm beginning to wonder now. Well, it's still very amusing, anyway. I know you'll keep me posted on this race—the odds on favorite of a few months ago seems to have lagged behind and where's the dark horse from Hawaii. The long shot is doing pretty well for himself, isn't he? Oh, but it's the home stretch and the finishing wire that counts. Let me speak seriously for awhile, will you, now that the situation seems to warrant it. Just a word of caution—don't be dazzled by the bars, the uniform and his well-to-do family. Look at the man behind those bars, inside the uniform—not just a swift, cursory glance, but a long, searching observation. I have nothing against the Capt personally since I don't know him from Adam, and who knows, he may be the piece that fits the puzzle, but the war isn't going to last forever, and a marriage should. The odds are against it in a hasty whirlwind combination, so take it slow and easy. There's not much to lose and everything to gain. I'd better take off this advisor's robe before I start growing whiskers.

MEDICAL DETACHMENT LOG

12–18 Feb 45—PX ration of three bottles of beer per individual distributed. Also candy and comfort items.

14 FEBRUARY 1945

Happy Valentines to you—I hope you received the flowers in time. This day crept up on me Indian fashion, so soon after the holidays and caught me napping. But, maybe the flowers did get to you in time— I hope so, anyway. It means a lot, doesn't it?, for it is a rather special sort of a day for us. Without going into any words, I think you know what I mean. I wish I could have even sent you a flowery card, but the French have no counterpart of St. Valentines here, so I'll just send you all my love with this—it'll have to do until I get home. Then maybe every day will be like a Valentine's Day. Let's try and make it that way.

I do feel a little guilty for not having written for three days and I don't have too much of an excuse. Some of us one day went to a funeral service for one of our boys—no, you don't know him, he wasn't a medic. This was held some 100 miles away and it was a long trip. The cemetery, an American one, was set in an olive orchard and we had our services in the bright sunshine with the breezes tugging at our locks. The crosses in beautiful but sad white symmetry shone in the sun and over all flew the Stars and Stripes at half mast. Once again as I did in Italy I was to experience the same sort of emotion that moved me then, a mixture of sadness and anger that these boys under the sod would never see day again, never know the joys and sadnesses of life again and never to realize that day for which they'd fought and died. The services, conducted by Chaplain Higuchi, were simple and a volley of three rounds were fired by a squad. It was all very touching and we rode home in comparative silence and I knew that I was not the only one that felt these same emotions as we stood there bareheaded in that olive grove.

On the way back we were caught by circumstances, the fact that we couldn't make chow at our place and if we ate in town we'd have to stay overnight because of the dark, our not being able to drive with headlights past the ridge into our valley. We decided to stay in town overnight and that we did, driving out before daylight and coming home as the sun lit up in rosy hue the distant peaks. . . .

Although we get the *Stars and Stripes* daily and Jimmy's *New York Times* comes quite regularly, I still hanker for a good novel. We've been hearing so much about Kathleen Winsor's *Forever Amber* and Erskine Caldwell's *Tragic Ground* in the papers because they've been bandied about by the Boston police. I wouldn't mind reading those. And I see where Erle Stanley Gardner's come out with *The Case of the Crooked Candle*. If you could get that in a cheap edition or Pocket book, I wouldn't mind reading that, either. I don't know which contemporary novels are any good for me because a lot of times the best seller lists don't jibe with my ideas about good reading. If you get a chance look around the bookshops, will you? Thanks.

Give my best regards to all that mad household but to you on this special day, all the love that you haven't got now.


16 FEBRUARY 1945

I received the camera yesterday in fine condition. While messing with it in joy I inadvertently opened the back not knowing a roll was in there, but that's just like me to do that and the whole roll isn't spoiled anyway. . . .

Before I forget I must tell you about the book which I just finished and which I was in such a lather about. It's Irving Stone's *Lust for Life* and is the novelized biography of Vincent Van Gogh the French Impressionist painter. . . . The man who can undergo what Van Gogh did as he did shows only his strength and honesty to himself. And that, I think is the greatest mark of all. "To Thine Own Self Be True"—how long has that burned itself into my mind and yet how dismally I have failed in that. I'm not upbraiding myself, merely stating a fact—nobody knows better than I. I'm very sorry, I started to talk about myself—the egotist in me. . . .

Everything is so quiet now with everyone asleep. Bambina nestles cozily against Jimmy and even she is fast asleep after having tired herself out as is her nightly custom, tugging at the blankets. The fire has gone out and yet I feel no cold, it is that warm. Spring must indeed be here. This afternoon we kicked and passed the football about enjoying the sunshine that shone down on us.

MEDICAL DETACHMENT LOG

19–28 Feb 44—Col C. W. Pence, Commanding Officer of the 442d Combat Team since the time of its activation was relieved from assignment as of 20 Feb 45. Regtl Executive Officer, Lt Col V. R. Miller assumed command of the Combat Team. 1st and 2nd Bns remained same area, while the 3d left L'Escarene for Peira Cava.

24 FEBRUARY 1945

Yesterday evening brought me four of your letters all at once. Your letters become more interesting by the day it seems. I told you this before, I think, but it won't hurt to repeat; an indefinable something has crept in between the lines. I still can't put my finger right on it. I just know it's there and that's what counts.

The enclosed snaps were from the first roll of pictures taken with my camera. Natcherly, I have to put my two cents in on the back of each. . . .

The *Nisei in Uniform* came, too, and we had very interesting reading there for all of us, identifying people and places. I was certainly surprised to see Sammy's puss staring out of one of the pages. I hope I can get to show it to him. Do you remember the four medics hauling a litter? That was taken in Shelby and shows Vic, Jimmy, Okubo, George Sawada and Dick Nomura holding up Kenso Osaki. I was there that day—only mainland boys being present for certain publicity reasons—they took a lot of others, too, including me, but naturally they picked the most glamorous picture. I'm glad that the WRA [War Relocation Authority] saw fit to bring out this pamphlet—every little bit counts. Incidentally, do you want the copy back? It wasn't so indicated, so I'll keep it unless you ask for it. . . .

It looks as if Sue went and done it—it was a surprise to me, but not a shock. The Captain must be quite a man and more power to him. He'll need all that if he's going to have darling Sue tied up with him the rest of his life—just another good man gone wrong. I guess with this all of her matrimonial problems are over, that is, for you to worry about. And you say that she won't be married until Sue graduates. When will that be anyway? . . .

I am sorry to hear of Harry's father passing away. When there is a coincidence of a wedding in the offing and death at the same time— periods of joy and one of sadness—one can't help but recall King Arthur's last words, "the old order passeth, giving way to new"—he had to go and he must have been happy in the knowledge that his blood will rise again in the offspring that soon must make its debut. In that sense, he will never die, will he? Please convey to Harry my best regards.


26 FEBRUARY 1945

The town clock clearly but softly tolls twelve bells and the three of us—Onodera (returned yesterday from the hospital), Mimura and I—have been chewing the rag on a multitude of subjects from hunting to beef cattle, here in front of the fireplace. There's nothing that is more cementing our friendship than these bull sessions that last half the night with its interchange of lovely experiences. . . .

When I think back over the day's activities, I'm appalled to find that I can't think of anything in particular that makes this day stand out from any other. That's the routine and charming existence we are leading. Maybe one day we get chicken for supper; steak, the next; maybe today the sun shone warmer, maybe it clouded over the next; maybe today I was CQ and maybe I was chore free the next; maybe we kicked the football around today, maybe the baseball, the next; thus, go the days with only slight variations to distinguish one from the other. In this fashion now the month draws to its close— where it went I'm sure I don't know. . . . Just as when you ask a guy, "what day is today" and he thinks back and says "today's Sunday" and you say "ah yes, so it is Sunday today." And then you think "so what—so what if it is Sunday today, what's the difference." And the answer comes back—there is no difference. I don't mean to say that this routine is one of a deadly boredom—to the contrary, it is a delightful, charming life and we enjoy it although I must confess that there are moments of impatience at life's crawling pace. But, mostly it is a life of graceful indolence—that we cram to the hilt with lively loafing. Here's a maybe representative day—get up lazily from my cozy bedroll possibly around nine-thirty after being forced to by the traffic and the fact that Bambina insists on harassing me, then a cup of coffee and breakfast whatever's on hand and some of the boys bring it back from the kitchen—a leisurely toilet with warm water heated in the fireplace—then maybe I'll read, or just talk or twang on the mandolin—comes lunch and rest in the sun after that—chop wood—kick the football around, read some more, play the mandolin again—lo it's suppertime—then comes mail call, if any, *Stars and Stripes* to read, play the mandolin again, write letters, bull session, make and drink coffee, sit around and chew the fat—bang, the clock strikes a late hour—sneak into bed and wait for sleep to catch up so we can begin another day anew. Maybe there's no future in such a program, but it's not a bad design for living in these times.

MEDICAL DETACHMENT LOG

> 1–7 Mar 45–Month began with the Combat Team maintaining usual
> defensive activities along the French/Italian border. Showdown
> inspection and preparation for movement were begun, all emergency
> rations, excess equipment, winter clothing shuffles back to rear.

## 1 MARCH 1945

Thanks for the package. I'd been expecting it and now I'm excited
about the rice. As you know we got paid yesterday and the boys insisted on making a pool with 200 francs from everybody. They want me
to send you the fifty bucks so you can keep sending the rice and *nihon*
[Japanese] stuff. They insisted on my sending the money—they do
love the stuff, even as I. So please send a package every week. I'll have
this money made into a money order and I'll be sending it soon, probably in the next couple of letters. As for the request, I'll write one
everytime I write so that it will be bona fide, such as this. Please send
me a big package of foodstuff as I've described above. Will that do or
do they ask for more? So hurry around like a good gal will ya and
keep the rice and stuff rolling.

## 6 MARCH 1945

We've been having a devil of a time with a huge crossword puzzle
this evening—all this evening—from the *New York Times*. What a
bad time it's given us, full of proper names and ambiguosities. It's
nowhere near completion and I've my doubts as to its ever being
done. I've given up my donations to the harassed group by the fireplace, cudgeling their brains in vain. . . .

And now that I haven't written you for a couple of days I've
quite a bit to tell about my two day pass at the rest center, my third,
incidentally. . . .

I went with Ike and spent a very quiet evening at his friend's place, a Mlle Lou-Lou, whom we'd met on the ski trip. The family's very rich and friendly and she told us exciting and unbelievable stories of her escapades in the FFI. She's from Paris and speaks English quite well in addition to being pretty. She told us of how they used to steal German cars for the FFI and of German reprisals and of their treatment at the conqueror's hands. She hates the Nazis from the bottom of her heart and can't understand some of our attitudes. You see, they'd been under the Nazi heel so long that only a dead German is a good one. As you can imagine she's learning a lot of American slang and she taught us some French ones, too. . . .

In the evening . . . we went to the newly opened army sponsored "Raynauds" (I've enclosed the card). It's a beautiful place with a small floor and a soothing orchestra. We kept in trim and our alcoholic level rising by imbibing cognac. Ogami and Ikebe saved the day when they came in to my great delight with a couple of gals—Mathilde and Marinette—for there was a dearth of women, only escorted women being admitted. I was soon chiselling dances off them and I had a roseate time as only I can have. As usual we were the last ones to leave the place and all of us feeling good we marched back arm in arm singing "Amour, amour, amour." Some of these French girls are really nice for they do not have any prejudices and we are just as good friends to them as anyone else. . . .

The boys have finally given up the brain-teasing crossword puzzle and are now cozily in bed, while I sit up by candlelight to write this. This is more like home again. Even though town is nice, it's still good to come back again where our relaxation and indolence can have full latitude. . . .

Harry, Abe and Kozuma (both 3d Bn) were passing by and they dropped in to see us. They're the same as ever, and natcherly we had to rib each other about our respective aid stations. That's always a favorite pastime. . . .

News still continues to be good on all fronts. When is Germany going to see the end of all this senseless conflict? I kind of shiver in anticipation of home when I think of the end that must be drawing near. To be home again and to be with you—sometimes the thought is overwhelmingly awesome. But it's better I dream in bed, so goodnight, darling.

MEDICAL DETACHMENT LOG

8–12 Mar 45—All forward areas relatively quiet, with usual defensive activities. Excess equipment, duffle bags etc being hauled to the new assembly area today. Beer ration distributed to all sections. Quartering party consisting of an officer from all companies left to reconnoiter for an assembly area 10 Mar 45.

12 MARCH 1945

There's not much else to say for activities over here except that latrine rumours are flying fast and thick, because of certain can't-be-disclosed activities. And such conjectures some of them are, too. It certainly seems as if something is afoot and just what it is I don't know. But we have interesting bull sessions and arguments about what's doing. You'll know soon enough, too.

It's now about seven months since we took Bambina into our circle and we've brought her up as best we knew how and now we are going to give her away. She's coming of age and with it goes added responsibilities since there can be complications of a litter and that will mean trouble if and when we move. Momoda and Ike are going to take her to their friends in Monaco. She's going to be a Monagasque now and we'll all miss her when she goes away, but it's for the best.

The Jerries threw quite a few rounds into the town today upsetting some of the tranquillity of the civilians and GIs. It's been some time since we heard some coming in—one guy told me they bashed in a few houses up "Whistlin' Alley" way.

13–14 Mar 45—1st and 2d Bn sections remained same and continued usual normal defensive activities, while 3d began movement to
rear bivouac area, Antibes, France, a distance of approximately forty
miles. Units of the French Troops, 2d Brigade began movement into
our forward prepared positions.

15 Mar 45—All sections completed movement to assembly area,
Antibes, France.

16 Mar 45—All sections spent the day in bivouac at Antibes, France,
in preparation for oversea movement. Showdown inspection of clothing and equipment was held. Typhus shots were administered, routine physical inspection was held.

## 16 March 1945

Sorry that I didn't write sooner, but we're in the throes of another
movement, not knowing but constantly speculating as to our destination. Do you remember that in my last letter I told you of rife latrine
rumors? Well, we still don't know nor will we know just exactly
where we'll be going. At any rate, we know we're going someplace.

All too sorrowfully we left our village home of three months and
longer and its comforts for we know what movement entails. And so
it was the usual packing and cleaning up. Our replacing outfit came
in and we pulled out and into this our new bivouac area.

We're now just a short distance from town in a broad meadow
and the whole outfit is tenting on the greensward with the resulting
colorful display. For the first time in a long time we're all together.
It's a very nice place since the weather is nice and the green grass
is a good thing to see. There are wild narcissi growing in profusion
although even now they are being trampled down by hordes of
athletically-inclined young men engaged in football and the like. All
the tents are pitched neatly row on row and we've put up our aid station tent, too, for a change. Morimoto and I are sleeping together in

Min and Tsuka playing the ukulele and mandolin, 1945. The men were passing the time while the 442nd was camped at Marseilles before embarking for Italy.

our respective bedrolls even as we did on the comfortable mattress which we shared together for so long. And now instead we have the cold ground and the cramped pup tent. Somehow, I don't mind that too much. The nights are not too cold and it's quite comfortable although I will always persist in sleeping on a hunk of ground with a hillock that hits the small of my back. We're more or less, all of us, busy with the routines of checking up all sorts of things. I don't think that we'll be here too long. Passes are issued but not as we've been accustomed to, but that's not too much of a drawback for me. I've had my share of the town and its pleasures. I am going in on pass tonight and probably for the last fling at I don't-know-what.

I've seen plenty of friends I hadn't seen for a long time and I've talked with about this and that. Sammy and Duffy just took off an hour ago for town and I just came back from K Co area where I went to see Harold—he's the same as ever and we exchanged among other things, skiing notes. That whole Celtic bunch was congregated, Pete

Kozu, Sol Kashiwagi, Fat Yana, Mas Watanabe and others whose names I've forgotten. [These men had played together on a team called the Celtics.] Everybody's all crowded into the meadow about six blocks square and so you can imagine the jumble of tents and vehicles not to mention the comradely *nigiyaka* [crowds and noise] of the place. It's only on rare occasions like this that we ever get to see and talk to our friends. We've slept two nights here already—and just to show you what a difference there is in me, I even get up for breakfast, but maybe that's because it's compulsory—do you think?

Of course, the biggest topic by far is the destination to which we are headed. Some of the conjectures are so farfetched that they are ludicrous, stemming mostly from wishful thinking. Of course, I can't repeat any rumours, but I've formed my own opinions, although I don't dare indulge too much in that direction for fear of being sorely disappointed. . . .

So don't worry at my seeming absence for awhile. You'll know it's not that for I don't have to tell you how much I love you and what you mean to me.

MEDICAL DETACHMENT LOG

17 Mar 45—Vicinity Antibes, France—warm clear day. 3d Bn section left by motor and train convoy for the vicinity of Marseilles, France.

18–19 Mar 45—Hq and 2d Bn sections, left vicinity of Antibes, France, by motor and train convoy. 100th Bn section completed movement to assembly area 19 Mar 45.

20 Mar 45—Vicinity St Pie au Pin, France—warm clear day, clothing inspection for EM—Exchange of franc notes to lire notes completed. Usual duties.

21–22 Mar 45—All sections completed movement to POE Marseilles, France. Boarded LST, waiting sailing order.

# 5 ITALY

*April–May 1945*

25 Mar 45—Arrived port of Livorno, Italia, by motor convoy, arriving PBS Staging area, West of Pisa, Italy. All aid stations set up. Usual duties.

Somewhere in Italy
26 March 1944

After what seems a long, long time, I am finally writing to you. I can't say that it was impossible to write to you during our many movements, but at times like these I have the greatest inertia in matters of correspondence. I think you could judge from my last letters that something was afoot and now you know just what did happen to us by glancing at the top of the page. Just what mental gyration brought us here we are still at a loss to know. We just know that we're here and we know as to the next step which can only mean, to us, the front lines, but what gets me and most of us is the why and wherefore of the whole thing. But, I think that most of us would rather fight on this front than the tough ground that Northern France would have held in store for us.

To get to this place (sh—secret) we utilized practically every mode of transportation (nope—no flying). I wrote you last I think about nine days ago—as you can see, a lot has happened in that nine days

Caricature of Min, 1945. This self-portrait was done at the beginning of the 442nd's second campaign in Italy.

from the narcissi-freckled meadow in France to this sandy staging area under the cypress groves in Italy. As you can imagine, everyone hated the thought of leaving such a paradise as Nice is, but the Army can't be that benevolent in its policies and there were plenty of sad souls when we departed, not only among us, but also in the civilian ranks and by this I mean the female contingent. You can imagine the last nights in this area—everyone trying to cram all the enjoyment possible into their system 'ere the Army carried us away to God only knew where.

Our first movement saw us crowded into what we'd thought would be nice railway smoking cars, but to our great disgust we were headed into empty freight cars, what an ignominious letdown. And the crowning blow was the sign on the cars, "Horses—8—Humans 20". That really took the cake! At that it wasn't so very bad. As the train wound its way along the beautiful coast and past many towns, we just dangled our feet out the open door and viewed the passing panorama with the realizations that this situation was previously known only to hobos. We were at our destination in a few hours, not too wearisome, immediately herded (how that word crops in!) into huge vehicles suspiciously like cattle cars into another staging area high on a plateau. This was our home for the next three days. This place was really immense and over all a constant haze-like film the dust blown up and thrown up by trucks. We were rather busy here getting organized for our next leg—discarding this and that and acquiring this and that—not to mention the usual chores pertaining to the Medics. I was glad to leave that place for the rocky, pebble-strewn ground was definitely not made for comfort when wooing Morpheus. And now we were more streamlined for our next hop.

Then one morning it was back on the trucks again and we making gay on the top of the cab of the trucks, hurling raucous cries at the mademoiselles and throwing lemon drops to the kids as we rode through town down to the port where our LSTs awaited us, mouths agape and ready to swallow us into its cavernous interior, which it did in due time. And this was one instance where rank has its benefits for the upper non-coms (why that's me) got bunks on the starboard side while the others had to throw their bedrolls down on the gloomy huge belly or up on the cold deck. These latter soon scurried down again after one night for the sea was not kind, constantly throwing spray and the cold wind sweeping the decks. We stayed one night in port and what a night that was. You see, the place is barb-wired, but after getting our places set and equipment settled, everybody roamed the port square and generally made gay with the multitudes that lined the fence either to gaze in curiosity or for gains of their own. In no time at all we were black marketing stuff through the fence and getting bottles of fermented stuff in. In some strange manner Hiramatsu and I found ourselves with a bottle of watery wine apiece for a couple of packs of cigarettes, for we'd acquired a great thirst after the meandering and bargaining. Although there was a movie scheduled in one of the boats, that was easily forsaken in a golden mood for an impromptu session under one of the lamp posts with some Hq 2 boys who'd brought out their ukes and guitars and were proceeding to get plastered with a multitude of bottles including cognac and the potent eau-de-vie. Naturally, I was not loath to join this merry group and also to imbibe their more potent liquors. It's too bad that I can't find words to describe these pleasant excursions. It was all a lot of fun and Hiramatsu and I finally rolled back to our boats, I to bed down in friendly confusion beside the others in the belly, dragging my bedroll down the hard way and finally sleeping (and letting the others sleep, too) on the plyboard and freezing through the cold night. Consequently, I did not even know when the boat left port to anchor in the harbor to await the others before the whole moved off. And this wasn't too long for we moved out in a neat procession with no fanfare whatsoever.

Life on the boat was merely a succession of hours until I could get my pins on terra firma again. You know that I never feel quite right on any sort of sea voyage and this was no exception, just eat, sleep and read until we finally come into the Italian port, battered as all hell, bringing memories of what we'd gone through over here. The huge jaw unhinged and we were disgorged into trucks which bore us to this spot, we passing some familiar spots on the way, now a bit changed that the surge of war has passed o'er.

This staging area is much much better than we'd ever dreamed of, having had some of Italy's finest. It's set in clumps of cypress trees and we are settled in pyramidal tents, in rows, and draped over wooden frames and with a wooden floor and best of all, we have wooden bunks. You see, we're initiating this particular area and everything is new and clean. We've a separate building for our aid station and tonight I'm on CQ and with the electric bulb burning brightly I'm sitting on my litter (I have to sleep all by my lonesome tonight writing this to you.) I have also just been informed that no mention of Italy can be made in letters, reversing the allowance previously made. Now with this much written, I'd hate to throw it in the ashcan, so I'm just going to hand this in to preserve the events while they are fresh. I'm going to write another letter which although innocent of all details, will pass censorship, but will be dull as hell. Captain says that he will keep letters mentioning Italy until they may be released and when that will be I don't know, but keep the innocent letter and match it with this one and then things might make sense. And I'll begin right away on this second letter, cause even then I have a lot of things to say.

## 26 MARCH 45

This is my second letter to you tonight, the other having proven unable to pass censorship, but it will get to you on some far-off date and when you get it, you will know the reason for this puzzle in correspondence. The maze of censorship at present lies heavily on our shoulders. Let's see it's been some nine days since I last wrote to you and these nine have been packed with experiences which naturally I can't divulge. I can't tell you where I am, how I got here, where we're going, why we're going and when. If you're worried about anything by the foregoing rest yourself, because truthfully, it is very nice here. We live in pyramidal tents, draped over wooden frames, having wooden floors and with genuine wooden bunks—what a setup. I'm CQing it tonight at this our aid station and we've even electric lights, too. I went to see a movie last night on the sandy field out here— *Brazil* it was—and I came away vowing not to go again for the picture is scarcely worth the discomforts undergone such as cold, cramped position, sitting on the ground, poor vision, bad acoustics etc. But, I'll probably go again.

I'm sorry that I didn't write to you sooner but we had been a trifle busy these past days although, I must confess that I could have written but in times like these I am overwhelmed by the greatest of inertia so far as correspondence goes. But you, you've been right on the ball and this another bad exchange for you. We've surprisingly had some mail in the past days and this poor lone letter will have to balance the eight that I'm answering tonight. So you see, you're getting gypped again. By the way, I saw Sammy and Duffy at the show last night sitting together proud as kings on their makeshift seats in the prime row. Naturally, we exchanged bantering comments. Sammy's still got his cookie duster and with one of his front teeth missing (it seems some horse or mule fracas knocked it out) he's quite the boy. He knows now of his mother's passing. I hadn't mentioned anything until about a week back when he visited me and told me. It seems Aya broke the news to him—he must have felt rather bad inside. There wasn't much I could say. He knew no details whatsoever, but when I saw him a few days ago he told me that he'd received a Red Cross message from his dad who told him about it. He was glad to know the details—ended some worries for him. No matter how nonchalant he may be I know that something has gone from his heart, a piece of his flesh is gone. But, he's a good soldier. I told him that you sent your condolences. He thanks you.

Incidentally, Haruo Kumakura's brother came over and introduced himself and said that Kumio wanted him to thank me because it seems that he dropped in on you in Minny and had a good time. I can't recall your mentioning that.

I suppose from your letters that Suzu is now Mrs. Kay. Yesterday, I suddenly remembered the date as her wedding day. I'm truly sorry that I couldn't grace the festive board and join in the gaiety. I'm sure that it must have been a very impressive ceremony and beautiful, too. And Suzu must have made a pretty picture. I guess that when that all important day finally came and it was all over, that all the work and worry and bustle that went into its proper making was fully justified. And now you can rest your weary bones for you must have been on the go all this time, if I know you. But, how happy you must be for all your efforts and I'm happy, too. Will you tell Suzu that and for the both of them the best that life can offer and it can hold much for those who would have it so. . . .

Of late, before dropping off to sleep my thoughts have been wandering home and to you. These are sweet sensations, all the more precious because of time and distance. To spare myself acute nostalgia, it's often necessary to blank the mind by will, but who can have such heroic strength for long? I only know in such moments that I love you so much my heart aches in its longing for you, till finally sleep, and it comes eventually, lulls the rampant thoughts.

MEDICAL DETACHMENT LOG

> 26–27 Mar 45—Vicinity West of Pisa, Italia, cold cloudy rainy day. Training schedule followed.

> 28–29 Mar 45—Warm clear day. Left vicinity Pisa, Italia, 28 Mar 45. Set up aid station, usual bivouac duties.

29 MARCH 1945

It was rather late last night when we came here into our new residence that I had no time to write you. Instead, after just hauling out my bedroll, I just flopped into it and got myself a good hunk of sleep. This place looked pretty good last night, but today's subsequent inspection proves it even better. It's a huge house and there are quite a few families living in it. The house is one in a cluster situated on a hill overlooking the fertile valley below. The fellas have a big room on the top floor to sleep in and the aid room is convenient on the ground floor. A doctor's widow occupies this one section of the house and she's been very generous in allotting us rooms. But, best of all is the general cleanliness of the place and the gardens both in front and in back. The front yard has many flowers—now in bloom in the warm sun are tulips, lilacs, plum blossoms and pear blossoms while in the backyard there are some beautiful camellias and some hyacinths.


MEDICAL DETACHMENT LOG

> 30–31 Mar 45—San Martino in Freddano, Italia. All sections await-
> ing movement orders.
>
> Month began with all sections bivouacked at San Martino in Fred-
> dano, Italia. Serious preparation to resume combat with battalions
> participating in night problems.
>
> All blouses turned in for "Eisenhower" jacket. Movies held at white
> area. Easter Sunday was observed with impressive service
> conducted by combat team's Chaplain. Our APO changed to #454
> from #758.
>
> 2 Apr 45—San Martino in Freddano, Italia—warm clear day.


2 APRIL 1945

We hit the jackpot yesterday when the mail accumulated during our movements finally caught up with us to our very great joy. And as usual you were right in there pitching as witness the seven letters and four cards that arrived from you. There were also. . . . Tama's Easter card and also Sue's enlightening and scintillating letter. Please thank them for me and I shall be replying, but the waiting line is terrific so they'll have to wait patiently for one of my treasurable letters. . . .

   As I write this in the doctor's airy study, on his sturdy desk, I can look out the tall windows and see the silver greened olive trees being playfully tagged by the breezes while the mellow sunlight covers all. And to the ears come wafted the strange mixture of Italian and Hawaiian pidgeon English. . . .

   What better use than to spend the sunny afternoon relaxing in the warm rays, or reading in the shade of the magnolia tree or shooting craps against the side of the house? How can one expect to withstand such wonderful distractions? Ah, but, today I was strong and since I went to Easter services yesterday morning and some of the spirit is still within me, I find myself at the desk scribbling away in a vain effort to reduce to nothing the mountainous correspondence.

As I said, I went to the services yesterday morning—Easter morning and althou' we got there late, I was glad that I went. The skies were overcast and mist encircled the vale when we went down in the early morn. The band was there and also a goodly company of men that came to worship. I've enclosed the program and you can see that it was well planned and we all agreed that the chaplain led himself right well in his sermon which was based on unenforceable obligations; I thought the sermon was excellent. . . .

Of course, on this Easter day it would have to be me on CQ and so I couldn't go to the movie at the Bn Motor Pool—they were showing Boyer and Dunne in *Together Again*. However, I think I did better in staying home, because while drinking beer and making with the instruments we were invited upstairs next door, whither we repaired. The signora played her accordion for us and we reciprocated with a few tunes ourselves. The best part came when she (a music teacher) played wonderful music for us on the piano. At first we just stood around her holding candles and we sang out of our songbooks. Later she hauled out the classical pieces and it was something to hear Strauss, Chopin, Beethoven, Liszt and a host of others again. After that impromptu concert, we didn't dare play our instruments. Natcherly, all this time I'd been imbibing freely of beer, which doesn't detract one whit of music appreciation, and I even had a twirling waltz with Micaela's mother. But, I should tell you of Micaela—she's a very cute youngster of about ten and she's quite smitten my heart and Tsuka's, too. We harass her at every opportunity, making her blush prettily on many an occasion—maybe that's why she's so appealing to us. We have a lot of fun with her as you can imagine. Last night we made her sing Lili Marlene together with

Tina, which is short for Albertina; she lives in our house, age about thirteen and properly demure, but she doesn't have the rascally personality that Micaela has. I'll have taken pictures of her so you can judge for yourself. . . .

We've been getting the *Stars and Stripes* daily, now in a four page edition here, and we scan it just as eagerly for the latest. Boy, the news is certainly good, isn't it? I wouldn't mind at all if the war were to end tomorrow.

Did I mention that while back in the last area, we met up with Minata, whom we'd left behind when we went to France. He's with a reconditioning outfit and doing alright by himself. He was pretty happy to see us, professing a loneliness for Buddhaheads and for rice, too. By the way, Hana, where's Franklin? You don't mention him much in your letters, nor his activities and whereabouts. When you write him will you tell him I said "hello"?

You know, I finally know Kay's last name—Kuramoto, isn't it? This I gleaned from one of your late pages. You did mention it once before and only once and I never knew for sure. He must be some guy—happily married now, I guess. . . .

As you can readily understand, coming to Italy after the glories of the Riviera was quite a comedown, but it's not as bad as it would seem either in thoughts or on paper. . . . Our Italian language is coming back although we still persist in speaking French when we are stumped in our conversations. But, we shouldn't find the regeneration difficult. At least, this isn't as tricky as the French tongue.

Medical Detachment Log

3 Apr 45—All sections in same position. Warm clear day. Gen Mark W. Clark, Commanding the 15th Army Group visited the 442d Infantry and addressed the members of the 100th Battalion. Bns in preparation for movement, duffle bags and excess baggage collected for storage. 3d and 1st moving up under cover at the out-

skirts of Pietra Santa, hiked the remaining distance some 4 or 5 miles, carrying on their back medical supplies, litters, individual full field packs, through steep and winding trails to the "jump-off" point.

4 Apr 45—Warm clear day. Regiment left San Martino in Freddano by motor convoy, arrived vicinity of Vallechia, Italia 3 Apr 45.

The following Special Order of the Day received by Allied Force Head-quarters, Apr 45. Soldiers, sailors, and airmen of the Allied Forces in the Mediterranean Theatre:

Final victory is near. The German Force[s] are now very groggy and only need one mighty push to knock them out for good. The moment has now come for us to take the field for the last battle which will end the war in Europe. You know what our comrades in the West and East are doing on the battlefields. It is now our turn to play our decisive part. It will not be a walk-over; a mortally wounded beast can still be very dangerous. You must be prepared for a hard and bitter fight, but the end is quite certain—there is not the slightest shadow of doubt about it that you, who have won every battle you have fought, are going to win this last one.

Forward then into battle with confidence, faith and determination to see it through to the end. God speed and good luck to you all.

/s/ H. R. Alexander

Field Marshal,

Supreme Allied Commander Mediterranean Theatre.

..................................................................................................................................

On April 3, 1945, the 442nd was detached from IV Corps and attached to the Fifth Army, Ninety-second Division. They were assigned to a ridgeline in east Italy. Their mission was to begin an offensive before the main weight of the Fifth Army moved toward Bologna. This offensive began at night because some of the area was visible in daylight. —DIANNE BRIDGMAN

....................................................................................................................................................

MEDICAL DETACHMENT LOG

> 5 Apr 45—Vicinity Vallechia-warm clear day. Regiment entered com-
> bat. 100th Bn and 3d Bn sections committed on line. 2d remained
> as regimental reserve. Resistance developed immediately and casu-
> alties passing thru 100th Bn and 3d Bn Aid Stations very heavy.
> Constant enemy artillery, mortar barrage, vicinity of forward aid sta-
> tions, made treatment and evacuation difficult. Despite mountain-
> ous and tortuous terrain, evacuation by litter relay train system was
> established. Evacuation took continuous marching of eight hours to
> complete a case. 1st day's battle casualties totaled well over 130
> cases plus many medical cases. Due to the fact that the aid station
> group anticipated heavy casualties all necessary arrangements were
> completed before the jump-off and the casualties were evacuated
> with minimum loss of time.

5 APRIL 1945

I didn't write you yesterday evening because I was tired and I curled up on this floor. I'd taken leave of the other house early yesterday afternoon to precede the others and we moved through the Italian countryside which is quite beautiful in its new dress of verdancy. . . .

Daytime found us this morning surrounded by mules and mule skinners and their accompanying stench. So maybe we'll be happy when we move out of here.

Things seem to be happening rather rapidly and when we went

up this hillside to visit the Regimental aid station, we could view the valley and the ridges and it was like a long distance grandstand seat to see mushrooms of smoke in the valleys and on the hills and to hear the reports of guns. This scene seems somewhat reminiscent of certain other situations. Spitfires were out fooling about in the blue sky, wheeling and diving and we could hear their unmistakable chatter on their downward strafe. This always does our hearts good. Spring is here and in its full glory, even as it must be in Minneapolis, but to us, too, the coming of spring brings portent of other things, for now the hibernation of Mars during the winter must also end with the spring sun. It must be very nice in Minneapolis with the advent of spring, that tang in the air to shake off the overcoat of winter.

## MEDICAL DETACHMENT LOG

6 Apr 45—2d Battalion section moved into lines, during the night of 5 April 45, meeting the same evacuation problems as other aid stations.

Litter bearers from Provisional Co, Company B, 317 Medical Bn and Partisans sent to 2d Bn section to help in the evacuation of the wounded.

7 Apr 45—Slightly cold day. Casualties passing thru aid stations somewhat decreased.

## 7 APRIL 1945

Hell, it's begun to sprinkle in this deep gorge with rocky crags towering on all sides and it can only mean more misery to the guys up front. We in this aid station in this house will not be too inconvenienced, but the guy in the foxhole won't like it one bit. At present, I'm in the rear aid station where the setup is pretty good. It's the good sturdy Italian house again which we've taken over for our benefit and we are nice and comfortable, thank you, comparatively speaking. The owners aren't about as nobody could expect when war moves in on them, but these houses aren't beat up, tho' terribly ransacked it seems, this deep gorge being a very good natural protection. Things seem to be pretty good up forward from all reports and that does our hearts good. The terrain is a forbidding one being loftily mountainous with crags and rocky peaks peering down at us. These our boys have had to assault and they've done well. Our battalion casualties have been light, thank God, although we were up till one last night. Evacuation down these very steep grades over the rocks is the main problem for us, but we're making out. We've two forward groups in the chain to relay the casualties down and I don't think that they are having any sort of a picnic. So we back here are quite lucky.

An unusual thing happened the first night we came here. I'd gone to sleep in a bare room by myself when an infantry man knocked and complaining of pain in his chest I told him to sleep beside me till morning so we could check him then. In the early hours of the morning about five, there was another timid knock on the door and strange muted voices. The infantry man got up and on investigation hollered at me to get up while he scrambled in the dark for his rifle. I slipped out of my bedroll in my underwear and pattered to the door to find four Jerries now humbly asking to be taken prisoners. You can imagine the scene—in the dim of night, I standing at the door clad only in shorts and socks, the rifle man behind me and four Jerries in alien voices saying, "Caput". Nonplussed is inadequate, to say the least. Still in my underwear, but now with my shoes on, I took 'em over to the aid room and woke the others up and we searched and asked them all kinds of questions while waiting for someone to come pick them up. Till then we learned that two were Poles and one a Czech—these three only eighteen, and the leader, a non-com, was a Berliner and thirty-one years old. They seemed quite content at surrendering, but this was

Forward Aid Station, 1945. Combat was beyond the hills; the wounded had to be evacuated down precipitous trails.

our first case of any Jerries surrendering to us and you can imagine that it was quite an experience.

We were treated to another sight yesterday morning and afternoon, too. Right behind this house flows a clear stream and from that a ridge rears up its rocky head; behind that towers another. Evidently Jerries were on this last ridge for all day they were subjected to merciless pounding and we down here had grandstand seats at the whole performance. First, the smoke shells throwing up huge white mushrooms of smoke, then the high explosives with their orange flash and gray eruptions and their crackling reverberations would run wild around these crags and gorges. This kept up steadily all day. The most awesome thing to see was the performance of the Spitfires that added to Jerrie's discomfiture. They came over wheel-

Surrendering Germans, 1945. These men awakened Min in the middle of the
night to surrender. They chose the right time—the next day, their former
positions were destroyed by the 442nd's artillery.

ing, wings in the sun and then one after the other go into their dive,
once strafing their guns chattering like mad, then unleashing bombs,
while the payoff was their firing of rockets. I don't see how the Jerries could stand such awesome but beautiful fire as we saw displayed.
The Jerries are off that hill now and I can't blame them for that and
it's a good thing that these four that came into us did when they did,
else they'd not be alive to tell any tales. It was a beautiful yet fearful
thing to see and a comfort to know that we rule the skies. I guess we
can't say that the Air Corps is not doing their part in helping out the
infantry man.

I can hear our familiar artillery Piper Cub in the air droning along
and our guns are still booming along, but this fine rain is certainly
a depressant in more ways than one. 'Nuff for today, darling, I'll try
and write as often as I can, but don't expect much.

MEDICAL DETACHMENT LOG

8 Apr 45—Warm clear day. Attack progressively continuing.

9 Apr 45—Left Vallechia by motor convoy and arrived Montignoso, Italia. Found for the first time all BN rear aid stations located in the same square.

Evacuation continued to remain over long and tortuous terrain, but a new route opened in the afternoon on Highway 1 reducing twelve-hour trip to two hours, relieving somewhat the overworked litter bearers who have been working long continuous hours including the men from Provisional Company, Antitank Co, antitank platoons, plus "paesanos".

10–12 Apr 45—1st Bn moved from Montignoso to town of Canevara, Italia. Red Section's casualties are being evacuated over hazardous mountain trails, which continued to be the major problem in this terrain.

Sporadic artillery air bursts in Massa all night.

## 10 APRIL 1945

Being at a relay post on our chain of evacuation here at this shell of a house, has its disadvantages and its advantages, too. I can't decide yet whether writing in pencil is one of them or not and also on Ike's borrowed stationery. We came up here yesterday afternoon, Ike, Onodera and I, to establish a collecting point. From here up only mules and foot troops operate, and if you could see this terrain, rocky, mountainous and precipitous, you can understand the difficulties of evacuation. We have relay posts stretching all the way up the hill to pack casualties down which, now, [are] thankfully at a minimum, for it is a terrific thing for the wounded to undergo and it's no joke for these emergency litter bearers, too. Only the stone walls and these crumbling, too, are all that remain of what must have been a house.

No floors, no roofs, no nothing. Just the stone walls are left and when we three cuddle up for the night against one wall, the stars twinkle brightly overhead, and interspersed is the flash of our big guns as they torment the Jerries constantly. We're still shoving the Jerries before us. Just what the exact situation is I don't know. Things happen fast, you know, and we just follow orders. In terrain such as this there can be no set procedure, we have to meet circumstances as they come and with our evacuation worries, there comes also many of its accompanying harassing details.

The rear aid station is below us down this gully to a town and most of the guys are there. We serve as the connecting link here between them and the forward station somewhere in the hills that tower inexorably in front of us. It's a rough narrow rocky trail down from here to the town and yet it's much better than the long haul by litter from the top down where the patient has to be tied down to the litter else he rolls off, so great often is the incline. But, as I've said before things seem to be going pretty good for the boys up there, else what a nightmarish headache we'd all be having.

After I wrote you last a couple of days ago, I moved up from that PBS rear station to another of these collecting points at the base of another towering hill where the litter trail wound down. I spent a night there and then we shifted the evacuation down the other side of the hill and subsequently pulled out baggage and all around the ridges to the other route, now made safe by the progress of the outfit. And so we moved into the town below yesterday and we three came right up here. I wouldn't at all be surprised if soon we were on the move again to evacuate by an easier route. You see, we have to change even as the boys forge ahead, for unlike being on the plains where there are none of these troubles, we have to take into consideration the features of the terrain. And so now with the slack time while Onodera has taken down a couple of patients, Ike and I sit comfortably in the shade of these stone walls to write to our respective wives.

Hayashi brought a sackful of mail in even while we were in the process of moving and boy did I hit the jackpot again. Seven letters from you. . . . There many other letters, too, from Nay, Mariko, Fumi, Jo (breaking a four month silence) and others. But, that wasn't all. There was also a piece of wedding cake (a trifle moldy) which Onodera and I ate with gusto, two birthday cards for which I now render many thanks to you and Mom. You will note that they came right on the nose today being that fateful day and I remarked to Ike and the Arab, "One fine way to celebrate one's birthday!" The very correct wedding invitation, futile as it was, also arrived and is now on its way back. And before I forget, I want to acknowledge the Minneapolis paper with its big lines on the wedding of a Japanese American couple. This helped to complete the picture of the wedding for coupled with your words, I can visualize the whole scene quite adequately. And I'm still sweating out Kay's profile, yet to arrive. . . .

Well, Kuramoto will soon find out what a delightfully wacky household he got himself entangled with and I don't think he'll regret that either. If he does, he's not the guy I'm thinking he is.

Tama's baby must be destined to be a girl—it's being just as contrary as any female can be. At any rate, that would be my guess and who knows it may have now arrived—possibly today by which token it labors under the handicap as having the same birthday as mine. . . .

I'm trying to send some money home to you which brings up Franklin whom you stated as being in Holland, and of having sent home a hundred bucks. He must have been shooting craps again. How's he making out and what's he doing, anyway? . . .

Yesterday's *Stars and Stripes* have made great mentions of the 442d in a first disclosure of this unit's operations here. Made us feel very good and with explanations and a picture of some POWs being marched back to a cage. If you read these articles you'll get the general idea of what's been going on. As it is, I'm just waiting for a go signal before I send you the issue or the clippings, preferably the latter if possible.

I've tried to take representative pictures right along as I've experienced them and usually you'll find the camera right close to wherever I happen to be. If I ever see these what a flood of memories they'll bring back and how much more simple does the story telling become, for a picture can take the place of a thousand words. I'm still sweating out a method of processing, but it's now in Mr. Collins' hands and he's Red Cross field director of the 442nd, working pretty hard on it and I think he'll be able to develop the rolls and then I can send them to you for printing. . . .

What a busy spot this is—this ruined building—for this is the junction of two trails snaking their separate ways up the two gullies and here jeep travel ends. Right next door, sits another unit's BN aid station with paraphernalia, all around us are Italian partisans who are the mule skinners and have made a temporary home by the rocks of the streams. Men and mules grazing all about us, jeeps pull up with stuff and jeeps go down, mule trains clatter up or clatter down and even paesanos run around here in their never-ending forage for food. And among all this we sit and wait in our easy leisure, just waiting for anything that may come our way.


11 APRIL 1945

As you can see, I've been able to get at my own stationery which also means that we've been moving about again. Regretfully, we had to leave our open-air residence amid the mules and paesanos and head for this place. You can also figure out that our boys have been pushing right along in a very confusing manner, at least to me. But, tonight everything seems quiet and we are bedded down in a big marble slab factory. I found a spring bed luckily, and my bedroll's spread out nicely on it, giving promise of a good night's sleep. Jimmy and I just got through playing on our strings and that was all right, too. In coming over here, we certainly passed through some battered places. Italy really knows what war is. I hope some of the pictures I've taken will give you an idea.

Just when I got yesterday's letter off to you, your letter of the 30th dropped in, also the Minneapolis paper and the long-awaited photograph of the elusive Kuramoto. He looks okay to me and the photo is now on the way back.

The enclosed lilac branch, now dehydrated and pressed is from the house of Micaela and Tina, some miles back now. At least, the fragrance is still there if not much of the original bloom. . . .

In another air mail envelope you'll find a mess of clippings which you'll find very interesting and tells in a few words what we've been going through. It also gives a pretty good overall history of the outfit. Be sure to read in acknowledged order and you'll notice the secrecy in the first two reports and then, boom, the 442d becomes unveiled and we get beaucoup publicity. And if you can synchronize my letters with the clippings, too, you'll get a pretty good picture of the situation. Yes, the 442d is still doing plenty all right for itself. The last clipping is of the new combat medics badge—nice looking, isn't it? We should be getting these soon. If only they'll authorize the pay, too, our happiness on this score would be complete.

I think I'd better bed down for the night—it's 11:35 already and one never knows what the morrow may bring. If I can dream of you, then of course the sleep is so much the better.


MEDICAL DETACHMENT LOG

13 Apr 45—Warm clear day. Regtl section left vicinity Massa by motor convoy, arriving Carrara. Intermittent enemy shelling of town in the morning. No troop casualties. In all some 1300 rounds of fire of all types was thrown in the Regtl Section during the day.

14–18 Apr 45—Casualties passing through Bn Aid Stations moderate. Enemy continued to harass with sporadic shelling of vicinity by coastal SP [self-propelled] guns.

After what seems a long time, actually only about five days, I'm writing to you again. You see, we're (the BN is in reserve now) now able to write letters again, having been restricted in combat time, this applying only to us medics. And a lot of things have happened I can tell you, but maybe I'll let that wait until I get back home.

I wrote you last from the marble mill by the river gorge where we had a day's rest. As you know now from the clippings sent previously and the ones enclosed here, the outfit has been going great guns and we had to catch up with the boys so the next day we were off again. On the way, Lt Doyon stopped the jeep and gave us the sad news of Roosevelt's death. To us it was all rather unbelievable until the subsequent issue of the *Stars and Stripes*. We lost a good man, but that can't stop this particular war one whit. I only hope that Truman's man enough to fill Roosevelt's shoes.

We rode on through one large town and then turned into the hills again to this village nestling atop a hill, so peaceful in the morning sun, to set up our aid station. We'd passed up our battalion GIs on the road and were the first 2nd Bn in this town, knowing that eventually we'd have to establish here, anyway. How deceptive it all was, our first view of this town, for all that afternoon and night the SP guns harassed us, but we were quite well protected by the wall and roofs albeit none too comfortably. It's amazing how we do get into situations such as these. And then, of course, our being at the spearhead of attack, the Jerries decided to counterattack on our left flank up the hill and it's a good thing that one company had come up as security because things certainly started popping all around us that early morning. Naturally, we were all petrified, but they were driven off up the hillside to our great relief. It was certainly one for the books and a new experience, hair raising though it was, for us. After that, however, it has quieted down here and we have watched the shelling and bombing of a strong fort to our NE with great interest, and we've seen from our vantage front how a good outfit operates as our men have taken this Jerry strongpoint in admirable fashion. We've had our share of casualties and plenty of Jerries have been treated, too. They still stink!

This is a typical Italian village, dirty and battered and now that we've been here four days we've managed to get pretty comfortable, having taken the best since we were here first. Since then others have moved up and it's quite a thriving community now. Today the 1st and 3d aid stations came in and we're all clustered on this street to make a *nigiyaka* situation. Hot meals came up for the 1st time today and was that steak and rice good! After all those Ks and Cs, I think anything would taste good anyway.

Mail has been coming in quite regularly and for that I give a salute salaam. I can't for the life of me knock the pile down and I'm frantic about the accumulation. It's getting to be a major problem. I was never so swamped before. . . . Will you please thank Mom for her birthday greetings and Tama and Harry for the Easter and birthday cards? . . .

It's good to know that some more perfume got home, but there's still some more, especially that last bottle which is a beauty. . . .

I had quite forgotten that a year had passed since Hack's death until reminded by your letter. Somehow it doesn't seem that far away and long ago and yet it must be. I often think that maybe it was better that he went when he had to than be embroiled in this horrible mess to meet a more violent death. But, I miss him.

MEDICAL DETACHMENT LOG

19–22 Apr 45—Warm cloudy day. Casualties passing through Bn aid stations moderate.

19 APRIL 1945

How goes it, gal? As in the last letter we're still in this mountaintop village, having a comparably easy time of it. Since that momentous first twenty four hours here, it has become a liveable place and we make the best of it. Our casualties (since our bn was off the lines) have been of nil. If only they could remain that way in combat too. . . .

Since this place seems to be the converging of all sorts of lines, I've seen all kinds of friends here. Of course, all our friends of the 1st, 3d Bn Aids—Abe, Squeaky, Ogami, Kitsu etc. are here and since the other day, Sammy's been staying with me. I saw him when he came down the road after being relieved of his chore of litter bearing and he's been with me the past two nights now. We sleep on litters in the aid station, a very bad place so far as sleep is concerned. Naturally, we shot the bull around and hashed over a lot of things on our common ground. He looks more rugged, unshaven and all, especially with that one-tooth-missing grin.

I'm rather surprised that you knew of the JAs [Japanese Americans] fighting in Italy. I guess that PRO's [Public Relations Office] on the ball. You'll be hearing more than just spearheading which seems to be our forte and also our crown of thorns. I have heard that General Clark asked for this outfit specifically from France to crack this line—that's why we're here—and I can say we haven't been idle at all. Even as I write this here where the tide of war has ebbed, further beyond, our boys are still in the thick of it. We have been moving, steadily, with objective after objective being taken and it seems we are ahead of our schedule—there are such things even in unpredictable war. If only the other elements could do the same we'd be very happy. As it is, usually we're spearheading out like a sore thumb and that meant that we have to worry about two sides and the front instead of just the front. That, my dear gal, in non buono. But, since this almost always seems to be our predictable lot, we bear it, even though this must inevitably mean a greater casualty list.

I didn't mean to talk so grimly since here in this town all is quiet and serene, excluding naturally all the artillery and cannon fire which is going out with special deliveries to the Jerries. Since the jump-off, it seems the whole Italian front's on fire and reports show that these Jerries in Italy are putting up a much stiffer fight than those fighting on German soil. That may be funny, but I'm inclined to believe it and that's no joke. Since we were in reserve, everything's been quiet and we've had time pretty much our own way, just eating, sleeping, reading, and loafing. The atmosphere and cleanliness is not much to brag about, but we certainly can't kick. . . .

You asked me about Harry Honda who'd phoned you. I don't know whether you know him, but I do. He's a Yakima fella—came to the U for awhile and was quite an athlete in his circles. He used to go around with Yone's bunch. It was nice of him to phone. . . .


21 APRIL 1945

Skipped you yesterday, but not because I'd forgotten you at all, only because I was too lazy to write. Even tonight, the inclination is none too strong, yet I know that I must write.

The radio report tonight tells of the Russians only four miles from Berlin and that they are only twenty-five miles apart from the American forces at one point. Isn't that good news? But here the enemy seems unmindful of the homeland trouncing, and keeps right on fighting, yielding ground only when absolutely necessary. Why don't they quit—that's one question on everyone's lips and here they're still fighting and dying and blood is being spilt. And all for I don't know what. Sometimes I get so damn mad and disgusted at this senseless conflict that my morale hits a low and today is one of those days and today has been a bad day, anyway. I can't help feel bad when I see our men come in bloodied and battered—our friends— and hear of friends who have given their lives on this rocky Italian soil. I think you will understand why I'm so depressed tonight.

We're still setting on our fannies here—the rear stations—we have parts of it at two other forward places. The situation is quite a difficult one, it seems, and I don't think that it will be any picnic. Evacuation of casualties from the ridges the battalion is fighting on looms again as the bugaboo. But that's the way it goes and we'll just have to cope with it as best we can.

Writing home, Italy, 1945. Min is leaning against the wall of a ruined Italian house, writing to Hana.

I'm sorry, darling, but I'm really in no frame of mind to do much talking tonight. I know you'll forgive me for this, but maybe tomorrow I'll be sprightly as ever. One gets these spells, as you may have noticed. So until the next time, I shall be seeing you in my dreams.

Medical Detachment Log

23 Apr 45—Warm clear day. Casualties moderate.

24–25 Apr 45—Warm clear day with Jerries on the run. Casualties passing thru aid stations very light. Left Tendola, Italy, by motor con-

voy arriving Caniparola, Italy. Set up aid station. Regiment in rest
area. Usual duties performed.

26–30 Apr 45—Warm clear day. Left Caniparola, Italy, by motor convoy 26 Apr 45. Arrived Genoa, Italy. Temporary stop, while reconnoi-
tering for CP. Left Genoa, Italy, and returned back to Sestrilevanti,
Italy. Bivouacked for the night.

Left the following morning by motor convoy arriving Busalla, Italy.
Set up aid station. Usual duties performed.

Month closed with German resistance in Italy broken, prisoners
were surrendering by units. Everywhere liberation celebration and
men received enthusiastically by the civilian population.


26 APRIL 1945

Sorry that I couldn't write to you for such a long time, but that was
unavoidable, we being a trifle too busy with this war business to take
time out to dash off a few lines. Right after I wrote you last from
that town on the mountaintop, I went up into the mountains to man
one of our forward posts down through which our casualties passed.
Because of the road being impassable, as yet in Jerry hands, we had
to take the trail in order to keep up with our men who were still
fighting over these rocky ridges. We'd litters spread all along the
trail, each squad relaying the casualties down to the next point,
and so on to the collecting point up to where the jeeps and ambulance could come to haul them to the rear aid station in town. We'd
paesanos, GIs, both colored and Buddhaheads, on this long chain and
as before, it's a good thing that casualties were not plentiful. The
boys pushed out of the ridge and surged into this next battered town
and I hiked over the tiring trail in, too, and boy was I corked! I never
was meant to be a mountain climber. By this time, the road was
open and we could evacuate over the road. But the boys weren't

idle—they were on the go the next morning, and in the afternoon Onodera, Kuge and I went on to follow the Captain up who'd gone on ahead on foot. We rode the jeep and luckily so, for the resistance being nil, they'd just hiked and hiked. We passed through about three towns and finally caught up with our boys on the road just a couple of miles from this big town in which we'd planned to bed down for the night. But, Jerry had different ideas, for we ran into some opposition and the outfit had to chase them out—the boys went in the next morning—but it was strange that we were right there with the forward elements; I can't recall a situation quite like this before. So, we'd stayed in a nearby house in satisfying comfort for that night. The Jerries in this region took quite a shellacking for, on this plain or small valley that we'd come into were great evidences of the disaster that overtook them—horses lay dead, flies buzzing over them in grotesque, obscene poses, all the world like overturned merry go round horses; the carts they were pulling lay scattered along the road and equipment was flung here and there. The strafing planes of the day before must have caught them on this level road and done a darn good job. Although hideous and malodorous, it did our hearts okay to know that the enemy had gotten a hard right to the chin. The Jerries in their withdrawal had blown bridges left and right and the engineers had quite a time making passable bypasses and fords across streams. What a rough ride we had going up there on the jeep over the bypasses. And at one time I was sure we were gonna be stuck wheel deep in the stream, but we made it okay. The Captain, on his jaunt with the forward elements, had gar-nered unto himself a motorcycle and he soon had it going and like a proud cavalier was putt-putting down the road. Even now he's still tinkering with this Jerry vehicle and it looks as if this is gonna be his method of locomotion from now on.

Now in regimental reserve, after the boys took this town we got together and came down off the hill back to this coastal stretch for a little rest. The plains here are fertile and with these green fields we can get vegetables to satisfy our gustatory needs, but as yet it is still too early for most things although just the green onions help out a lot whene'er we cook. You can imagine how glad we were to pull back. We'd gone in the 5th and pulled out the 25th—so it was twenty days without stop for us. On the way back we came back on the roads with all the destruction by them, and we viewed the terrain we'd gone through and familiar houses, trails and landmarks with a fond recollection of the time spent. Altho' now peaceful—in the passing of war, we could remember when it was not thus. It's begun to rain here now and that's not so good. I had to interrupt the writing to go down for cokes (two bottles rationed out), incidentally, these cokes are not like those back home both in flavor and sparkle, but it's still better than none. PX rations seem to be here, too, and there's plenty of beer for tonight. Chow (noon) was served and we got our mail, too, at the same time. Four came from you—I'm answering with this solitary letter. But, as I write this, things seem to be happening again to our great disgust and I think that we are moving again, probably tomorrow, to where we don't know for sure, but we have been hearing plenty of latrine stuff and I'm inclined to believe it. At any rate, you can read about it in the papers while we go out and do it. We're more or less disgusted about moving for we'd anticipated this rest, but as I said before, we don't have much sayso about this. Still, for this little rest we've had we're grateful, for it has brought us out of the ridges, the hills and the mountains and going over them was definitely not a small jaunt. That last day on the road the boys went a long way coming down from that ridge into the town they'd been assaulting. From there it was just march, march to them as the Jerries had retreated quite a ways. Now that the 5th and 8th are running around in the Po valley and going hell-bent these Jerries on this Ligurian coast are busting their fannies out, else it's the same finish-off story for them again. All of which doesn't make me sad in the least. And of course we read with great avidity, the Russian fight in Berlin and the expected junction of the Americans and Reds in the south. From this angle it seems as if the Germans aren't going to do any surrendering, but expect to be torn apart piece by piece. What a stupid, useless tragedy! We all ask ourselves when are they going to stop and still the silent voice answers back— "nevermore." Well, if that's the way it is, that's the way it is. But we still don't like war one little bit.

Your two packages of rice and *nihonshoka* came some days ago, but we've been too busy moving and separated to cook it up. We may tonight depending on the situation. Thanks, that's the kind of stuff I like. These came while I was up in the hill, but they kept the packages at the station for me. Mail came up via the relay posts as did the supplies and I received one *Newsweek*, keep them coming. . . .

In another envelope I've enclosed a *Yank* clipping which is self explanatory, the town I mentioned some time ago, about making entrance into possible and not getting a chance to get huzzahs for the actual march into it, is mentioned. The rest I picked up in the hills, you'll note their condition. Two are Jerry propaganda stuff. The one on General Doolittle is interestingly perverted and the other, on a V mail facsimile, gives quite a detailed wealth of procedures for those who would care to simulate sickness to avoid combat. I thought this quite interesting. The last is one of ours, informing the Germans on how to capitulate. I've some other stuff I'll be sending later on.

I just reread your letters and I enjoy reading them very much— they've the bounce of home life and I can picture all the things going on around the house. When you talk of wash nights, Mom's cooking, Kay's cooking, Mildred, Helen's cookies, Tama, Sue, the raincoat and the rain that compels you to think of raincoats, and juggling office figures, I have the feeling that I'm right there and I know what's going on at home. I can tell you that it does me no end of good. And now I won't have to worry about that last batch of perfumes— that was the last for some time, if any.

All the boys took off on the jeep for a shower, but I can wait, besides, I took a bath yesterday in one of the cold streams we forded, so I don't feel too dirty although I know you'd differ with me. And how, you would!

1 May 45—Busalla, Italy. Chilly cloudy day. Three casualties treated at Regtl Aid.

1st Bn Section at Isola Del Cantone, relieving 2nd Bn Section at vicinity of Balzaneto, Italy. Housed in Jerry barracks. Men enjoying shower facilities and passes into Genoa.

## 1 MAY 1945

Things are happening at such a rapid pace that it's impossible to keep up with them; yet we are trying. I think that you know what I mean. Since the fall of Bologna and the onrush into the Po Valley, the German army seems to be at the disintegration point. You read the papers and know what the overall situation there is. As for us, we too have to read our *Stars and Stripes* to find out what's going on. Everyone is more or less bewildered at the situation and trying to figure the next move. Now that the Brenner pass is sealed, all the enemy in Northern Italy is doomed and the end is in sight for them. This accounts for the mass surrendering of Jerries that one reads about and we see. The enclosed clipping will help you to understand the circumstances. It has now become a very peculiar type of warfare in which the main object is to pursue and to round up. We've done so much traveling that it amazes us, and at such a tempo. We are all rather incredulous at the rapid turning of events, but, of course, we're all very happy about it, too. Let me tell you about my personal experiences so you can tell for yourself.

The last letter of about five days ago (and you will know why I didn't write subsequently as you read on) was written when we'd pulled back for a deserved rest. A fine rest it turned out to be, for with the crumbling of the Po defenses, so too did the resistance on this Ligurian Coast. The Jerries had to pull out else their retreat would be no more. As it was, that's exactly what happened, for now there are plenty of Germans hopelessly trapped. Somebody had to help chase them up this coast and we were one of them, bypassing everything in our dash up the coast. So it was no rest for us at all, though we stayed there two nights, it was on the alert, so there could be none of that blissful relaxation. As our bad luck would have it—by we, I mean Ike and I—we had to ride the trucks up, the others going on the jeeps and trucks. I'll never forget that first day—everything in the nature of bad luck happened to us. First, we were sitting pretty on a roomy truck when it was found out that one truck too many had been filled, so we had to hop onto this fateful truck. This one, driven by a harassed partisan, had gone into a ditch once already that morning, hampered in its action by an unwieldy, heavy trailer. On this we had parked ourselves and to make the place more crowded, the captain had thrown his motorcycle on it and what a headache we found that to be later on, due to its occupying needed foot space and bouncing around on its stand as we jounced forward. We made our way with the rest of the convoy in a good enough manner, but we soon came to our first nemesis, an innocent-looking, but wide stream which we had to ford. The trailer was our doom, for with the water swirling above the hubcaps, the truck bogged down despite frantic turns of the wheels and there we ignobly remained while others passed along splashingly. We remained behind for a good two hours until we finally unhooked the trailer and lurched forward onto the other side. The truck had to go back for the trailer with a chain to pull it out, all the while remaining on a shallower level. So finally we were off again, everybody giving the poor partisan driver a very bad time with all sorts of comments. We were far behind now, but we plugged along and now the driver finds himself out of oil and the motor overheated and we had to park for awhile. After going on again, we borrowed some oil from some tanks that passed on the road. After we thought our troubles were over, we had to stop once again due to lack of water in the battery, but the climax came when the motor quit altogether on a hill and calmly froze up tight and we couldn't move nohow, nowhere. Boy, were we burned up by then. Luck was with us this time and we collared a passing Service Co truck and were happy to know that we had a dependable vehicle and a dependable driver. And now with the darkness coming on and here we were apart from the rest. We finally caught up with them and everything was messed up as no one knows where to go for the night. And I was feeling lousier than a dog from a mean headache of the ride. To top it off it began to rain. And I was mighty happy when Ike and I bedded down in one strange barn on a mess of corn husks and slept away the weariness of the day. The next AM saw us taking off again, but this time, we rode in the ambulance and we rode and rode, with frequent stops. It was all a trifle strange after just moving along so slowly and now we were chasing the Jerries as fast as the vehicles could move. As the convoy moved northward, people would line the roads and village streets and clap and throw flowers. Naturally, we were not immune to these blandishments and had a swell time. By this time as we approached a large city, the weather had turned fine, and we scrambled upon top of the three-quarter for better view and to give the admiring throng an object of applause. The people in this city really gave us a royal welcome and we enjoyed every minute of rolling through the streets. At one long stop we got plenty of drinks and acquired ourselves a huge Italian flag which we promptly flew from the roof and I suspect that it was partly the flag that gave the Italians cause for cheers. But, you can't say that we didn't incite them to it, either with loud cheers and gesticulations ourselves, such as "Viva Italia," and "Viva Partigiani" etc. By the end of the day we were quite tired from our exertions, but it was really like something out of the books, to be hailed like conquering heroes and bask in the warm smiles and cheers of the populace. Through one narrow street, I recall, we had to crawl through the people so packed the streets to view the caravan. Naturally, our throwing out candies, cigarettes, etc. had quite a bit to do with our popularity, but we don't like to think of it that way. You know how human ego is. And so for the night we slept in a huge house by the stables on the cold stone floor, expecting at any moment to pull out. But it was morning 'ere the ambulance went off with a couple of fellows (patients) to try and find the collecting station, everything having moved so fast that nothing was set and communications at a loss. We got rid of the patients and now tried to catch the rest of our vehicles up this Auto Strada—a kind of super highway, but in name only. We finally did, but no sooner than that we had to pull out again, and after numerous stops and gas and indecision and waiting, we came to this city where we've been hesitating for this our third day. It's a nice place and we're fixed up very comfortably in this hotel. This has been our first rest ever since starting and it was not premeditated, for we've been expecting to pull out at any time but we haven't as yet. This kind of thing is the nuts for we don't know when we'll go, where we're going and that causes a lot of boring waiting. We've been expecting to leave any hour and yet here we've been for three days now. But, we haven't wasted any time in seeing the town. We can't stay out too long since everything is indefinite, but we've all been shopping for things and I've three pairs of silk stockings and perfume for you which I'll be sending soon. It's a comparatively modern city and has quite a few shops. Today Ike and I borrowed a couple of bikes and had a nice ride around. Now that we know that we're staying at least for supper, we're going cycling again this afternoon. This city has not seen much destruction—they should be happy for that. The place is much cleaner, the people much better dressed and well mannered and the signorine much prettier than those of the South, for which we are happy. To make us happier we've replaced our diet of Cs and Ks with the cuisine of the hotel restaurant and that's much better to our liking. The fresh eggs in the morning (four this AM) are okay altho' we can't say too much for the manner in which rice is cooked. Onodera, Higgins and I have a room for ourselves with a bathroom (sorry, no hot water) and the former and I sleep on the wide bed under sheets while Buck takes the floor which is to his liking.

Mail finally caught up with us yesterday and I have two of your letters that I'm answering. . . .

The very glad news seems to be the one of Tama's becoming a

mother. I'm glad that the trying and expectant times are over. And it turned out to be a girl after all. I guess it had to be what with all the expectant waiting it caused. And now I finally have a niece; that's always nice after having so doggone many nephews. Be sure to tell Tama that I send best wishes, will you?

And I'm still in desperate need of getting my rolls of film processed. Then if you could see these prints you'll know of some of the things that have happened to me. I guess this spells *finito* for today. And I seem to have done all the scribbling about myself. But, you don't mind, do you? In these hectic times I'll try to write when I can, but all we do is wait, so please don't be disappointed if letters are few and far between.

MEDICAL DETACHMENT LOG

2–3 May 45—Left Busalla, Italy by motor convoy, arriving Alessandria, Italy. Set up aid station. No casualties reported. Usual duties performed.

THE SURRENDER OF ALL GERMAN RESISTANCE IN ITALY AND THE END OF RESISTANCE IN THIS THEATRE WAS OFFICIALLY ANNOUNCED 2 MAY 1945.

3 MAY 1945

As I sit on my iron cot and ponder on how to begin this letter, a partigiano is sitting in this hospital ward room and really giving the mandolin a workout, the boys are in the center of the room, shooting craps again, others are writing letters even as I. The *Stars and Stripes* just came in ten minutes ago, the two inch headlines screaming of the complete capitulation of the German forces in Italy, which became official as of twelve noon yesterday. This is what we'd all fought and bled for, what we'd gone through all sorts of hell for and yet, it all comes as an anticlimax. For us the war was actually over sometime ago, altho' it was never official. The Captain told us this noon of the unconditional surrender and because of the total events up to this point it was no surprise, for this we had conjectured. I suppose you've read all about it now. The official end of this Italian campaign caught us in this town of Asti which I may mention now. We'd moved up here yesterday morning after leaving Alessandria, the town we'd stayed in for some days as I told you a couple of days ago. We didn't want to leave the place, but the next morning bright and early we drove out of town in a brisk sunny morning, about twenty-five miles to this city. It is not a small town as we discovered in our meanderings yesterday afternoon. I've postcards so you can judge for yourself. Right now we are occupying a couple of rooms in an Italian military hospital which has a few patients. We're in one corner and the boys all sleep in this airy double exposure room on hospital cots and mattresses. We're not too far from the city center and we could make it by walking if we had to. So it's quite a comfortable setup, and we're taking advantage of it by getting cleaned up, airing bedrolls, sending out laundry, etc. For you see, even if the war is over here in Italy, we are still in the army and the Captain just told us today of the tightening of military regulations which means the stringency of garrison discipline and that's not to our liking. And now we'll have to sweat out going home or wherever we're going or whatever we're going to do.

Your April 24 letter came today with its usual cheeriness. . . .

Today I sent off a package to you containing a lot of junk. There's a bottle of Italian perfume, the bulk of it is Jerry leaflets and pamphlets. . . . Oh yes, there are a mess of postcards to give you an idea of what we've seen. . . . Do you recall my telling you of entering the big city on our drive northward where we got plenty of cheers and applause—well that was Genoa, but we never stayed long enough to get anything. From there we came on into Alessandria. The next bunch of cards—watercolor cards—are of this town of Asti. . . .

Do you remember the thirteen rolls of exposed film I've been carrying about? I had them developed and printed and they came out pretty good. I'll send them to you as soon as I can—quite a batch I have. We all had quite a good time recounting the memories these shapes inspired.

I hope you'll excuse the listless scribbling and general overcastness to this letter, but I'm not feeling too good tonight—a touch of the sniffles so I'd better hit the hay pronto. I notice in your letter you mention Carolyn Sue in the same breath as Tama so I'm assuming that that's her monicker and right purty, too. Please forgive this dull missive.

## MEDICAL DETACHMENT LOG

4 May 45—Cold cloudy day. Left Alessandria, Italy, by motor convoy and arrived vicinity Novi Ligure, Italy. Set up aid station, with usual duties being performed.

Red, White and Blue began displacing to Novi Ligure, billeting in an old army barracks.

5 May 45—EM settling down once again to garrison life. Passes to Genoa started.

6 May 1945—Warm sunny day. Church services for fallen comrades held in regimental area, conducted by Regimental Chaplains. Address by Col Miller.

All sections billeted in barracks in Novi Ligure, Italy, taking advantage of periods of rest and recuperation. General rejoicing and celebration prevailed throughout the evening, when names of men going on rotation were received.

## 6 MAY 1945

When I last wrote you we were still at the hospital in Asti, and then one day we got orders to move and one rainy day we came back this forty-odd miles, past Alessandria, to this town that we'd passed on the way up, Novi Ligure. Don't ask me the why or wherefore—we're just as in the dark as anyone else. This town is supposed to be pretty big although I haven't seen it yet. This is our third night here. The 100th and 2d Bn are quartered in these buildings built right around a central square. Training schedule including reveille and retreat starts tomorrow and incidentally, the medics are scheduled to give typhus and smallpox vaccinations tomorrow which fortunately I shall miss, catching the morning train for Genoa. 3d Bn is just a half mile down the road so we're all together. Squeaky and Vic Izui came over to take a shower, but they were frustrated in that effort, the engineers next door having decided that Sunday was not a day for labor. I'm CQ today and so I've been stuck here all day and have been rather busy treating scabious guys and making a makeshift preparation. . . .

Your letters have been coming in with a joyous regularity. . . .

You mentioned Junie Kawamura in your letter. I think I may have mentioned that he was injured when we were up near Sospel. The Special Service forces were around for some time. He was in the hospital near Cannes for some spell, but we couldn't get around there. I'm glad to know that he's okay and at home. He must have told you some of the wonders of Nice, eh?

We still don't know what's in store for us. With things going so smoothly over here in Europe, it's hard to see combat for us on these grounds, but CBI [China-Burma-India Theater of Operations] beckons. I can only wish that we'll be able to go home if they decide to ship us off. But, for the time being we're doing nothing in this peaceful town, we eat good and sleep is fine, but I still want like hell to go home to you.

MEDICAL DETACHMENT LOG

7–12 May 45—Training schedule commenced 7 May 45. EM paid for the month of March. Typhus and small-pox shots administered to the regiment.

2d Bn section left Novi for Cuneo, Italy, 8 May 45, on a special
mission.

## 8 MAY 1945

We've had quite a busy past forty-eight hours since I wrote you last,
so I'll tell you everything as it happened to me. As I told you, I was
going on a day pass to Genoa. That evening I got my Eisenhower
jacket and it's a mighty sharp jacket, too, and I fit it good. We stood
reveille the next morning and then we were marched to the train station just a few blocks away and off we were at nine sharp pulled
by the electric train. . . .

The first thing we did was grab a trackless trolley to the city center. This is quite a large town having about half a million and there
are some modern buildings and a couple of tall ones. . . . There were
a couple of theaters in town, GI sponsored, and we went to one in
which we saw a mess of Army release newsreels. One especially was
very interesting since it was devoted to Japanese Americans. It began
with a memorial service in a relocation camp for the Nisei dead and
presentations of awards to the next of kin, and then went into the
Nisei fighting in Italy. It was darn good, showing the 442d and 100th
in action in Pisa, Anzio, Livorno, etc. and we recognized some of the
boys in the scenes, such as playing with kids and cooking up chicken
hekka. Another surprise was a closeup of Dick Nomura, dusty as all
hell, giving an explanation of how and why he volunteered. It ended
with the station citation of the 100th by General Clark and his ring-
ing speech. We all felt, I am sure, proud of this newsreel—I wish you
could have seen it in its entirety as we did.

But getting back to Genoa—we just walked around rubberneck-
ing and I did some shopping. . . . I did see Harold Horiuchi on the
streets fooling around just as we were. The Genovese papers came out
with headlines of a total German surrender and we were treated to
some beautiful fireworks all about the city. Regardless of how inaccu-
rate this was at least it brought about a beautiful display. . . .

We got back at almost midnight and what a surprise to find out that we were pulling out the next AM at six, and all the trucks and trailers all packed up. After a very short sleep we were up again in the dark and getting organized. The proper hour found us on our way and we got to this, our destination, Cuneo, close to the French border and at the foot of the Alps about noontime. . . . We've taken residence in what evidently was a former Jerry barracks because of 1) the filth accumulated 2) the typical Jerry smell 3) the scattering of Jerry literature found. It's all cleaned up and burned and that was no mean job. We're all sleeping in a large room—lined up dormitory style—on steel heavy cots. I've yet to test the comforts of this. Being filthy dirty and dusty from the jeep ride, Mo and I took a cold shower and it was an invigoration. Tomorrow, we'll probably have hot water showers, but the main thing is I feel good tonight.

I still can't figure out what we're doing way up here. The only fighting now is in spots and none in Italy, but we're supposed to be here for some obscure purpose and so long as this life is uncomplicated I guess I'll have to be content to let the Army run things the way they want to.

We'll probably start getting mail tomorrow. You see the 2d Bn is hell and gone from everybody, the rest of the regiment still being around Novi and that complicates things because of none to good communications. However, we were surprised to learn that a couple of Piper cubs, close by, are attached to us as a means of liaison—that's a new one on us.


9 MAY 1945

Another day gone and it's another closer to that one when I shall be seeing you again. . . .

Mail came in today and I had a couple in my allotment . . . and by golly, practice must make perfect for yours are just that and maybe you don't think I'm in favor of that!

Golly I wish I could see Tama's offspring, the delectable Carolyn

Sue, who must still be a red bundle at this writing and homely as all dickens although I know Tama and Harry would object strenuously to this description. What with you and Mom fussing around I've a mean hunch she's gonna be one spoiled infant, but at least this way one has more fun. By the way, why don't you take pictures with that 127 camera that I sent back home when we first landed in Italy last year. This is the camera that Hack won in that raffle and sent to me. Thinking about Hack certainly makes me feel sad although I don't think of him often. I'm glad for that, but when I do I can feel the void that his passing created in me.

We almost moved out of these barracks today, but they decided agin it when they found out the contemplated move down the road was to a TB Hospital. That cut that off quick happily. It looks as if we're going to stay awhile.


## 11 MAY 1945

Now that I've a couple of cans of 3.2 [beer] under my belt and a cigar sits jauntily in my mouth at an acute angle, I can sit down here in the aid station (yeah, CQ again) and write in peace to you. . . .

We're still in the Cuneo barracks and now with the thorough renovation that the grounds have undergone, the place looks nice and clean and inviting. Summer seems to have moved upon us and the afternoons are quite warm. We all wear fatigues daily (a sure sign of garrison life), but when we go out we must wear OD's, jacket (Eisenhower) and this is the payoff, neckties. The 442d in neckties—that's really something. . . .

I'd gone into town yesterday. . . . There was a celebration for the victorious (blah) Partigiani who so valiantly wrested the city from the Germans (excuse me, while I laugh up my sleeve). . . .

Right now the hottest subject for debate and cusses seems to be the immediate future of the 442d and the new discharge system that the army proposes. We've been figuring up points for this and points for that, but alas, I don't come close enough to being eligible for immediate discharge, altho' I must confess that I hadn't dreamed of shooting that high. But, still one can dream. I just came down previous to writing this from the room upstairs where the air is thick with talk about the 442d and its destiny, which involves CBI, occupation, G2 [Military Intelligence Section], combat, rear echelon, etc., in other words everything imaginable that could possibly happen to the outfit. It's naturally all very interesting, but still in the speculation state. As for me, I repeat, all I want to do is go home. If I'm sent to CBI okay, but let me go home first—that's the main thing. Then I'll feel much better about going again. We're all inclined to doubt that the 442d will go into combat as a unit again. I myself have been thinking of home and G2 at Minneapolis, but don't think that I'm going to volunteer to go into overseas duty. It would be awfully nice to be stationed at Minneapolis, though, wouldn't it? (notice the wistful note in my voice)?

It seems that after all the efforts in getting comfortably settled, there are rumors of moving out again. That does my blood pressure no good, I can tell you. At any rate, I'll try and write tomorrow, darling, so now I bid you goodnight with all my love thrown in as bonus.

MEDICAL DETACHMENT LOG

May 13, 1945

The following letters were received by this Hq from our leaders:

*TO THE SOLDIERS OF THE FIFTEENTH ARMY GROUP*

*With a full and grateful heart I hail and congratulate you in this hour of complete victory over the German enemy, and join with you in thanks to Almighty God.*

*Yours has been a long, hard fight—the longest in this war of any allied troops fighting on the Continent of Europe. You men of the Fifth and Eighth Armies have brought that fight to a successful conclusion by recent brilliant offensive operations which shattered the Germans forces opposing you. Their surrender was the inevitable course left to them they had nothing more to fight with in Italy. You have demonstrated something new and remarkable in the annals of organized warfare: you have shown that a huge fighting force composed of units from many countries with diverse languages and customs, inspired, as you have always been, with a devotion to the cause of freedom, can become an effective and harmonious fighting team. This teamwork which has carried us to victory has included in full measure the supporting arms which have worked with us throughout the campaign. The services that have supplied us have overcome unbelievable obstacles and have kept us constantly armed, equipped, and fed. The magnificent support which we have always had from the Allied air and naval forces in this theater has written a new page in the history of cooperative combat action. Our exultation in this moment is blended with sorrow as we pay tribute to the heroic Allied soldiers who have fallen in battle in order that this victory might be achieved. The entire world will forever honor their memory.*

*The war is not over. The German military machine has been completely crushed by the splendid campaigns waged by you and our colleagues of the Western and Russian fronts. There remains the all important task of inflicting a similar complete defeat on our remaining enemy—Japan. Each one of us in the Fifteenth Army Group must continue without pause to give the full measure of effort to that task wherever we may be called upon to serve.*

*I am intensely proud of you all and of the honor which I have had of commanding such invincible troops. My thanks go to each of you for your capable, aggressive, and loyal service which has produced this great victory.*

*Men of the Fifteenth Army Group, I know you will face the task ahead with the same magnificent, generous and indomitable spirit you have shown in this long campaign. Forward, to final Victory. God bless you.*

*Mark W. Clark*
*GENERAL USA COMMANDING.*
*HEADQUARTERS*
*FIFTEENTH ARMY GROUP*
*3 May 1945*

*PRESIDENTIAL MESSAGE*

*I take great pleasure in conveying to each American officer and enlisted man in the Fifteenth Army group the following message received by me from the President of the United States.*

*On the occasion of the final brilliant Victory of the Allied Armies in Italy in imposing unconditional surrender upon the enemy, I wish to convey to the American forces under your command and to you personally the appreciation and gratitude of the President and the people of the United States. No praise is adequate for the heroic achievements and magnificent courage of every individual under your command during this long and trying campaign.*

*America is proud of the essential contribution made by your American Armies to the final victory in Italy. Our thanks for your gallant leadership and the deathless Valor of your men.*

*Harry S. Truman*

# 6 ITALY

*May–December 1945*

When the Germans surrendered, the 442nd was scattered all over northern Italy. They assembled near Brescia at the Ghedi airport, where they processed 80,000 German prisoners of war. After the 442nd was relieved by the Eighty-eighth Infantry, they were sent to Leghorn, where they guarded POWs and supplies.

—DIANNE BRIDGMAN

......................................................................................................................

NEAR GHEDI, ITALY
19 MAY 1945

The 442d does get around, doesn't it? We're hell and gone from where I last wrote you in Cuneo. You ask "what are we doing up here?"—wait awhile and I'll tell you. . . . Before going any further get hold of a map of northern Italy and follow us on this long trip. We headed north from Cuneo, I, the Lt Herman and Higgins driving in the front and in the rear were Ike, Takeshita, and T. Masuda. We were following G Co and catching all the dust, but luckily most of the way we had good roads. We pulled through Torino, a big city, quite damaged as we got an unsatisfactory view in the darkness of late evening. Night fell and we pushed right along with the proper stops for natural desires and such. The night was not cold and I kept awake to keep Buck company. It would have been impossible to sleep anyway. I remember one stop where we stayed an hour when the trucks gassed up and we opened rations and Tsuka and I played on the mandolin and guitar till we got the go signal. Dawn found us on the outskirts of Milano, a big city that we could see only in the distance. We turned up, went through Bergano and into Brescia. The sun was up above the horizon now and we drove down through Ghedi, to this our destination, in the hot morning sun about nine o'clock. This destination is a huge open field which evidently was once an airfield with its surrounding areas. The whole regiment is lined up here, right in order down the line all on this one side of the road. It took us all day working in the now hot sun to set up our tents and the aid station just as they wanted it. It was then we found out what the regiment is doing here. We've the unenviable job of processing the thousands and thousands of Jerries that surrendered in northern Italy. The huge field opposite us is used for that purpose. Convoy after of convoy of Jerry vehicles roll onto that field into certain numbered spots and the men and vehicles are all subjected to inspection before being taken away. It's a terrifically huge job and there doesn't seem to be too much confusion. Whoever said the Jerries didn't have vehicles didn't know the truth—to see all these trucks, busses, trailers and sedans, etc rolling in here at all hours and continuously. There was no stop except for darkness. The way they work this setup is this, as I found out later. These groups of Jerries come in led by the captors, and park in a numbered section. They dismount and spread their stuff in neat order and teams of our men go through every bit of their equipment and personal stuff, weeding out certain things. And then comes the medical aspect of the job, the whole kit and caboodle has to be deloused and what a job that is. They've trained Jerry teams of two in the spraying of the DDT powder on clothing and the person. And then they move through the inspected lines of Jerries doing their stuff and after that's over then they can pack up again into their own bivouac area somewhere close by. There are so many Jerries and vehicles that it's unbelievable that a couple of weeks ago they could just as soon have killed us as not, and vice versa. Today they're just bewildered humans. It only goes to show how time makes fools of men. That, in the brief, is the job that we're doing here. There are a lot more complications, but no sense going into that. You can't imagine the situation. All these Jerries and vehicles moving onto the field in clouds of dust in every portion of that huge field waiting to be processed. Even as I write this three enormous searchlights swing over the grass to give light to the processing that still goes on, and it's now 10:30 PM. It's really a terrific job. We see Jerries all over the place, some work around our areas, they march by on their way to help the processing, they roll in to be processed, and they come in on every possible type of vehicle. I've never seen so many in all my borned days.

We've had hospital units moving in, too, their vehicles all painted white with the appropriate red cross. Their nurses ride by in their white busses and they looked rather severe. There have been Jerry WACs coming in, too, and they are quite the object of discussion as to their function, most of us believing that they follow women's oldest profession. With all this continuous activity you can imagine that everybody is quite busy. We medics are plenty busy, too, what with aiding in the delousing by supervision, the profiling of our own GIs to find out fitness for the army, and now they are shoving injections upon us. This naturally, all falls on top of the regular sick call duty. So we are not idle.

But, I've been getting ahead of myself. After getting set up, the first day of arrival here, we were filthy with the sweat and dust of the long trip, so after lunch we hiked over to an irrigation ditch and we had a very nice cold cleaning up. That evening there was a movie on and we all went to see *None But The Lonely Heart*, a rather peculiarly morbid feature but with certain merits and certainly fine acting.

The second day dawned hot and bright and three of us, Mo, Ike and I went on the delousing detail. We had, each, certain groups of Jerry delousers recruited and trained, and we watched them as they went through the inspected lines, and did plenty of delousing our-

Processing surrendered Germans, 1945. 442nd soldiers inspect German clothes and equipment while the German soldiers wait in line.

selves. It's quite a dusty process as you can imagine. We've hand sprayers and we go over every inch of the clothing and squirt all over under the Jerrie's clothing that he's wearing to his great discomfiture. All of them are quite submissive and glad that the war's over. Naturally they're not happy they've lost, but they cooperate. Maybe some of the officers are arrogant, but we saw only one of these. And what a motley looking crew these Jerries are—ranging in all sizes, shapes and age from eighteen to fifty-five or sixty. This only goes to show how deep they went into their manpower barrel before capitulating. And you should see the junk they carry and the assorted un-uniform clothing. There seems to be no standard clothing such as we carry and wear. Some have hard loaves of bread, cans of food, all sorts of cigarettes in huge quantities and the cheapest sort of knick-knacks. . . . I loved going through their stuff and looking at what they had. They are all quite curious as to their fate as anyone would be, but we don't know either. These come from different outfits, and they're brought here in these small groups and processed a little at a time. There must be a huge mass just waiting for this somewhere. They are all rather well disciplined but submissive. At least for them the war's over. I wish I could say the same for myself!

This morning after sick call, the companies came in for profiling and it still goes on at certain convenient hours. This individual inspection and questioning involves time but mostly on the Bn Surgeon's part as only one other man need help him, and I did today. This afternoon, Ike, Mo and I got to go on the swimming excursion and we had a swell afternoon. We hopped on the trucks right after lunch and the convoy wound north through Brescia, thence east to Lake di Gardi. We swam close to the old moat and the water was blue green and clear and clean. We escaped the camp and heat this afternoon in the swimming and the rowboat through the waters. We got home in time for supper after the hour's ride through very scenic countryside. If I can get to go again, you can bet that I'll jump at it.

Comes once again all the finicky details of garrison life that descended with the finish of combat. It became worse daily and sits astride us like a huge burden. It's annoying to say the least and do we bitch about it?! Just to show you what I mean—aside from reveille, retreat, inspection—there's the policing to be done and worst of all, they tell us to the smallest detail of how to keep our tents in order. Every item has to be rolled up inside our bedding, towels, equipment, clothes etc, every day for inspection and the duffle bag in front of that. I guess you can't understand the complete situation not being in our shoes, but it is *rerusai* [troublesome]. It makes us all very sick in the stomach. . . .

The days grow hotter and hotter. The sky is always blue, though fluffy cumulus clouds are always on the horizon. The sun beats down all day and in the noonday heat it can be quite destructive of all energy and initiative. I hate to think of what July and August will bring and I certainly hate to think of staying here that long. The sooner we leave this treeless place the better.

My goodness, I just counted and this is the tenth page. I did get kind of carried away with my scribbling and all about what I've done only. Let's talk of something else. Mail has been coming in regularly though not too many for me. . . . I got the packages of rice and all I need now is *okazu* [a main dish]. Incidentally, send just that from now on, will you, till further notice because we've been getting rice fed to us quite regularly. So please just send me the *okazu* in your next package.

We don't know how long we're staying here. Some say long and some say short. At least the consensus seems to be that we'll be moving up toward Austria way. Don't ask me why—I just thought that I'd pass on a choice bit of latrine rumor.

I hope that this letter gets to you before our sixth anniversary date. I hadn't forgotten it at all. I wanted to write you a special letter since Cuneo, but the movement foiled that, and I want to say something to you, only for you, at the end of this letter. I guess the only way to say anything right is to say it simply, and this is it. I've never had happier moments than those that I've spent with you. Our marriage is something that you and I know is perfect and others can only look on in admiration; I can honestly say that I'm only looking forward to the time when we can take up our lives again together and live it as it should be lived, for you are the one, the only one for me and need I say this—I love you—the most precious thing that I have and I'll always try, though I know I fail at times, to live up to you.

P.S. Don't mind the incoherency—just realize its sincerity.


22 MAY 1945

Sorry that I didn't write you yesterday as I'd planned, but there are so many distractions among which are 1) we are quite busy what with one thing after another 2) it's so hot that one doesn't feel like writing in the day 3) movies and band concerts at night are a distraction, it being after midnight when we come back 4) the days are so long that time is deceiving and first thing you know, it's time to go to sleep. I think that's enough of alibis; quite a mess of 'em but you know that I'm only procrastinating anyway. . . .

In spite of the fact that I had delousing to do yesterday afternoon, Ike and I went off swimming, and what an experience. Instead of the usual Service Co truck to haul the boys out to the lake, they'd gotten their mitts on some of these Jerry busses that were in their huge motor pool. . . . All these busses were driven by the Jerry drivers and it was a peculiar feeling that we should be riding on their vehicles and driven by them. I wonder if the Italians that saw us on the road quite knew what the score was?

Before we took off on this swimming, I'd requisitioned for four Jerry laborers to fix up a gravel floor for the aid station, and we put them right to work having them haul the gravel from the dump to the station and spreading it out. While we were gone, Mo even had them dusting off the guitar and uke. And so now we have a nice crunchy clean floor of pebbles and it looks good, too. It's nice to have these guys doing the work around here. In fact we all love to see them working and you can understand why. . . .

Jerries are still coming in, but not it seems as in such a continuous manner as to having the dust darken the sky as it was in our first days here. We must by now have processed thousands upon thousands of Jerries and still they come in. I still can't get over the peculiarity of the situation, seeing all the enemy vehicles going by, Jerries working around here, marching by, etc. They outnumber us so overwhelmingly that it's not even funny. Somehow it all seems so grotesque, that I can't describe my feelings, especially as I sit in the aid station by the side of the road, and I can look across the vast field across the way and see the hundreds of collected Jerries, patiently waiting to be handled, and seeing all that goes on around here.

I thoroughly enjoy your accounts of home so much that every time I read, a warm glow comes into my heart knowing that you'll be waiting for me at home, and I can see home and you in it, doing all those things so familiar and dear to my memory. And Mary Mary, quite contrary, it seems your garden's growing all right from your sayso. I'd still like to come home for a garden salad. And then little Carolyn who must be quite an important and established member of the household by now with her overwhelming demands. All this is home, and to say that the biggest wish within me is to be there would only be a gross understatement.

## 25 MAY 1945

Our job here is not still entirely through for as I look out where the great spotlights stab the deep blue of the sky, I can see pearls of lights as convoys, probably Jerries, move in, but the flood seems to be over. They're still coming in however—what a mess of Jerries we've gone through. Still, it has its good points because we profit from it in many ways—Jerry busses transport us, they work around here, we get silk stockings, cameras, souvenirs, liquors, radios, etc. Tonight we were all issued a bottle a piece of confiscated liquors and there will be plenty of drunks around now and the Jerries had plenty, too. If you could see the warehouse all filled with the stuff taken off them, you'd wonder, too, what all that junk was for. The Army has a technical word for all this stuff—"war trophies"—it sounds better than "looting" and we benefit from it.

## 26 MAY 1945

After lunch and a short nap, Higgins woke me up and I went, purely for the ride of it, on the garbage detail with him and the driver, an irrepressible personable boy called Forty, who's the driver of the ton-and-a-half. We took the camp refuse out to a small village and because of two previous visits, the townspeople were waiting for the truck and when we showed up how they came running in anticipation of digging in. . . . We just couldn't keep 'em off the truck for the kids and women swarmed all over despite our frantic efforts, they just couldn't be denied the chance to grub around the littered mess looking for anything of value. That's how destitute they are here . . . there was a strain of the pathetic in the eagerness of these poor people.

Our garrison life still keeps up and from the way they're prettying

Italians scavenging 442nd garbage, 1945. Villagers waited for the truck every afternoon; they searched for anything of value.

this place up with wooden-framed tents and brick walls and borders, you'd think we were here for a long stay. Another harassing phase in the constant practice of retreat parade which we have to undergo. Twice a day we go through the gyrations with the able aid of our band. Just what they're prettying up for, I'm sure I don't know, but this I do know, we're all nasty as hell.

You asked me about discharge once—well, you know that at present par is set at 85 points. And my figures tally up thusly:

| | | |
|---|---|---|
| 24 | months in the army | 24 pts. |
| 12 | months overseas | 12 |
| 4 | campaign stars | 20 |
| | TOTAL | 56 |

Kind of sad, but that's the story. One main bitch is that the combat man gets no priority although the army considers citations and awards a criterion. In my opinion, that's a fallacy for how many can get awards regardless of all the fire and hell they've gone through. Too late now, but don't expect my discharge for some time yet. This is commonly called TS in this man's army.

28 May 1945

Six years today and I haven't forgotten the date but somehow except for the knowledge within me, there is no way that I can celebrate this milestone of our life together. Today only makes me realize what a contradictory and relative thing time is, for all at the same time it seems that I've known you and held you dear for a lifetime and yet it has seemed such a short time for all the happiness we knew. And when I realize in the latter sense, that life has really only begun for us, then I know that life holds meaning all the more. I'm not good at this sort of thing trying to put down in black and white just what demands expression from my heart. For this I'm sorry, but I'm sure that you know what it is that I'm trying to say and please make allowances. . . .

Life here still goes its quiet, unhurried way. The Jerries have stopped coming in and consequently processing has ceased, to all intents and purposes. We're more busy with the routine things of the army, drill, calisthenics, parade etc. But, most of these things we're immune from under the cloak of medical matters, all except the latter, which we have to undergo every afternoon.

San Pellegrino, Italy
30 May 1945

Perhaps you're wondering about the above new location of this writing. . . . Hayashi kicked me out of my warm blankets at 6:30 to tell me I was the lucky one on the four-day pass to the Regimental Rest Center here in San Pellegrino. . . .

It's peaceful and relaxing here. Trees line the streets, and there is the quiet serenity to the place that makes for mental repose. Our Hotel Como is nicely chosen and we have good rooms with luxuriously soft beds. Maid service is available, we dine in a white tableclothed, sparkling silver-wared dining hall. Reading material is available and for those athletically inclined, ping pong and a swimming (I've got to see it) pool just around the corner with convenient showers. . . .

I shall leave you for the night on paper, but never in my thoughts.

SAN PELLEGRINO, ITALY
31 MAY 1945

I borrowed myself the padrone's bicycle right after chow, and heading out the gate and up the road, I pedalled my solitary way. The road runs along the rushing stream which is constantly bickering with the boulders. It picks its way through these hills, past farmlands and houses, through the next town, and disappears into the hills. It was so very nice just pedaling along, looking at the eye-pleasing panorama that slowly unfolded itself with each turn of the wheel. I labored up grade and coasted down grades, always the crunching of gravel against rubber accompanying me. There were many others on the road other than I, out for exercise and relaxation. And as I saw couples riding by, I couldn't help but feel in the complete restful pastoral atmosphere, that here in this old world, these people have something that is lost in cosmopolitan America. These people have certain values of life which they feel have deeper meaning than we have as yet to grasp. Regardless of how much farther advanced we are mechanically, I can't say that we are up to them in the philosophical way of life. We're so busy trying to get someplace, that we lose sight of the beauties along the way, after all, isn't life the means to an end and not vice versa as we are inclined to view it? Too, as I rode along, I couldn't help but visualize you riding beside me, pedaling together, and enjoying every minute, just exactly as it should be. Ah, but it is nice here and relaxing.

Near Ghedi, Italy
5 June 1945

Right after noon chow, it was so hot . . . that we asked the Lt for the use of the truck to go swimming, and the whole load of us got in and ambled off to Lago di Garda. It's just as beautiful as ever and we had a wonderful time, for we got ourselves two huge rowboats and we had races with the inadequate oars and defective oar locks. I was hoarse from laughter when I saw everybody trying to row so hard that they pulled the oar out and tumbled over backward. I did that myself three times, and each time I couldn't move up from the weakness in my stomach from laughter. Needless to say, our boat won twice what with the expert stroking and coxswainship of a Washingtonian. I saw Sammy there, too, enjoying the cool green waters. . . .

The Medics' softball team was playing a pretty important game so I was out there after supper to root them on to a lopsided victory over Serv Co which folded up unexpectedly. Now we're tied with AJ Co for the lead in the Special Companies league. The winners of the Bn leagues will fight for the regimental championship and the winner will go to Milano for the 5th Army championships—that's one incentive for the boys' playing.


7 June 1945

I saw the companies of the 3d Bn moving in sections down the road to see the "must" film *On to Tokyo* and, of course, I noticed Sammy's toothless grin among the faces. I saw Fudge Fuji marching along too and hollered at him. This is the first time I've seen him over here and I think he'll come over to see me soon. Now with another three hundred or so that joined the first bunch of replacements, the total comes to over six hundred that have come to the 442d this past week. The first bunch has been reassigned, and I wouldn't be surprised if there were plenty more that I know in these bunches. Slop Aoki surprised me one night when he came over. Do you remember him? Hatchan's kid brother. He told me that Ish is here, too, somewhere. Eventually, at this rate, I should meet all my friends in the army this way.

A lot of our eligible men have gone home or are on the way, due to the point system. At present only some 100th medics have gone home, but this next batch, scheduled for soon, will take away quite a few of our medics. The gaps left will be filled by the Regimental Aid Stn, probably going to be broken in as a clerk—a not enjoyable job.

Some more Jerries have come in the past two days and the scene across the road is one of activity. There's rumors of another second batch of eighty thousand coming, so we may be around awhile, but this AM I heard latrine whisper of our being replaced by the 88th— just what would happen to us being one of calculation only.


## 11 JUNE 1945

Four truckloads of 442d boys left for home on points and I went down to see my friends off. How I wished I could be on that list! I hope some of them will be able to come around and see you so that you can feed 'em and maybe get some firsthand information about me.


## 14 JUNE 1945

We have been preparing to move and we are scheduled to go out tomorrow. . . . Our new destination is Lecco, near Lake Como, and we are going there for a rest. It's beautiful country up there, but we're still bivouacking, but this time on green field. . . .

The 442d Combat Team seems to be slowly breaking up. First the 522d separated from us and fought in France while we toiled in Italy. A few days ago the band went to Florence, why I don't know, and now there's an announcement that the whole 232d Engineers will go back home as a unit and then disband there. It's official and not a latrine rumor. Of course, you understand that disbanding doesn't mean being discharged. When I heard that, I wondered what the ultimate fate of the 442d is. We've still cannon and antitank and the infantry battalions. Maybe, we'll all go home together, I hope.

LECCO, ITALY
23 JUNE 1945

On the 21st I went to Milano as planned. . . . I'd noticed that *Madame Butterfly* was playing at the Teatro Pucini so I rode out that way on the trolley, dragging another with me. A Miss Atsuko Ito was singing the title role and that intrigued me, so we bought tickets. . . . I was very curious about Miss Ito and her abilities, but when she once began singing there was no doubt at all. She sang beautifully, with volume and clarity—in fact the whole performance was the best I'd seen and heard of *Madame Butterfly*. The tenor was very good, too, but the star was definitely Miss Ito and she was the darling of the crowd and it did my heart good to hear all the applause and clamor for bows and encores. Somehow, to see a *"nihonjin"* [Japanese person] receive the plaudits of the audience does my heart good. She was superb in "One Fine Day" and did the people love her?! She was extremely graceful in her role and I was proud indeed, and I must have shown it for many of the other listeners seemed to [be] quite amused and curious at our presence. Squeaky Kanazawa was right behind us and after the performance we decided to go and see Miss Ito altho' I was *"hazukashii-wa"* [shy]. But, she received us very graciously and we had a good time conversing with her. She's about thirty-five and is married to an Italian. She has been studying voice in Milan for eight years and Cho-Cho San is hers over here. Born in Japan, she met her husband while he was teaching Italian in NY. Incidentally, he speaks Japanese beautifully—even better than Miss Ito who is so unused to Japanese that she gets stuck and lapses into Italian which is very queer indeed. She speaks only a smattering of English and what with our poor Japanese and Italian it wasn't too easy, but she had just as difficult a time as we did. There's another girl, a Nisei from California—Miss Hasegawa, who's been here twelve years and sings at La Scala, but of course, the latter is now destroyed by bombardment. She, too, sings Cho-Cho San, and she may sing for the 442d one of these days. After the delightful visit with Miss Ito and her husband we took leave. We were the first JA soldiers she met with and she was certainly surprised to hear of our doings. I'd like to hear her again 'cause she's much better than Koyko of the San Carlo—remember? Of course, here there is not that race prejudice encountered back home and, an artist as she, is only judged on her merits and that she has aplenty—altho' she did express a desire to see America. I'm enclosing one of her autographed photos. The others and libretto I'll send later. . . .

Incidentally, your talks concerning G2 have come to pass. Someone is here now for examinations for that particular branch and their offer is certainly an attractive one. They are looking for three hundred volunteers but it still remains to be seen if they'll get 'em. Examinations are being held now—interviews that is—and HQ Co will have them tomorrow AM. Their offer is this—these three hundred will be sent home, get a forty-five day furlough and then school at Snelling for six months or nine months, the former being the minimum. And then they say that there will be more time spent in the US, so there will be at least a year spent back home 'ere being shipped out to CBI. I've been wrassling with the offer myself, but haven't come definitely to it, but I don't think I'll commit myself. I'd rather sweat out going home from here and when I do get back, depending on the disposition of the 442d, I may go into G2. At least, by then the chances of war ending sooner will be much greater. At least, that's the way I've been figuring. At any rate, since this is just as important to you, I'll let you know how things go.

26 JUNE 1945

Today's an anniversary for the 442d. A year ago today we went into combat and about this time, 9:00 PM, we were having one of the worst times of our whole sojourn here. That's a day I'll never forget as long as I live, for I can't remember when time dragged by so slowly. I don't think I ever told you about our first day. We were all rather wide-eyed and anxious about the initiation, and as the morning progressed we followed the companies in the slow trek advancing through open fields and vineyards, just as if there were no war whatsoever, for there was no shelling at all, and we were quite happy that war could be so pleasant. It was a bright sunny day and we kept moving forward slowly without opposition. But, what a rude awakening awaited. Just as we'd stopped at the edge of a field in clump of trees and waited for reports, we heard our first shell and it being the first one to greet our ears, we'd no idea of the barrage to follow. It landed some 300 yards behind us, and then others followed in regular pattern even coming forward toward us. We'd been dug in, but we were ordered to move out in the field and that was our mistake, for as we scurried out from haystack to haystack, we must have been observed by that 88 as we crossed the road into the ditch on the other side, a narrow thing about two feet deep. We worked forward into a culvert and from this ran a rocky gully running up the side of the gentle hill. The whole Bn CP was soon stretched all through that narrow gulch filled with boulders of all shapes and sizes. Meanwhile, the 88s were still coming over and now we were pitifully pinned down, the whole lot of us stretching flat in whatever position offered the best protection. The gully itself wasn't shallow enough to give us adequate protection, and the terrifying shells came in clusters that sent fragments whining, shaking the earth and clipping branches and leaves off overhead that fell on us to remind us that they were coming close. Thank God that you'll never know the abject terror that we knew in those first moments, nor come to realize just how deep a love one has for life. There never was a better thing to cling to than Mother Earth and there must have been uttered many a prayer. Since 88s have a [flat] trajectory, they were falling all about, but not into the ditch—I hate to think what would have happened if mortars had been trained on us and came raining straight down. However, it was inevitable that the hard-luck shell would come over, and it hit us in one spot of the gully which widened and shallowed out. It came with disastrous results. A call came down for medics from above the gully and I worked up past the huddled men to gaze at our first casualties. Two men were dead—one our Capt and the other a PFC. Four more lay injured. Realizing the inadequate protection of this gully, we picked up the casualties after first treating these injuries, and staggered up the rocky gulch for a hundred yards, which deepened at one portion. Here we scooped out protected places for the wounded and took better stock of their injuries. All were litter cases, and two were badly hit. We piled rocks about them [to protect them] from any flying missiles and then ourselves tried to spread out and get our own protection. It was impossible to dig into the rock and so we piled up the smaller ones along both sides and prayed that nothing would come in, for the 88s were still coming in barrages. We couldn't evacuate at all, it was too hot—there was an open space in the gully that offered the enemy visibility and each time a man came up towards us, another mass of shells would come over. The hours passed and still we couldn't move—two of our medics worked up the gully and made a long roundabout trip back to the aid station and came back with plasmas. Evening was falling. We gave the men plasma—moving them out to center of the gully so we could work—we decided this as we figured that with cloak of night, we could get out, so held the plasma, figuring that the men would need the effect of it for the trip back. Just as we were in the midst of the transfusion and I was holding up the bottle allowing the precious liquid to flow in, the Jerries opened up again with their hottest and most prolonged fire. What an awkward situation. Now the shells screamed even closer and ground shook and we could hear the fragments whining off or clipping branches, and dust would come down as the ground trembled. And our patients had been moved out of their rocky hole and here we were holding up bottles of plasma. It was a dreadful moment. I recall flattening myself, still with the bottles aloft; I didn't give a damn how silly I may have looked. And now the plasma was almost all in. Impatiently I jerked out the needle, threw the bottle away and pushed the litter close to the wall and hurriedly piled up rocks about him and jumped head first into my scant rocky retreat. You must remember that during all this the shells were coming over in deadly regularity—a short quick s-s-s-t and then bang as the shell exploded. What terrible moments war can hold. It so happened that this particular barrage was the worst of all—we figure about forty shells came over all about our particular spot in a space of a few minutes. The funny thing about it was that it was more fearful while huddled into our "hole" than when I was actually helping out the patient. I guess I had more to worry about then. And funnier yet was the fact, (funny when I look back on it) it wasn't funny then, that when I jumped for my scooped-out hole, another was in that tiny confine, his place being further up the gully, but the urgency of the moment [had] thrown him there and can you see the two of us burrowing into that small space into the most contorted positions to get closer to earth. There certainly was no humor then, I can tell you that. The barrage finally lifted, and calling on some infantry men for help, we began moving our patients out, for now darkness had begun to fall. We worked hurriedly as you can imagine, never quite knowing when again we'd hear that terrible whine of shells. We were the last to leave—the four of us on this one casualty who, because we'd only three litters, had to be lugged out on a shelter half. As you may know there is no place to grab on the smooth canvas and what a rugged trip we had, stumbling over rocks and dragging the protesting patient over the field till we finally hit the road again. I thought I'd never see the road. God had somehow seen us through and to top it off, a jeep came by us as we stumbled along and we went back to the aid station which we'd not known existed till the plasma had come back. It was nothing but an old stinky barn and the men we made comfortable in the hay right next to the huge white cows contentedly chewing on their hay. We'd no way of transporting the wounded out, for everybody had mysteriously disappeared. We were never more so disgusted in all our lives—we alternated cussing the officers with tending to the wounded. We'd sent word on down with the jeep—we just waited and waited in the dark night, completely baffled. Now hunger caught up with us, for we'd eaten nothing all that afternoon and night, and fatigue crept in with the mental and physical strain. After a terrible four-hour wait the ambulance showed up and we came back to the collecting station, and after a hot cup of coffee, tumbled wearily into the malodorous hay in unconcern and slept the sleep of the utterly fatigued. All that night the "Long Toms" (our rifled 155's) boomed and flashed, but we disdained that for the sweet arms of Morpheus. Now you can see how we can never ever forget that first day when we received the baptism of fire. There were other days, terrible days, to follow, but I won't go into that now. I got rather carried away in this relating, so you'll excuse it. But, now that it's all over here I thought maybe I'd tell you a story, for now you won't worry about it, and the date egged me on.

To get to pleasanter subjects, I was lucky to get to see the Frank Sinatra show yesterday evening in Milan. We'd a quota and I got in on it. The show was in a huge open-air arena and there was plenty of room and not hot at all. Ike and I rigged up a very nice observing position with a bench and hurdles and were much entertained by the hot 34th band that came down for the occasion. I guess it was not only curiosity, but also the attraction of Phil Silvers, bespectacled comedian, and Fay McKenzie (beauteous babe) that drew me to the stadium. But, I'm certainly glad that I went for I was entertained from start to finish. Silvers was excruciatingly funny, McKenzie pulchritudinously pleasant, and the show very fast-paced. As for Sinatra himself, he's okay and in my book a very good entertainer. I can see why some of the bobby soxers are so thrilled because there's a personal quality to his delivery and that distinctive caressing feeling in his voice. He knows his timing and he's quick on the mental draw. He was also very obliging, singing plenty of songs, and there were plenty of cracks in the dialogue and songs about his physical condition and the swooning business. I came away with a distinct feeling that I'd been very pleasantly entertained and happy that I'd come. I couldn't ask for more than that. . . .

A pleasant surprise awaited me when I got back from swimming. Minato had rejoined the outfit. You see he'd left the 442nd our first month in combat after being rather hard hit and now he's come back, almost a year later. As you know we'd met up with him in Pisa when we returned from France, but just for a day. He says a lot of our Class B (non-combat) men are coming back, even as he, and he also brought a wonderful rumor that I'd very much like to believe, that we're scheduled to go home soon, in maybe a couple of months now. How I hope he's right, but I've been hearing rumors of a longer stay so I don't know what to believe. Natcherly, I like to believe the best and that's what I usually only listen to and argue for.


## 28 June 1945

The medics were called for the G2 interview today and we all rode over to Regimental, all making cracks at each other about Okinawa Japs, etc. The whole thing was very simple. A Capt McClanden or something had been sent over from Snelling to take three hundred back with him. When my turn came, I went in and saluted and he, looking quite bored it seemed, asked my name and the amount of Japanese schooling and where. I answered these and when he asked whether I cared for this sort of work, I replied "Not particularly." That was all there was to it. I think that only Ben Yamanaka volunteered and he's fit for the job. But there's still the examination to pass yet. Although the lure of forty-five days and school at Snelling so tantalizingly close to you is certainly a temptation, I think the better bet is to sweat out going home over here. By the way, this Capt McClanden, whom we chatted with one day, knows Kay and the other officers. I guess Kay would know him, too. . . .

I'm sorry to hear that your mom had a stroke that sort of incapacitates her. I hope she'll be alright. Be sure to tell her I send my best. By the by, I saw Richard and Harry H at the interviews and Dick has his hair crew cut and makes himself looking like a resident of *Nippon* [Japan]. We threw the bull together and Harry seems to be making out alright.

3 JULY 1945

Dear *Sensei* [Teacher]

*Ikaga desuka?* [How are you?] When I read of your going on probation of three months as a Japanese instructor at the U I was very happy indeed of your good fortune. I hope you consider it so, else I wouldn't think so either. Now, if ever I should happen to go into G2, I can begin by taking lessons from you. Congratulations, but I hope you won't have to sweat too much over it. Let me know how things go along, won't you?—dear *Sensei*. Gee, but I'd like to be in your class—how I'd love to heckle you and see you blush and stammer in confusion. Remember one time at the U Open House where you talked on nursing?—dear *Sensei*. I know you'll get along in this alright, though—it shouldn't be too difficult for you.

Tomorrow's the Fourth of July already and I suppose that back home the rigmarole of festivities is planned. Well, it's no exception here, for there's going to be a parade through town tomorrow, and citation ceremony. I signed up to go to Milano tomorrow, but no dice, they cancelled all passes and so it seems that I'll be in that parade. Hayashi told me yesterday that I'll have to be there anyway because it seems they're going to give me a Bronze Star for something or other I did in the last campaign. Just what I don't know. I thought I'd tell you this, not in a sense of bragging, but because you're gonna hear about it sooner and later and might get blown-up ideas about it. You see, although I'm glad that I'm getting the award, the why is not too clear and Bronze Stars in this outfit have ceased to become too important. But at least, it'll look good on my blouse and it's five more points to my 56 to give me 61.

NEAR LEGHORN, ITALY
14 JULY 1945

It's with a sense of shame and contriteness that I begin writing this letter, for I have neglected writing to you for such a long time, as long as I can remember, for I really have no excuse whatsoever. I hope you'll forgive me for the negligence. . . .

If I recall I wrote you last on the night of the third, just the eve of the Fourth of July parade and citation ceremony in which they were going to give me the Bronze Star. That was the first lucky break for all that were being cited didn't have to march in the parade, and we just walked down to the field and practiced a few times before the companies came marching back from their hot, dusty trek to way the other side of town and as usual the usual number of kids and adults trailed along to see what was cooking. The ceremony was brief. After the companies were properly lined up the line of us moved forward and as our names were read off we individually went forward and Col Miller pinned our medals on us. I wasn't too nervous and Col Miller as he pinned me, asked if I was a medic and when I responded in the affirmative he gave me a story on how the medics all deserved medals and thought that they didn't get enough recognition. It was all quite simple and went off sans hitch. I've found out just what the medal was for—the enclosed is the official citation and we all had a big laugh over it. It all sounds heroic as hell, but it wasn't like that at all—it seems that you have to write citations up in this glorifying tenor to get it. I'll tell you about it, so you won't get the wrong impression.

We were at Castelfoggi at the time, the mountaintop village above Carrarra where we stayed for about a week, while still trying to clear off Fort Monte Bistion. I think I wrote you about the air attack and shelling of that strongpoint. In the big shipment of snaps I sent you, it's where the partigiani posed for me and where the tanks were in the street. At any rate, as I told you, we moved up into this town ahead of the infantry, figuring that we'd be there eventually and so we made the long hop, passing our boys on the road on the march forward. It seemed peaceful enough that morning we moved in, the first elements of our battalion. At that time only a platoon of M Co was there, throwing mortars up the side of a nearby hill. We got set up, the other elements pulled in, and then the Jerries began throwing 88s at us all day so that we couldn't freely move about either inside or outside the buildings. This continued all night and in the early dawn the Jerries counterattacked in battalion strength, and we were awakened by the small arms fire that began in the eerie half light. B Co had moved in as flank security and unquestionably they saved us all from capture. I was quite scared and just burrowed down into my bedroll further as the machine guns chattered. M1s sang bullets through the streets and burp guns seemed to be going off right next door. After what seemed a long time but was actually not, the fight moved away slowly—we could hear the firing recede from very close by to the hill. We were up by then and finally all firing seemed to have ceased. As we peeked out we could see on the distant hillside the Jerry litter parties waving huge white flags as they carried their wounded away, slowly but patiently now dipping into a gully, but reappearing and finally over the crest of the hill. But, before this, there was a call for medics for there were our casualties at the bend of the road a couple of hundred yards ahead. Kuge and I grabbed a litter—remember this was almost right after the firing had ceased—and trotted forward up the dusty road towards the casualties. I can't exactly recall my feelings at the moment, but it had all happened so fast that as I went forward I did have time to think and I know that there was some trepidation in my heart. We came to the bend of the road and there some of our boys—Baker Co boys—had dug into the ditch there and though at the time I didn't realize it, concentrating on the wounded, four of those boys were dead and silent and unmoving in their own dug graves. As we patched up the wounded, there was an eerie silence after the uproar of an hour before, and while my hands were busy, I glanced up to see a German rifle trained on us from only twenty-five yards away, and was I flabbergasted, for there in a gully were three or four Jerry litter squads patching up their wounded even as we were ours.

Our guns were on them and theirs were on us. What a peculiar situation, and I could find no words to describe my mixed-up emotions at that time. They carried flags just as we, while their aid man had a huge red cross plastered right across his chest. But, we weren't wasting any time here, and as soon as our man was ready we lifted him and began the trek back. Now I could see things better. The one man—Jerry, waved his flag while the other groups, about three—all in the same ravine patched up their casualties. As we went by the waving Jerry shouted "Hello" and that only made the situation that much more flabbergasting. During all this I can't recollect fear, being too busy and as we slowly wended back, the litter on our shoulders, the patient complained of his leg injury and pain, and incongruous though it may seem, I began to count cadence to keep our steps in rhythm to cut down the bouncing. Imagine counting cadence—one, two, three, four—at a time like this, though it wasn't incongruous at the moment. About twenty-five yards before we came to the shelter of the buildings on the narrow street, a bullet came out of nowhere and knocked a chip out of the corner of the house before us. It was when this stray came near that I began to realize that this was definitely not good for my health, and only till then, and so we speeded up and brought him back to the aid station. Half an hour later they were all on their way back towards a further echelon. And that was it—if you can make more out of it than the WD did, then you're a better PRO (publicity). So don't get too big ideas of how they pinned the BS on me. In the 442d you know that these are almost a dime a dozen. Incidentally, I've sent the medal home, keeping only the ribbon to wear on my shirt or blouse. . . .

We'd known about moving out in a few days and as usual the 2d Bn had the hind end of the deal. We were going toward Leghorn to take care of PW cages 336 and 337, the 3d went to Florence, Pistora, Lucca, and Montecatinei and the 100th went into Leghorn. We were given the lousiest job in the lousiest place and it's not the first time; so we're scattered all over the place. . . .

This camp has pyramidal tents to our liking, but it's dusty as heck and is set up to take care of the two PW cages here. Our boys took over this morning from the 473d Inf Regt who've been here about three months now. They were on our left in the last push—also attached to the 92d Div.

Morimoto and Futamata had preceded us here on a quartering party, and when we got here, Jimmy gave us a healthy hunk of rumors or facts, as he says. At any rate, an AEF [Allied Expeditionary Force] station announced that the 442d and 473d are now placed on the status of "strategic reserve" and that we'll be going home soon. Just what that "soon" indicates is what gets us. We know we're going home some time or other, but "when" is the big question. At least, our moving here to Leghorn is a move in the right direction. And I hope the implication of the announcement is absolutely correct. But, don't put too much stock in it.

About the G2 business, I think I told you of my interview. The men have already been picked and will be leaving us today at noon to await shipment. Yamanaka is the only medic leaving and he was over this AM to say goodbye. He's an original member and has been with E Co as aid man all the way through. He's a nice and quiet fellow, and when he gets to Minny he'll look you up so please treat him nicely. I gave him your address. When I think of their leaving it certainly makes me want to go too, but I guess I can stand it a little longer.


16 JULY 1945

The Jerry prisoners from PW 336 do most of the work around here and you see them all over, of course most of them are under guard. They work very well and I'd take one of them to a half dozen Italians any day. Evidently they are rather satisfied at the treatment under our hands—too bad our men couldn't do the same. There are two of these huge cages, 336 and 337, here and the 2d Bn is concerned with the first. Our men have taken over and you see them patrolling the barbed wire fences and manning the machine gun on the towers. The

Jerries live in pup tents, orderly, on the dusty ground and get meals twice a day. That's one reason so many volunteer for labor outside, for they get fed three times, just as us.

## 22 JULY 1945

This recent report of deactivation and schedule of our going home by Feb of '46 is certainly a discouraging thing, but at least I'll be that much further away from CBI. I think I'd rather have it that way. So for a little while longer, honey, I'll guess you'll have to have your picnics and dinners without me, but wait till I get back, we'll have one merry celebration.

## 24 JULY 1945

There hasn't been much of anything doing around here, that's why I didn't write last night. Just lie around here and think about nothing in particular and do nothing in particular. . . .

I don't know just what this "strategic reserve" is that we're scheduled to be in when we get home in February, but it certainly sounds important. Of, course, this February business is tentative and I'm optimistic enough to believe that we'll still be home by Christmas at any rate. I've five dollars on it. While we're more or less waiting to be shipped home and doing odd jobs, the army wisely contrives to establish things what will keep the GI occupied and halfway happy. I think I told you once from Lecco about all of us signing up for various schools. Ike and Bobby Takeshita are leaving in a couple of days for a three-month course in Italian culture and fine arts at Florence—the main idea is not to absorb the culture, but to be away for three months and that's not a bad deal, but I'd no hankering for it so I didn't sign up. I did sign up today for a month's course at the GI study center in Florence in certain sciences. I may be lucky enough to be chosen, but I'm not optimistic about that. I'd much rather go to technical schools, but nothing has shown up as yet along those lines. . . .

Did I tell you that we have laundry service now? I guess not—anyway twice a week Supply sends out ten pieces for us, to be washed and pressed by the Jerries for only twenty cents. In anticipation of being able to wear CKCs I sent a suit out. Wherever we go it seems we're the only ones in ODs yet—if we do get to wear khakis, it'll be about the first time overseas because the ODs are a sign of combat men with all the PBS and rear echelons wearing the CKCs. I'd rather wear the latter for summer anyway.

You asked me about our luggage in camp. I think that it would be best if you were to get it shipped to where you are now, if WRA is going to clean house. There wouldn't be much point in shipping it anywhere else. Then, if you needed, you could draw from it and if not, just leave it in storage somewhere.

## 25 JULY 1945

Nay wrote me the other day and she told me that she's headed for Portland, Ore. on the seventeenth to a poultry ranch, the kids being all excited about it. They'll get pretty good food, I hope—they're expecting eggs and milk and such. Mom and Pop are staying till the end of Hunt in Oct or Nov; they may go to Ogden or to Portland depending on how Fred and Nay make out. I think they'll be all right.

## 29 JULY 1945

Coming in again late as usual, but I'd better get this off before I have to take off tonight to go to some kind of gathering. Jimmy and I are going to take our instruments to play for Capt and his female friend or friends. It's not at all to our liking and we're sort of ——— off about it, but he's insistent. Can you imagine—hauling me, a mainlander, to sing Hawaiian songs for his advancement along amorous lines. That's why I'm drinking gin and juice right about now as I write this to fortify myself for the ordeal. I'll tell you how I make out. . . .

We don't know what's in store for us, the 442d, as yet; just now we're all living the life of Reilly. Of course, the infantry boys take guard, but other than that, there isn't much doing, so it's very restful and calm.

I've heard ugly rumors about my name being sent in on a list to be MAC. I asked Tak Nakamura about it but he claims ignorance. I sure hope they don't shanghai me into it. You see Momoda, Morimoto have points high enough to be close to discharge while poor me, with measly 61 have not much *tanoshimi* [wishful thinking] in that direction. Well, if they call me up and order me, I'll just flunk the damn exams. I'd hate like hell to be shanghaied as was Kuge, out of the outfit, for direct shipment to the CBI. It's unfair and I don't go for that at all. I don't know what I'm getting hepped up about—it's only talk from Kuge's lips anyway, but I thought I'd let you know to get the lay of the land a little better.

## 6 AUGUST 1945

We just read an article in *Stars and Stripes* about Pfc Naito's being refused into the Spokane VFW [Veterans of Foreign Wars] and it's caused a minor furor, it being plastered on the front page with a commendation of the Nisei from Gen Truscott's and Col Miller's backing up of the boys. Of late *Yank* and *Stars and Stripes* are going great guns for us, and it does us good. If only the people back home could have the same viewpoint as the GIs who shared some of our miseries. I guess it's up to us to show some of these narrow-minded bigots when we get back home.

## 9 AUGUST 1945

We seem to be pretty well set on moving again somewhere. That's definite, for there's some Italian troops and 92d troops waiting to take over our two PW cages. Just where we are slated to go, whether it's just a movement of the 2d Bn or of the whole scattered regiment, no one seems to know. But one thing we're pretty sure of and that's that we're not going home for we are all pretty well resigned to staying till Feb 1946. I wish that we would go north, even if northern Italy; it's much nicer that way than here.

I think I wrote you that Nay has moved out to Oregon. She's written me from there already and they're pretty busy and not well organized at the writing, but the living accommodations are pretty good. If you want the address it's: Rt 4, Box 80, Sherwood, Ore. I guess Mom and Pop are pretty insistent on going to Seattle around October with the Horis and staying at their place. They seem pretty well set on it and I can't see any reason for stopping 'em. Gee, I'd like to see the two of them again. I sent Pop a wonderfully carved cigarette box from Lecco on Father's Day—couldn't think of anything else for him. . . .

Do you know that I have as yet to see Carolyn's picture—why don't you get busy and take some pictures with that 127 camera that I sent home over a year ago. I would like to see what that little rascal looks like. . . .

I hadn't realized that Suzu was graduating already until you so informed me. So she finally made it; she must have made a nice figure in cap and gown. Sorry to hear about Kay's operation on his leg. It seems everything's happening to the newlyweds. I presume that Kay is on his way to the Islands by now, but you didn't mention whether Suzu went along or not and whether he or they are coming back and when. I'm assuming that this is just a leave. By the way, how does Suzu like the life of a married woman? I haven't heard from her for a long time.

## 11 AUGUST 1945

There's been stories that the war with Japan is officially over, but I'm not too sure although I'm inclined to believe it. Some officers have been passing these reports along. The only one I know was the offer of surrender with a stipulation for the Emperor's recognition which was reported in today's *Stars and Stripes* and which we heard over

the air last night. It may be that the war is officially over at this
writing—and I hope so for Japan's sake. She couldn't have stood the
atomic bombing and other air attacks on top of the Russian push in
Manchuria. We are all glad that the war's at a recognizable end, but
there isn't the feeling of spontaneous jubilation and celebration. This
is merely because so far as we ourselves are concerned, there will be
not much of an actual difference in our status. This is according to
the *Stars and Stripes* of yesterday, reporting the necessity of ships in
the Pacific. In other words, at the present time Feb '46 is still our tentative departure date.

I'm glad both for Japan's sake and the thousands of our boys,
sacrificed to be, that this world conflict draws to an end. I didn't
think, altho' we hoped, that Japan would swallow the bitter gall
of pride and capitulate. If she wanted to survive she had no other
course. When we read of the destructive force of the new terrifying
atomic bomb, we can be thankful for humanity's sake that so far
only two of them have been used in this war, and to our advantage.
So it is in all probability that when you read this, that the world-wide
war will be at its end and thank God that he's seen fit to call it quits!
We're all waiting for further reports on the situation.

We're getting reveille these mornings and it's at seven o'clock, an
hour earlier than we are accustomed to rising, and it's not to our liking at all. We still don't know what's going to be our next immediate
assignment although right now there is some redeployment of our
far-flung companies. All COs of 3d Bn are congregated around the
CP in Pistoria now, and we are all together in these groves of trees.
Whether we go north or south is still speculation, but from the latest
latrine, I wouldn't be at all surprised if we were to get the hind end
of the deal and be strung along toward the South and we'd all rather
be up along the green Po Valley with the many cities which we may
visit. . . .

Some forty or so more fellows left today on their way to MIS
[Military Intelligence Service]. It seems to me that they were more

or less shanghaied into it, but they were asking for more volunteers. Even if the war in the Pacific is over now I'd rather sweat it out here rather than find myself in the Orient or South Pacific long after the thing is over.

## 14 AUGUST 1945

With the now imminent surrender of Japan, there may be a revisal of program, so far as we are concerned. Please, honey, remember that what I'm saying is only conjecture to make buoyant my optimism. At any rate, being the unique unit that we are, with all the combat days and publicity behind us, the Army may be prevailed on to give us a break and send us home so that a lot of the boys can go home and help their parents out of relocation centers which close in November. At least, there's logic behind this (as if the army cares about logic!) The story from the chaplain (notorious rumor monger) is that the chief of chaplains of the 5th Army is going back to plead for this our cause to the staff or Gen Marshall. It's a good story and I hope it's true, because after all, I would like to go home, you know. By the way, where did you get this rumor of our coming home in Oct? You wrote this before we ever talked it up, and knowing that your last rumor of MIS came true, it only bolsters up the optimistic theory. Maybe, darling, if we pray hard enough for this it will all come about, but please don't take it too much to heart, although the prospect is so dazzling that I can't think too much about it or I'll burst wide open.

## 15 AUGUST 1945

It looks as if peace is finally with us after having fled this earth for so long. It's strange to know that there is no war going on anywhere. The surrender kind of crept up on us and I think that no one a half a year ago could have predicted that it would come so soon. But, how thankful we can be that the holocaust is finally over. But, for us, of course, the primary question is "When do we go home?" We are all taking an optimistic attitude that in the case of the 442d, we will be given a break and be sent home earlier than scheduled. It seems to be one of the prime topics for discussion here and I think you know why. When I lie in bed after I've blown out my lamp and I'm enclosed in my own world of mosquito net and try to imagine my being with you again, I just get all filled up with something inside, tightening me all up with a warmth—and now that this time is some time in the near future, that engulfing nostalgia becomes just that much more acute. Last night I heard a beautiful rendition of "My Heart Sings"—beautiful lyrics and it tells just exactly how I feel and when I closed my eyes I could feel and see and hear you again, always so close to my heart.

## 17 AUGUST 1945

I've been doing a lot of reading lately since we have plenty of time and we do manage to get plenty of GI booklets—mostly new ones, but also the standard classics of fiction and non-fiction. My most recent delight was found in G Graham's *Earth and High Heaven*, a contemporary novel (I've read so damn many historical novels lately) on love and intolerance, with the scene laid in Canada. It woke me up on the Jewish question since in the West this is not as strong as on the East coast. And also the subject could so apply to us Nisei—to me the best part is where David, Marc's brother, tells him of Marc's own failing in his struggles. I'm inclined to agree with him in our own case and you should read it, for I found it quite absorbing.

## 23 AUGUST 1945

Yesterday morning Hayashi, Mizakami, (H. Co cook whose folks lived next to my folks in Hunt) and I took off on a jeep to visit the cemetery at Follonica a 100 km away to the south. To add to the discomfort, we had a flat to harass us on the trip. The reason I went down was to see what the place looked like since a year ago when I made the last pilgrimage and also to pay respects to our many friends. I gave a prayer for each—Bill Nakamura, Geo. Sawada, and Bako Kinoshita. The cemetery was neat and orderly under the warm sun, the white crosses gleaming brilliantly in beautiful straight lines. Grass had grown, but with the summer and drought, it had turned brown, but they are going to irrigate soon. We left flowers and we all took pictures (though prohibited). I took snaps of individual graves, for maybe the folks would like to know where their brave sons now lie. We didn't linger long and as we came back we looked again and saw the stars and stripes waving in the breeze over the orderly white crosses and felt secure in the knowledge that these that were near to us were in good hands. . . .

By the way, the WD [War Department] finally gives us combat pay, but from Aug 1 and so we don't get that back $120 I was expecting, still that $10 extra a month will come in handy.

## 26 AUGUST 1945

The past week has seen the 2d Bn, once clustered in this grove, scattered all over this coast. One day H Co and the ATR [Antitank Rifle] ptn of Hqs moved out to Naples, then G Co moved down to Grossetto, Fox has gone somewhere, and only a handful of E Co remains, while Hq itself has been cut to a mere half, so that it is pretty deserted around here.

## 29 AUGUST 1945

Although I have pretty well decided to go to school on the Bill of Rights deal, I'm still not sure of where, so maybe you'd better stay put for awhile till I make up my fool mind. I don't think you should worry about housing until I get home and don't buy a house cause I don't know whether we'd stay in Minneapolis.

American cemetery at Follonica, Italy, 1945. Min and his buddies made a special trip to see where their fallen comrades lay. Min's friends George Sawada, Bill Nakamura, and Bako Kinoshita were buried here.

## 1 September 1945

Lucky Hayashi and Higgins leave us tomorrow on their first leg of the long journey home and eventual discharge. There's about ten guys from the 442d in this bunch all above 85. Gee, I wish I were going with 'em. The way things are going all my original buddies'll be gone and I'll be left with the new ones that came in later. It makes me feel kind of sad to have them go one by one, or two by two, after having known them so deeply these past two and a half years. Anyway, a part of me will go with them when they go—isn't it always thus? I'll give Hayashi your address and he may, this is a long shot though, get a chance to drop in on you—I hope so.

## 4 September 1945

Golly, but I'm glad that my birthday gift got to you in time and everything done up proper and probably better than I could arrange it. I only wish that I could have been there. I couldn't think of anything better. You see, when I was up in Lucca that day with Ike, we saw this artist's work and we just went in to look around—his portraits were so good that we couldn't resist having Shiz and your pictures done. He finished in about a week and then I sent it right on to Mildred, because I figured I'd get a better frame back home. And I'm certainly thankful to Mildred that she arranged everything so wonderfully. The reason I didn't have Tama or Suzu do it was because I was afraid that somehow or other you'd get wind of the whole thing. But, best of all, I'm so glad you like it. . . .

I hit the jackpot in mail these past two days. You blanked me yesterday, but Mom and Pop wrote me in *nihongo* for the first time and then Fumi wrote me a nice long letter all about her life—yes, they miss the old days, too. Pop and Mom, as I told you, are going on to Seattle about the end of September. As is the usual, mail came in while I was in my afternoon nap and what a pleasant eye opener— two from you, Mildred's, Mariko's, and one from Yosh Mizuta, a classmate of mine through grade and high school and kid playmate, who'd been with the 442d Hq and 2d Co and volunteered for MIS and went back about a month and a half ago. He wrote me from Seattle and he's having a swell time there, some of the 442d boys there being treated royally by Seattle organizations on the strength of their achievements and the fact that Capt Crowley—E Co's CO— was speaking on our behalf. It certainly is good to have men all over the country working so hard for us. . . .

With the announcement of VJ day, things began popping over here since there's been big plans for a parade and it came off yesterday. The 442d led the mile-long procession and had the honor of being color bearers. By manipulation, I was CQ for the day and stayed behind and listened over the radio. The commentator certainly praised the boys up. . . .

Remember that I told you some time ago that the 2d Bn had won the Presidential Unit Citation badge? Well, the 3d Bn got theirs, too for the "Lost Battalion" action and today was the day. Gen Truscott of the Fifth Army came down to pin the blue ribbons on our guy— dons. I managed to squeeze out of this, too, unexpectedly, altho I did go down. I got a job photographing the activities for the Bn, and so I had a good view of everything and close up, too and what a lot of snapping I did. You'll have to wait until the pics are done to see what kind of job I did. Now all the battalions have unit citations, the 100th getting theirs some time ago. F and L Cos get to wear clusters on their badges for their "task force" activities in Bruyeres. Can you beat this—one RCT with five unit citations in it—that's pretty darn hard to beat, you know. . . .

There's been great rejoicing over here with the announcement by the WD lowering the critical discharge score to 80 and the addition of service from VE day to VJ day in our case coming to eight points. And now I have 69 points which though still ineligible is now in a hopeful state. . . .

So I'm rather hopeful of being home by Xmas, even if the unit doesn't as a whole.


9 SEPTEMBER 1945

There isn't much to announce over here except that it looks as if the unit won't be going home as a whole until next year, but the redeployment program is going along fine and I'm still hopeful of being home for Christmas—just the thought of that gives me goosepimples. Morimoto got his Bronze Star as did Iijima, yesterday, and so he's high point man with the aid station, for with the extra eight points from VE and VJ day he now has a grand total of 92. He'll probably be leaving the middle or latter part of this month and is he tickled pink?! He's already getting set for it and goes about with such a self-satisfied expression on his face I could kick his behind. The list of guys on the new list of 80 and over for the medics encompasses practically all the guys that came over together. And the guys have no reservation in rubbing this in—jokingly, of course, but I still feel bad about all the guys going home without me after being through so much together. Anyway, with Ike getting his BS he and I have the exact number of points and he and I will at least be going home together, all the way to Minneapolis, too. Dick, with Robin and Ellen's precious 24 accompanying points should be home for Thanksgiving—ah, Thanksgiving, this is how many that I've had apart from you? I remember that day when we were out on bivouac when you came into Hattiesburg.

So Tama's sick again and complicated with pregnancy. I didn't know. I guess she believes in a big family—good for her, but I hope that she'll be able to take it better on her second try than on her first. If it'll do any good tell her I gave her a cheery hello, will you—maybe just thinking of me will make her laugh. . . .

Evening saw Tsuka and I twanging away in old-time fashion on the mandolin and guitar. And for the first time in a long time, we cooked up some rice and had a swell late snack on that with *foonyu* and some K and C ration stuff.

I haven't heard from Suzu in such a long time, but I guess she's the same irrepressible one.


21 SEPTEMBER 1945

The *Stars and Stripes* of today has some more good news about the discharge points going to be lowered to 70 by Oct and then 60 by Nov 1, but in this MTO [Mediterranean Theater of Operations] the worry is whether the shipping will ever catch up with the schedule. Here Sept is almost over and our 80 pointers and above are still with the regiment. Even patient Morimoto with his 92 is still sitting on his fanny. The repple depple is all filled to capacity with waiting men just waiting for boats and so our boys will have to wait till the others are cleared out. We had nine men (Lefty Ichihara, one of them) with ages above thirty-five and they went to the 27th depot a couple of days ago, but they had to come back because there was no room at all for them. So you can see how the situation is. It's my opinion that the regiment has fouled up the whole works—they should have been on the ball and sent the guys out earlier, before the other outfits sent their 80 pointers out. So if you read about the lowering of point discharges, just remember that before you can get too elated that there's the mechanics of the thing to be considered, but I'm still pretty sure of being home for Christmas, and incidentally, if you're contemplating any sort of a package for me, I'll be home to receive it, so don't send anything over.

Here everybody's harassing the army to send their sons home and they can't find the boats to do it. In the Pacific they're even converting battleships and carriers for transports, but we have none of these in the MTO. The ETO [European Theater of Operations] has huge transatlantic liners that can be used in addition to their Liberty ships and such, but does this theater have any? Just a precious few, and none as huge like the two Queens, *Mary* and *Elizabeth*. Anyway they're trying their best and I keep saying to myself that a couple of more months won't make too much difference, but you and I know that I'm only trying to find solace in the waiting.


25 SEPTEMBER 1945

I suppose you saw the pictures in the papers and read about the presentation of the 442d contribution toward a Roosevelt memorial of some sort. Sgt Kuwayama made the presentation and gave a speech. It's good stuff this and I hope it gets around—I think my one buck is in that fund, too.


29 SEPTEMBER 1945

Did I tell you of the formation of a 442d football team? Well, they've been at it now for about a week. . . . I think that we'll make a creditable showing for what we lack in weight we can hope to make up in skill, speed and spirit. There's gonna be a first scrimmage this afternoon which I'll be out to see along with a few sundry medications in case of banged noses and bruised shins. . . .

I was relieved that Tama's home again altho but a shadow of herself. And Kay's coming back should help out just with his presence. It was good of him to bring back such nice Hawaiian gifts for you. I'll bet he had a swell time back home and I can imagine how happy 'lil Suzu was over his return.

I'm afraid that, though I've given the guys going home your address, that most of them will not be able to drop in because they are usually rushed cross country to San Francisco. But, there's always the chance that some will be able to make it.


9 OCTOBER 1945

I'm feeling like a virtuous and dutiful boy tonight and the reason for the halo around my head is that this is the third letter I'm writing and the last, too, incidentally. I haven't done this in months and it may be another long time 'ere it will happen again. I wrote to Sat and Rose in Renton and Kiki. You see I just yesterday heard from the former and I hastened to write because I'd neglected them, too. I told you of them moving to Seattle with the folks and now they're staying at the Renton housing project which I can't seem to recall unless it's the one lining Empire Way which turned off Rainier Ave. In case you want to write them, the address is 1934 Renton Highlands, Renton, Wash. I told them how busy you'd been with your classes, *Sensei San*, so don't fret over that. They haven't told me too much about their life as yet, but it does my heart good to know that Mom and Pop are once again enjoying the pure air of freedom. And Sat's bought himself a 1940 DeLuxe Ford in which they rode to Seattle, so when we go back to see them, we'll have something to ramble about in. . . .

Did I tell you, I don't think so, that Frankie H got a letter from Higgins and he's in San Francisco together with Hayashi awaiting a boat for Hawaii. It seems that they flew transcontinentally and so couldn't get to see you at all. They wasted no time getting there and now they're cooling their heels waiting for a boat to go home on. Remember that first batch that left from Ghedi—well, those guys were still waiting for a boat when Higgins and Hayashi got to Frisco, but latest reports indicate that their wait isn't too long now. Lucky guys!

Our biggest preoccupation seems to be in the progress of our football team and we go out every day to watch them go through their paces. . . . Incidentally, Capt Ushiro, feeling the need of exercise, is turning out for the team. He went out a couple of days and he's a quarterback, but he doesn't know signals as yet, so he's not much, but his high school playing may stand him in good stead later on, if he stays on the team. He's a mighty tired man it seems these nights though.


12 OCTOBER 1945

The *Stars and Stripes* carried a story yesterday of the three-hundred-ship tie up in New York by a longshoremen's strike. That all made us so doggone mad because we could certainly use those boats to take the fellows home. Here our depots are brimming with anxiously waiting men to be discharged and the longshoremen tie up three hundred precious boats simply because they're peeved about something. No wonder the MTO redeployment is set back so far. I guess there must be a side to the strikers, but I don't see how it could outweigh the consideration for the boys who fought for them that they could strike. This is the kind of stuff that makes us always the maddest. Can you blame us? Especially when all that it's doing is lengthening the time when I shall see you again.

The game between the 442d and 228th Ord colored boys turned out to be a rout as we trampled over them to the tune of 26–0. . . . I was rather busy at the game doing a medic job for the banged-up guys. The funny part of the game was when the Capt went in, in the dying minutes and intercepted a pass and went over for a touchdown—I wonder who was more surprised, he or us.

### 13 OCTOBER 1945

Even though the 442d is the lightest team in the league, we're still on top with two wins—we haven't played strong opponents, but you know how the 442d is. It'll take plenty to lick us. The 92d Div and UQC are our chief opponents—can't see anyone else who could beat us. We're hoping that over-confidence on their part will help us lick 'em. . . .

The medics of the 442d has got itself a decoration, that of the Meritorious Service Plaque, so that we medics can now wear the golden laurel wreath on the right sleeve by the wrist. This was rather unexpected to us, but we're not declining the honor at all. This is the first recognition that the medics as a unit has achieved.

The Michigan–Army game's on the air now on a shortwave broadcast and I just can't concentrate anymore—you'll excuse me, darling.

### 28 OCTOBER 1945

Momoda, Oscar, Morimoto and Onodera already left for Naples together with many others with whom I'd been so close for lo these two and one half years . . . to actually feel their absence now makes me forlorn. Golly, but they were all swell guys. And then on top of that, more guys are leaving tomorrow, the 76–79 pointers, and this embraces all the original Hawaiian members of the 442d with whom I'd begun training in Shelby. The Hq boys are happy as hell, a whole mess of 'em going and they all expect me to go along with 'em or thought that I'd gone along with Morimoto and Oscar, et al. Can you blame me for feeling so bad when all these comrades are slipping away, probably never to be seen again? All these guys with whom we shared life and death so much. You see, we've been giving flu serum shots to these guys going home and you know all of them, maybe not by name, but by face and for a man that's enough. And that only accentuates the feeling of being left behind. Mike Hagiwara's going too and he's rather dazed about it—can't actually believe that he's on his way home. I wonder if I'll feel that way when my turn comes to go. I know one thing and that is that I won't be reluctant!

The aid station along with Hq Co 2 . . . moved in with Baker and Dog companies of the 1st into Leghorn. . . . We're all housed in a big building that once was a factory of some sort and it's a huge dormitory life. Chow is served in segmented metal trays and there are German orderlies and Italian civilians working. It's a much sweeter setup than we'd had for the past three months in tents, not to mention the fact that we're much warmer here. The hot showers are right in the buildings along with everything. We sleep in double deckers and our aid station is being fitted out handsomely in white. The best feature of life here is the spacious dayroom occupying one whole floor with billiard tables, ping pong tables, library and a dance floor. Movies are shown every night, since we are at the wrecked port quite away from the center of the city. I haven't lived here long enough to know how things will go, but it looks alright to me. . . .

And dear *Sensei San*, how's your new classes coming along—those with the bright eager youths of the ASTP [Army Specialized Training Program]. Golly, the way you talk you make yourself so old and you're not that at all. I know you and I know that you're young in heart and that's what counts. By golly, I wouldn't trade you for all the so-called youth in this world. Why lament for the passing of years—there are so many many more spreading out for us in front of us. I can't wait to take up those threads of life together again with you.

All except this business of getting up at 6:00 AM. That is definitely out. What an ungodly hour to awaken and putter about. We'll see about this when I get back. . . .

I hope that I haven't been too much of a sentimentalist tonight, but I think that you understand exactly how I feel. Goodnight, my darling, and never forget that you're the dearest thing to my heart.

## 1 November 1945

I don't feel like doing much and I don't as anyone will testify. What with compulsory flu vaccinations being given now, and us running around to the scattered platoons of the scattered company, it's a little busy. And don't forget that with everyone going home, our aid station boasts only the scant personnel, five to be exact, and we catch CQ every fourth day since one guy goes to school daily and only catches CQ on Sundays. On top of that, just moving here, we're fixing this place up rather cozily, painting and arranging. All in all, we're pretty busy, but I'll be doggoned if I feel like doing anything. What a frame of mind to be in. But that doesn't prevent me from enjoying fish and rice as we ate last night—Frankie Harada and Eddie Sasaki cooked up at their motor pool home and I naturally barged in and it was a very satisfying meal. Zeke [Ike's nickname] and I went to sleep on a full belly and very contented.

## 7 November 1945

Golly, darling, I hope this letter gets to you in the quickest time possible because this is gonna be a happy letter and I've been that way the past four days and pretty busy too, so I couldn't write to you. I must sound a little mixed up, but you'll know the reason why in a minute.

Darling, I'm finally coming home. Redeployment has been going along in a smooth fashion since once they started moving a couple of days ago the 70 pointers shipped out and you know what number comes next—yes, 69, that's me. I expect to move out of this outfit at the beginning of next week, Monday, perhaps (this is Wednesday) and so I'm really up in the air about it as you can imagine. . . . Gee I can't tell you how happy I am to be leaving. Ike and I are the only ones left of the original 2d Bn members and you know how I felt about their going. With our departure, Ike's got 68 and we should be leaving together for Minneapolis, there'll be no original man left at this aid station. When the 63s and 64s leave then there'll be no

EM left of the original 442d in the whole regiment. That's another reason that I'm so happy about leaving. All these strange faces around here doesn't make me feel that I'm a member of the unit anymore. I'm so happy that my head's been in a cloud of late and I don't care what happens at the aid station—I'm not of much use there. So don't write any more letters and don't send any packages—the reason is obvious. . . .

Last Saturday was the big football game of the year for us as we played the 92d Div Buffaloes. We played a good game, but their weight was a little too overpowering and they beat us 14–0, their shining black light being one fullback, John Moody, who was the difference between the two teams. We were the underdogs, but they certainly knew that they were in a good fight and one thing was certain, win or lose, the fans are all for us. I'm also enclosing some pictures of the game that I took. I was sitting by the bench as is my wont because of my duties as a medic, taking care of injuries. I think the pictures are self explanatory. . . .

Gee, just think, darling, I'll be home for Xmas, just as this guy on the radio's singing about. It's still too much for me to believe. Home for Xmas, oh, darling, I can't think of anything that fills me so completely. Just to be with you again! I'd better stop now before I get maudlin. Gee, I love you so doggone much.

10 NOVEMBER 1945

I guess the time has finally arrived—that gala day is come when I am on my way home at last. As I told you, we'd been anxiously awaiting orders for our movement. Indirectly we'd heard that 65 and above would be leaving Tuesday, that's the 13th. Then this evening Hasegawa (yes Harry—who's now acting 1st Sgt of medics) phoned and gave me the straight dope on it. We are scheduled—Zeke and I—to actually move on the 13th to 1st Staging Bn near Pisa. . . . Doesn't it make your heart tingle? It does mine. I still can't quite grasp the fact that I'm going home—doggone if I can. But I'll get the impact of it when I get on that old boat. Harry's supposed to let me know a little more detail by phone as soon as he can and you can imagine how anxious we are about that.

After this kind of news, there isn't really much more I can say—everything seems so anti-climax. The things we say or do somehow seem all unimportant in the face of the imminent departure. I don't know a lilt seems to be running through me all the time nowadays—you can't catch me in a bad mood. Of course, Zeke's just as happy as I am. After all he's just a newlywed of three weeks or so—he's got a lot to catch up on. I've been married much longer, but I've also plenty to catch up on, too. Don't you agree?

I could tell you about the fish and rice I ate tonight just before writing you, the lousy movie we came down from, the book I'm reading—all this, but somehow now that I know I'm going home it seems so trivial and I feel a little foolish telling you. Zeke and I were just now talking about what we'll do when we get to Snelling where we'll try to get our discharges and oh, the plans we're making and of course, you and Shiz are right in them. I am getting delirious, aren't I? I think I'll stop now before I get hysterical. I'll probably dream about it tonight.

1ST STAGING BN, PISA
14 NOVEMBER 1945

So far as I'm concerned, I'm about ready to go home now. The news that I have for you today isn't too good though. Yesterday afternoon we were processed and went through all sorts of forms and stuff. The most important finding was that it's here that we are assigned separation centers. It was somewhat of a shock to find out that Ft Snelling isn't on the list as a separation center regardless of what Zeke read in the papers. Here we are all set to be rid of the army right in Minneapolis and they tell us and assign us to Camp McCoy in Wisconsin to be discharged—why that's not even in the same state. . . .

There has been nothing definite as to when we'll sail and nothing is of greater importance to us right now than that. I hope that Zeke and I make an unfitted Liberty Ship which will mean more comfort and better food, if we can't catch a carrier. However, one of the boys that processed us yesterday said that we'd be leaving in four or five days and that's not bad, in our estimation. Koseki, that rumor monger, in fact told us this AM that Group 1 (that's us) is leaving tomorrow, but I take that with a grain of salt.

I'll keep you posted on everything that happens in my tender young life—you are interested aren't you? Hang on till I come home.


18 NOVEMBER 1945

Here it's Sunday, today, the day that we'd thought a week ago that we may be shipping out and we're still in the same boat as when we first came here and possibly in a worse fix, at least mentally. This is the seventh day of our incarceration here and it's not good. . . . there was a letter from Mariko waiting. . . . almost got sent back. She's moving to Evanston, Ill. or do you know this already? Her address is 816 1/2 Foster Street. She didn't explain about the movement. She gave me a big dose of news too about our friends in Japan [Seattle Nisei caught in Japan during the war] of whom we hadn't heard for so long. Her source was Floyd Yamamoto who's in Tokyo now. Yuri Aoki Hayashi died of TB in '43 or '44 and Nachi's remarried to an Oakland girl. Sono Hoshi was still there, and Tish Matsushima's in a TB sanitarium, and also that Fred Shimanaka had been killed on Saipan (I certainly hope this one isn't true) and that Tosh Funakoshi was a soldier somewhere in one of the fronts. What a mess life can be and what strange destinies fate deals for us!


21 NOVEMBER 1945

Some more dreary news for you, honey, but no more dreary than it is for me. I don't know how I'm the one that should happen to get caught in this unholy sort of bad luck, but there it is. . . .

Hqs here has no idea when we'll move out of here and no boats are scheduled to come in either. In fact, some other high-point haole boys got so mad that they went up to Hqs and bitched and as a result they moved out to Naples to catch the boats and carriers that are coming in. When I heard I was depressed indeed, and went to talk to Zeke's brother-in-law, the 442d Chaplain—Geo Aki's his name and told him of our unfortunate circumstances and he came up here this morning and had a talk with the office and he was told that they were cutting orders now for the casuals to move out on Saturday to Naples. . . . Golly, I hope we're on these orders. We'll find out tomorrow anyway. What a snafu deal we got—no kidding—this is the kind of stupid mismanagement and disorder that makes me so mad about army life. . . . At least in Naples we'll be sure of boats coming in because that is the center of redeployment and if we catch a carrier that's better yet because it only takes one about seven or eight days to make the crossing and a Liberty will take about seventeen or eighteen days. . . .

Tomorrow's Thanksgiving and I don't feel in a very thankful mood—I guess you can see why. The only thing that'll be different that we'll probably get a mess tray all jammed with turkey and mashed potatoes and cranberry sauce and fruit cocktail and olives and all the trimmings—and when I say "jammed" that's exactly the right word.


22 NOVEMBER 1945

In contrast to the dolorous letter of yesterday, today I come bearing much better tidings. We're finally moving out and it came about in this manner. Yesterday, I told you that they were cutting orders for our movement to Naples on Saturday. Well, they pushed that up one day and this morning the announcement came of the movement tomorrow (Friday) instead of Saturday as I thought. Even a matter of one day is heartening to us. . . . After anxiously scanning the bulletin board with the other expectant guys, I finally found my name and Zeke's. . . . I hope that we won't run into any delays at the 7th Repple where we'll be going, but even that's overlooked in the joy that we're getting out of here. If we leave tomorrow morning as is scheduled (breakfast 6:30—assembly at 7:30) we should be in Naples on the 24th, Saturday, and with two carriers scheduled to come in on the 23d and one each on the 26th and 29th, not to mention the transport *Vulcania*, we stand a good chance of making a fast trip home. All I can say now is that I hope all these calculations come to pass—the army's gotta treat us right sometimes!, but one never knows.

What a Thanksgiving day! We had the feast all right—enough turkey and all the things that go with it, but doggone if I could get into any festive mood about it. . . . Cooked up rice tonight and had that with our evening chow, heated up, and that was much more enjoyed.


7TH REPLACEMENT DEPOT, NAPLES
24 NOVEMBER 1945

This is the first chance that I've had to write to you since I last wrote that night, so long ago it seems, in Pisa. We've finally made it down here and everything is much rosier. . . .

It was almost noon when finally we dragged into the train station, the same train station that we'd first hit when we came here a year and a half ago. This 7th Repple is on the ball though and from then till supper we were in their hands and we'd a hustling time all day and we got plenty done, too. . . . We've had some very encouraging news officially and after the hedging we got up in Pisa it's a good sign. Not only that, the efficiency of this place makes everyone feel as if they were getting someplace. Just before beginning the processing the Capt in charge told us that all of us would be in the states by the 9th or 10th of Dec and that was certainly heartening.


26 NOVEMBER 1945

Hello, honey, I didn't write you yesterday as I should have, but I didn't have anything to say. . . . The day after we came the carriers

*Randolph* and *Langley* left and now they're loading the *Monterey* and the *Wasp*, they should be pulling out of the dock tomorrow or so.

You see, it works this way. When you come in, you're only one molecule in this gigantic depot and you just go when your turn comes, regardless of the points and that's why we were really snafued up when we wasted eleven days up at Pisa before being shipped down here, else we would right now be on the high seas. After a few days here, you're assigned a certain shipment number and put on the alert. From this point on then all we have to do is wait till the shipment is called—a very simple thing on paper, but to us that calling out is the most important announcement in our lives. All day long we hear numbers being called out and preparing and guys leaving the hut and we can just look on—we haven't even been assigned shipment numbers yet and we know that we have plenty of time yet. All we can do is bide our time and wait our turn, but how tedious waiting becomes. I'm fully expecting to wait at least ten days 'ere we get called. Yesterday, I was a trifle depressed because of the strange circumstances concerning the 442d medics that have come down before us. When Morimoto and Momoda came down their shipment numbers were different from everyone else's and we've reason to believe that they went on unfitted Liberties. And then of this last batch—the 60s to 64s, only about three medics were left behind while the others all left. And then they told us that the medics were left behind to take care of the GI personnel on unfitted Liberties and that's why they have to wait for these and not go on the speedy carriers. When I heard that I really lost fight and that's one of the reasons I didn't want to write last night. . . . But, this evening we were happy to find out at the ARC where we went for coffee that these medics were going on carriers tomorrow—Isozaki on the *Monterey* and Oguri on the *Wasp*. They'd been here thirteen days. So now I don't actually know what the score is, but I'm happier to know that what we'd feared isn't exactly right. I guess all we can do is just wait.

## 29 November 1945

The redeployment outlook is not so favorable today and my morale isn't any too good and here's the reason for it. . . . Most of the fellows that came with us are on alert already, but Zeke and I aren't. Recall what I told you about discrimination on medics? It seems rather apparent here and I am expecting to go up to higher Hqs to find out the exact score on this if I'm not alerted today. . . .

I was on a Jerry chasing detail today which involved my getting up at 5:15 AM and going to the PW cage to bring back a mess of Jerry PWs that work in the 290 area. So in the pitch dark of night I was aroused by the cook and jumping into my clothes I stepped around the corner to the Co orderly room and picked up a carbine and managed to get a clip into it and trudged off into the darkness for the compound. What a time I had before I finally found it—I must have been wandering about the beer garden wilderness for a half hour before I got set right and got my detail back to the area here. But you can imagine the incongruous situation—guarding the Jerries with a carbine and the only thing I know about it is the end the bullet comes out from. At any rate, it's a simple detail and now all I have to do is take 'em back after supper.

I think a new batch of alerts will be posted this afternoon. I'm praying that I'll be on it; if not, I'll have to do something about it. Wish me luck, darling, I really want it badly now.

## 30 November 1945

After the letter I wrote yesterday morning, I waited for the posting of the new alerts. None came—and in the afternoon about three, out of patience, I went to the Troop Movement Office to find out if new alerts were to be posted. He was just typing out a new sheet and on inquiring I found out that my name was not on this list either. He also didn't know of any discrimination in the redeployment so far as medics were concerned. I went then to our Co orderly room and made an appointment to see Hqs about it, and then Zeke and I went to the ARC for coffee. One 442d Sgt told us to see a Lt Hunter in personnel at Hqs and having nothing to lose, we went over to his office. He mildly upbraided us for not going through channels, but he listened to our queries just the same and then phoned the upper Hqs about any discrimination against medics since this was the first he'd heard of it. He got the answer alright and so did we. It's absolutely true that a certain amount or percent of medics is always held back so that there will always be medical attention on all the boats going out. So what we'd feared and heard about is actually the case. Now there's nothing that we can do about it but just sit back and wait until we are released, and that's an indefinite time although they did try to reassure us that the medics that came in on the 24th (us) would have their orders cut in a couple of days. This doesn't mean much to us though. Now for sure we know we're not going on the *Bataan* which leaves tomorrow, as loading has already begun. So Zeke and I, though none too happy about it, are trying to be philosophical about it and just sit on our tired little fannies and wait and wait and wait.

1 December 1945

I was awakened this morning by loud noises and harsh voices and found out that all the hubbub was about the enclosed *Stars and Stripes* article. Please read it now and you'll know why all the shouting.

Do you realize what this says? It only means that I won't be home for Christmas unless something drastic comes up. We're all pretty sore about it and I'm heartsick. . . . It's all so discouraging, isn't it? Everytime I think of the fouling up we got when we shipped to Pisa and to realize that if not for that we'd be in the States makes me just writhe inside with anger, but that's not going to do any good.

Of course, everyone here, the thousands, are just as sore and concerned as I am. The furor this morning must have been reenacted all over the depot. The things said about the Army would have curled the ears of any and all brass-studded Generals and I was in there throwing a few choice words myself. Now everyone's hoping like hell that Navy beats the pants off the Army football team today. Our wrath even extends to the gridiron.

I think that I've caused enough damage for today—don't forget that I feel as bad if not worse than you about this and I can't write anymore without going into a harangue. Maybe tomorrow I'll feel a little better. Goodnight, darling—even though now I'm pretty sure that Christmas with you may not come to pass—just to know that you'll always be waiting for me helps me tremendously.

STARS AND STRIPES

Naples, Nov 30—Two Essex-class aircraft carriers, the *USS Lake Champlain* and the *USS Wasp*, have been diverted to the European Theater for redeployment, according to dispatches received from the Chief of Naval Operations in Washington at the Naples port today. The two carriers would have moved approximately 11,000 MTO veterans back to the US according to previous carrying records of the ships.

Originally scheduled to make three trips each to the MTO the carriers were ordered to Southampton England. No reasons were given for the change.

The *Lake Champlain* would have been the first carrier to return to Naples on the magic carpet run and would have arrived here on Dec 8. Under the new orders the *Randolph* and the *USS Langley* due here on Dec 14 are the aircraft carriers next scheduled to return. The *Wasp* was slated to be back in the Naples port on December 18. The dropping of the two carriers from the Naples run slices in half the number of troops the magic carpet program would have taken from the MTO before Christmas.

10 DECEMBER 1945

I've got very good news for you today and I'm not moaning about anything. Just as soon as I found out I couldn't help but sit right down and write to you. This morning when I got up and read about

the carrier *Randolph* coming in on the 12th I decided I'd better
do something about my not being on the alert. I dashed over to Troop
Movements who had no record of me at all, so I went over to the
Records section and there's where I got the good news. I'm on orders
12–70–S and this order is a special medic order and embraces the
medic cadre for the *Randolph*. When he calmly said that I was
stunned and I could feel myself getting warm all over. I could have
cried with joy. Isn't it the best of news? The *Randolph* is scheduled
in the 12th and should leave in two or three days. Giving seven days
for the crossing, we should be in the States by the 21st—maybe
that'll give me a chance to get home for Xmas. It's possible that they
may allow us a week's furlough at home for Xmas before discharging
us. If they don't give us this consideration, I don't see how we can be
home for the holidays, because time at the POE, on the railroad and
separation centers will take about a week. Being always a believer in
the goodness of man, I'm preferring to think that they will be gracious
enough to grant us this bit of holiday cheer. You think that we deserve
this much, don't you? I know you do.

## 11 DECEMBER 1945

It doesn't seem possible at all, but overwhelming printed evidence
seems to be that I'm finally going to leave this depot and be on the
way. After the exhilarating news of yesterday, I've been all keyed
up . . . according to the best minds present, the thing to do is get a
delay-in-route and from the POE just take off on one's own to home
and after the holidays report at the separation center (McCoy) and
the army will recompense five cents a mile for the distance traveled.
It seems that a furlough will involve more time (and believe me, it's
a mighty important thing right now) and have to be obtained at the
separation center while a delay-in-route takes no bother and time. So
that's what we're planning to do when we get into NY or wherever
it is that we land. If I do have time I'd like to drop in on some of our
NY friends, but the main thing for me is to be home for Xmas—my

this year's gift to you. Don't worry, I'll send a telegram or phone as soon as I get into the proper place. And it'll be just about the time you read this, so get excited about it, will you?—at least, I am. I can't get over the fact that next week will see me in the States. What a wonderful thing to contemplate.

About Zeke—what a time we had. Out of a clear blue sky he found out yesterday about 9:00 PM that he's on the advance party for the *Harrison*, a Liberty, and loading this AM at 9:15. He came rushing over to tell me and he was so disgusted and low in morale about this terrible blow which meant, by the Liberty's long journey, that Xmas was an impossible goal. Of course, I got sore at the whole thing and I put my coat on and we went over to Troop Movements to bitch. Remember that it's night and he's scheduled to fall out at 8:00 tomorrow AM and his orders were already out. It was a discouraging thing, but we trudged over and getting no satisfactory reply, only discouraging rationalizations we went to Headquarters and bitched some more, but no officers were present and we'd no alternative but to wait till this AM. Zeke went over and giving the Capt his story, he was allowed to see the Col who turned out was a right guy and knocked Zeke's name off the *Harrison* list. It was this afternoon that Zeke found out for sure that he's now slated on the *Randolph* so we'll be coming home together and you can't imagine how happy we are about it. All of us, for out of that Pisa bunch he was the only one so ill-fated and he had everyone's sympathy. I'm glad that a good warm heart can cut through red tape and dispense proper justice to those that merit it.

13 DECEMBER 1945

I'm not a little excited tonight—you can guess the reason why. This is my last night in this place. We're loading tomorrow in the early afternoon. The order finally came out this evening. We fall out, the 1st advance loading, at 12:00 noon and by 2:00 we should be boarding the *Randolph*, our home for the next week. Other loadings will come in rapidly and by Saturday morning, the 15th, we'll be all on and the 'ol boat is expected to pull out sometime in the afternoon. They don't waste any time, do they? Zeke will be on the last loading and Duffy and Harry on the 4th and 5th respectively. So we'll all be on it. I'm expecting to send you a cablegram tomorrow morning after I turn in my sheet and stuff to the supply. It should get there in a couple of days, but this letter should explain everything. I'm all set to go (and how long have I been?) and tomorrow morning I'll just repack my stuff a bit and then off we'll go after early chow at noon. There's no sense in my recounting the days prosaic activities—it'll all be eclipsed by the news of my going home. And so this is finally my really last letter and am I happy? No words can describe that and after all this forlorn waiting I can't believe that I'm really really going. I like to believe, and I've every reason to believe that the army wants to get us all home for Christmas and that means a fast trip across the ocean and all the facilities for rapid homesending. Pray for all this and darling, I'll be home for Christmas, just about the time you're reading this, if everything turns out right. So until I see you and hear you again, God keep you and I love you so much. P.S. I'll let you know when I get back.

TELEGRAM

1945 DEC 15
WE SAIL 15TH ON *RANDOLPH* DUE IN NYC ABOUT 22ND
MIN

# EPILOGUE

RECOLLECTIONS / HANA MASUDA 1990

*Because of the rough seas, the* Randolph *was delayed. When the seas subsided, the ship was able to reach New York. Then the men were sent to Camp McCoy, Wisconsin, to be discharged. I expected Min to be home New Year's Day. The thought of seeing him again filled me with overwhelming happiness and excitement. I had visions of greeting him in my new outfit, my makeup flawless, and with every strand of hair in place. However, it wasn't that way at all.*

*New Year's Eve Mom and I were busy preparing Min's favorite dishes—makisushi (rice with seasonal colorful vegetables wrapped in seaweed), octopus, teriyaki chicken, soya bean soup, chicken with vegetables (Japanese stew), and shrimp. The kitchen was an absolute mess, with pots and pans, knives and chopsticks scattered here and there. We cooks blended in well, with bobby pins in our hair, beads of perspiration instead of makeup on our faces, and aprons over our housecoats.*

*In the midst of all this activity, the doorbell rang. I opened the door thinking it was our friends coming to help us cook. There stood Min with his face beaming in a big smile. My first words of welcome were, "Min, you weren't supposed to come home 'till tomorrow!"*

Min kept repeating "It's so good to be home," and twirled me around again and again.

Next morning I cooked Min's favorite breakfast of orange juice, eggs sunny-side up, waffles, and Spam (which I had saved especially for him). Then Min said, "Anything but Spam." I later learned that Spam had been a GI issue.

Min didn't talk a lot about the war. He always gave careful, complete answers when I asked specific questions, but otherwise he was concerned with getting on with his life.

But there were other reminders of the war. I'll never forget the first night a siren sounded when we were asleep. Min jumped up and hid under the bed. This reflex action continued for several months.

The period of readjusting from being independent single people to a couple proved to be hilarious and puzzling—especially for me. Shopping for two, cooking for two, thinking as one part of a couple was confusing.

One evening I was having a grand time. I had met a girlfriend after school so we could have supper together. It was after 9:00 PM when I got home. I had completely forgotten about Min until he opened the door. He said "Where's my supper?" and I said, "What supper?" Another time I planned to go to the ballet with friends. I got my ticket in advance, but none for Min. We were able to get him a ticket at the performance, but while I sat in the middle section with friends, Min sat in the balcony, alone. Later he said, "It's a good thing I have good eyes."

Min adapted more easily than I. His sense of humor and gentle cajoling helped in many embarrassing situations. Min's former professor, Dr. James M. Dille, was at the University of Chicago when the war ended. When he found out that Min had come home, he wanted to see him again. We both went to Chicago, and Dr. Dille, who was going to go back to the University of Washington, persuaded Min to also return to the UW to begin studying for his PhD.

## Recollections, Minoru Masuda, 1970s

Back from the war and reunited in Seattle again in 1946, we buckled down to salvaging what remained and to start all over again. I returned to graduate studies. My folks again ran the small hotel in downtown Seattle, with my older brother taking charge. When I came home from the army, I had sworn that I would never come back here to Seattle because it had been the scene of one of the most bitter memories of my life, but I guess my roots were deep, and I came back because I felt that this was my home in spite of what happened.

I have never repented the decision to volunteer. In retrospect, the war record helped all Nikkei in their postwar struggle.

But there are many sad memories of friends who fell in battle, young, fresh-faced, eager, beautiful lads with whom I had volunteered, men from camp or those from Hawaii and other places with whom I'd trained in the heat and cold of Mississippi. What a price they paid for all of us. And if that is how loyalty is measured, then America got more than its money's worth in their sacrifice.

Compiled from a speech given by Minoru Masuda, "Evacuation and Concentration Camps," n.d., Minoru Masuda Papers, Box 1, Acc. 54–12, University of Washington Libraries, and an article he wrote, "Japanese Americans, Injury and Redress" *Rikka* vol. 6, no. 3 (Autumn 1979): 15–26.

# AFTERWORD

Minoru Masuda earned his PhD in physiology and biophysics in 1952 at the University of Washington. He joined the faculty there, serving in the Department of Psychiatry and Behavioral Sciences in the School of Medicine. He was an expert in a variety of biological, psychological, and sociological sciences. His primary research was in psychophysiology and psycho-endocrinology.

Min and Hana became the parents of two children, Tina and Kiyoshi, born in the 1950s.

During the sixties and seventies, Min became known as a spokesman for minority rights. He was active in the Japanese American Citizens League, serving as president of the Seattle chapter in 1971. He was a member of the Asian American Task Force of the Seattle Community College District, the Nikkei Retirement Coalition, the Nisei Veterans Committee, the Asian American Counseling and Referral Service, and the Asian Americans for Political Action. He was chairman of the Pride and Shame Traveling Exhibit and Program from 1973 to 1975. He also was active in the community, serving on the King County Mental Health Board, the Washington State Advisory Committee to the Department of Social and Health Services, and the United Way Mental Health Committee.

From 1979 until his death in 1980, Masuda was the principal investigator for the Nisei Aging Project in the University of Washington Anthropology Department. This project reflected his deep concern about his fellow Nisei. The purpose of the project was to investigate aspects of the life experience of older Nisei, such as health, employment and income, living arrangements, kin, and community involvement. The study was supported by the National Institutes of Mental Health.

In 1980, Masuda received the Charles E. Odegaard Award from the Friends of the Equal Opportunity Program at the University of Washington. Also in 1980, he was given the Community Achievement Award from the Seattle Urban League. He was posthumously honored as Japanese American of the Biennium in Humanities and Education by the national Japanese American Citizens League in 1980.

Minoru Masuda died of lung cancer on June 12, 1980, at the age of sixty-five. Hana died in 2000.

DIANNE BRIDGMAN

# APPENDIX

## *People Mentioned in the Letters*

### FAMILY

Sahei and Kida Masuda, Min's father and mother
Ruth ("Nay") Nomura, Min's sister
Satoshi ("Sat") and Rose Masuda, Min's brother and sister-in-law
Hack Masuda, Min's younger brother
Kiki Momoi, Min's younger sister
Tomi Koriyama, Hana's mother
Franklin and Yoshi Koriyama, Hana's brother (a member of the
     442d) and sister-in-law
Kay and Suzu ("Sue") Kuramoto, Hana's brother-in-law and
     younger sister (Tama's twin)
Harry and Tama Murotani, Hana's brother-in-law and younger
     sister (Suzu's twin)

### CLOSE FAMILY FRIENDS

Mayme Chin, longtime friend from Seattle who visited Hana and
     Suzu in Minneapolis during the war
Ethel Fukumaga, Hawaiian who met Hana at the Aloha USO in
     Hattiesburg

Joe and Mary Higuchi, University of Washington friends

Mariko Inouye, UW and skiing friend

Dennis, Mariko's son

Sam and Aya Kozu, investment club and skiing friends

Fumi Yoshida Lee, nurse at Camp Minidoka

Helen O'Connor, Hana's Minneapolis landlady

Yone and Gloria ("Glo") Ota, childhood friends

Dr. L. Wait Rising, UW Professor of Pharmacy

Roy and Jo Sakamoto, investment club friends

Yoshiko, Roy and Jo's daughter

Setsu Suzuki, Seattle native who first met Min and Hana in
    Hattiesburg

Shigeko Uchiyama, Seattle friend who shared Min's and Hana's
    interest in opera


THE UNIVERSITY OF WASHINGTON "PHARMACY BUNCH"

Don Kazama, served in the 442d

Dick and Massa Nomura, Dick served in the 442d

Fred Shimanaka, worked in Tokyo when the war began, drafted into
    the Japanese army, died later during the war from natural causes


FRIENDS IN THE 442ND

*Mainlanders*
Augie Aratani

Fudge Fuji

Futamata

Mike Hagiwara

Sammy Hokari

Harold Horiuchi

Lefty Ichihara

Isaac ("Zeke" or "Ike") Iijima

Vic Izui

Squeaky Kanazawa
Haruo Kato
Junie Kawamura
Kitsu
Ed Kiyobara
Pete Kozu
Tosh Kuge
Kelly Kuwayama
Maekawa
Minata
Yoshito Mizuta
Tak Momoda
Jimmy Morimoto
Mukai
Speed Murakami
Oscar ("Kenso") Osaki
Osozawa
Waka Sagami
Sammy Sakai
Howard Sakura
Eddie Sasaki
Munro Shintani
Eiji Suyama
Bobby Takeshita
Wachi
Mas Watanabe
Ben Yamanaka
Bill Yanagimachi
Haribo Yanagimachi

*Hawaiians*
Masato Hasegawa
Hayashi
Higa ("Higgins")

Higuchi
Hiramatsu
Lionel Ikebe
Walter Inouye
Kamo
Yosh and Haruo Kato
Pete Kozuma
Ogami
Onodera
Sakamoto
Taira
Herbert Tsukayama ("Tsuka")

*Killed in Action*
Yosh Kato
Bako Kinoshita
Bill Nakamura
Yohei Sagami
George Sawada

# NOTE ON SOURCES

M inoru Masuda's World War II letters to his wife, Hana,
are located in his papers in the University of Washington
Archives. This collection also includes excerpts from the *Medical
Detachment Daily Log*, used to provide context in this book. In
addition, publications of the 442nd Combat Team are found in
Masuda's papers: *The Album*, a yearbook-style account of training;
the *442nd Newsletter*; the *442nd Combat Team History*; and a pamphlet entitled *Go For Broke* (cited below). I used information from
these sources to compose the brief notations on the strategy and
action of the unit.

Hana Masuda wrote her recollections in 1989–1990, as the need
for more explanation of her activities during the war became apparent.

A reader who wishes to learn more about the 442nd Combat
Unit should consult *Go For Broke: A Pictorial History of the Japan-
ese American 100th Infantry Battalion and the 442nd Regimental
Combat Team* by Chester Tanaka (Richmond, California: Go For
Broke, Incorporated, 1982); *Unlikely Liberators* by Umezawa Duus
(Honolulu: University of Hawaii Press, 1987); *I Can Never Forget:
Men of the 100th/442nd* by Thelma Chang (Honolulu, Hawaii: Siga
Productions, Incorporated, 1991); and *Honor by Fire: Japanese Amer-
icans at War in Europe and the Pacific* by Lyn Crost (Novato, Califor-
nia: Presidio Press, 1994).

For more information on the Japanese American experience in World War II, the following books are useful: *Prisoners Without Trial: Japanese Americans in World War II* by Roger Daniels (New York, New York: Hill and Wang, 2004), and *Years of Infamy: The Untold Story of America's Concentration Camps* by Michi Weglyn (New York, New York: William Morrow, 1996).

Densho, the Japanese American Legacy Project, has obtained the oral histories of Japanese Americans who were interned in World War II. The videotaped oral histories, historical photos, and teacher resources are available on a most impressive Web site, www.densho .org.

# INDEX

football, 252–53, 254–55, 258
Fort Monte Bistion, Italy, 236
44th Antiaircraft Artillery Brigade, 132–33
442nd Regimental Combat Team: activation of, xv–xvi, 158; deactivation of, 227–28; volunteering for, xv, 8. *See also* 2nd Infantry Battalion; 100th Infantry Battalion; 3rd Infantry Battalion
France, xvi, 31, 91, 227; army of, 168; black market in, 95, 173; landscape of, 92, 97, 130, 133, 137, 168; liberation of, 101; weather in, 93, 94–95, 96–97, 100–101, 103–4, 107, 114, 118. *See also* French people; *names of individual cities and regions*
Freddano, Italy, 178
French Alps, 108
French people, xvii: assistance from, 95–96, 102, 108, 121; and language barrier, 92–93, 96, 97, 99; women, 92, 104, 134–35, 166
French Riviera, xvi
front line, 51, 56–57, 61, 70–72, 77, 80, 118, 129, 171, 182; medics on, 201, 127, 128, 140
Fuji, Fudge, 226
Funakoshi, Tosh, 260
Furuno, Yeichi, 62
Futamata, 86, 113, 147, 239

G2. *See* Military Intelligence Section
Gavorrano, Italy, 38
Geneva Convention, 37
Geneva Red Cross, 37, 49, 72–73, 238
Genoa, Italy, 197, 209
Germans, xvi, 37, 55, 61, 144, 149; amity with, 72–73, 106, 237–38;

empathy with, 217–18; medical treatment of, 46, 53–54, 113, 193, 216; occupation by, 36, 45, 47, 49, 75, 166; retreat of, 81, 91, 157, 181, 185–86, 194, 199–200; surrender of, xvi, 184–85, 197, 201–3, 205–6, 209, 212–14, 215–16; war tactics of, 57, 95, 101, 104, 108, 110, 132, 145, 146, 167, 192, 194–95. *See also* prisoners of war
Ghedi, Italy, 215–16, 226
Gibraltar, 33
GI study center, 240
Grebefosse, France, 115–16, 119–20

Hagiwara, Mike, 78, 256
Harada, Frankie, 257
Hasegawa, Masato, 12, 13, 15, 258–59
Hattiesburg, Miss., xviii
Hawaiians, xvi, 8, 16, 255; National Guard unit, 9, 12, 32, 85. *See also* 100th Infantry Battalion
Hayashi, Sgt., 20, 27, 77, 124, 188, 224, 235, 246; discharge of, 248, 253–54; illness of, 22–23; medical duties of, 103, 112
Hayashi, Yuri Aoka, 260
Higa ("Higgins"), 48, 53, 76, 82, 149, 151; discharge of, 248, 253–54; duties of, 112, 117, 215, 222; and music, 88, 106, 150
Higuchi, Chaplain, 41, 42, 45, 52, 74, 78, 97, 161
Higuchi, Joe, 81, 119
Higuchi, Mary, 81, 119
Hiramatsu, 173–74
Hokari, Sammy, 13, 19, 54, 108, 163, 194, 226
homecoming, 271–72

photography, 140–41, 143, 147, 149, 161, 189–90, 206–7, 211, 250

Pianodiquarto, Italy, 85

Pieve di St. Luce, 49–50

Piombino Port, 82

Pisa, Italy, 84, 177, 263

Pomaia, Italy, 49

Pompeii, Italy, 35

Pope Pius XII, 36

Post Exchange (PX), 23, 37

prejudice, xvii, 3, 7–8, 16, 78–79, 166, 229, 242, 246

prisoners of war (POWs), *186*, 189, 239–41, 242, 264; medical care of, 46, 53–54, 216; processing of, 215–22, 224, 238, 239

Puyallup, Wash., xv, 5

Pyle, Ernie, 126–27

Racism. *See* prejudice

radio, 66, 137; German programs on, 139

railways, 10, 18, 21, 35, 91, 94, 170, 209; conditions on, 19, 172–73, 209

*Randolph* (carrier), 266–71

reading, 63, 66, 157, 161–62, 246

recreation, 11, 23, 134–35, 142, 162, 166, 256; drinking, 15, 31, 75, 77–78, 132, 144, 150, 174; gambling, 93, 124; movies, 19–20, 26, 31, 57, 59–60, 64, 68, 142, 150, 151, 175, 217, 220, 226; shopping, 136, 141, 209; swimming, 63, 219, 221, 226. *See also* music; rest periods; *names of individual sports*

Red Battalion. *See* 100th Infantry Battalion

Regimental Combat Team (RCT), 18

religion, 42; services, 12, 13, 41, 45, 52, 98, 133, 179

rest periods, 50, 56–57, 60, 70, 107, 115–16, 120, 124, 129–30, 133, 199, 201, 207, 227; areas for, 56, 58, 66, 85, 91, 141–42, 145, 165, 197, 224–25

Rome, Italy, 33, 36, 38–40, 65

Rosignano, Italy, 46

Russians, 195, 199, 213

Sagami, Waka, 144

Sagami, Yohei, 143, 144, 154

Saint Peters Cathedral, 39

Sakai, Sammy, 51, 62, 169, 176

Sakamoto, Jo, 40, 189

Sakamoto, Roy, 19, 40, 93

Sakura, Howard, 14

Salerno, battle of, 32, 84

San Martino, Italy, 178, 181

San Pellegrino, Italy, 224–25

Sasaki, Eddie, 257

Sassetto, Italy, 43, 62

Sawada, George, 68, 163, 247

Scandicci, Italy, 71, 79, 82

Seattle, Wash., xv, xviii, 3, 156, 253

2nd Infantry Battalion (White), xvi, 44; in combat, 32, 137, 142, 146, 149, 158, 168, 182; commendations for, 62–63; training of, 13, 15; troop movements of, 36, 46, 50, 52, 56, 101, 115, 119, 123, 129, 138, 162, 207, 209, 242, 247

segregation, xv

Septemes, France, 91

Sestrilevanti, Italy, 197

Seventh Army, 91

Shimanaka, Fred, 241, 260

Shintani, Munro, 52

ships, 21; conditions on, 22–24, 32–33, 82, 91–92, 173–74; postwar transport on, 252, 260–63, 266–69